PERSONALITY
COMEDIANS
AS GENRE

Welcome to the world of personality comedians. W. C. Fields, arguably America's greatest native-born comedian, on the set of *Poppy* (1936).

PERSONALITY COMEDIANS AS GENRE

Selected Players

Wes D. Gehring

Foreword by Dennis E. Hensley

Contributions to the Study of Popular Culture,
Number 61

GREENWOOD PRESS
Westport, Connecticut • London

Library of Congress Cataloging-in-Publication Data

Gehring, Wes D.
        Personality comedians as genre : selected players / Wes D. Gehring
    ; foreword by Dennis E. Hensley.
            p. cm.—(Contributions to the study of popular culture,
    ISSN 0198–9871 ; no. 61)
        Filmography: p.
        Includes bibliographical references and index.
        ISBN 0–313–26185–7 (alk. paper)
        1. Comedy films—United States—History and criticism.
    2. Comedians—United States—Biography. I. Title. II. Series.
    PN1995.9.C55G427 1997
    791.43′ 617—dc21   96–47536

British Library Cataloguing in Publication Data is available.

Library of Congress Catalog Card Number: 96–47536
ISBN: 0–313–26185–7
ISSN: 0198–9871

First published in 1997

Greenwood Press, 88 Post Road West, Westport, CT 06881
An imprint of Greenwood Publishing Group, Inc.

Printed in the United States of America

The paper used in this book complies with the
Permanent Paper Standard issued by the National
Information Standards Organization (Z39.48–1984).

10 9 8 7 6 5 4 3 2 1

Copyright Acknowledgment

The author and publisher are grateful for permission to reprint the following material:

Wes D. Gehring's poem "Film Comedy is . . ." which originally appeared in a special edition
of *Literature/Film Quarterly* 23, no. 2 (1995).

To
Geraldine Chaplin
and
Richard Dyer MacCann

"Film comedy is . . ."

laughing at this "cockeyed
caravan" instead of
turning on the gas,

realizing the "boy genius" was
no genius when it came to
homogenizing the Marxes,

wondering if a reference
to Carmen Miranda should
have occurred in *Brazil,*

hurting your sides instead
of those people talking
during Charlie's "Oceana Roll,"

knowing the "Great Stone Face"
still managed an Oscar load
of expression with those eyes.

—Wes D. Gehring

"Charlie's Revolving Door"

In Chaplin's *The Cure*
Charlie enters but can't
Escape a revolving door:
    Too fast
    Now past
    Too fast
    Now past
    Too fast
    Now past
And amidst the fun is
Another Charlie metaphor
For life.

          —Wes D. Gehring

CONTENTS

ILLUSTRATIONS

FOREWORD

There is a marvelous piece of editorial satire inserted into Chapter 4 of Mark Twain's *A Connecticut Yankee in King Arthur's Court*. The Yankee, having been transferred from 1889 back to 513, finds himself seated in a crowd before comedian Sir Dinadan, who has just launched into his comedy routine. The Yankee notes:

> I think I never heard so many old played-out jokes strung together in my life. He was worse than the minstrel, worse than the clown in the circus. It seemed particularly sad to sit there thirteen hundred years before I was born and listen again to poor, flat, worm-eaten jokes that had given me the dry gripes when I was a boy thirteen hundred years afterwards. It about convinced me that there isn't any such thing as a new joke possible.

And of course, the Yankee (Twain's alter ego) is right. There are no new shticks. Even today.

When Jim "Ernest" Varney dresses and talks like a hick, he's standing in the shadow of Will Rogers. When Lily Tomlin dresses as Edith Ann, she's mirroring the antics of Fanny Brice doing Baby Snooks. When Robin Williams spews a rapid-fire monologue, he's copying the blitz-paced delivery of Groucho Marx. When Jim Carrey does a pratfall, he's carrying on the antics of Buster Keaton.

So, knowing this is true, we may well wonder, why do audiences keep coming back to see the same old stuff all the time? The answer is simple: They are looking for *variation on a theme*. Although the routine is old hat, the person making the delivery is fresh, new, and surprising; and that makes the material seem original and distinctive, too.

This proves to be a double blessing: The old-timer who grew up watching Groucho in *Duck Soup* on Saturday at the Bijou can now enjoy that same style of frantic repartee by renting a video of Robin Williams in *Good Morning, Vietnam*. Likewise, the kids who grew up watching Robin Williams on TV in "Mork and Mindy" can now discover the same sort of fast-paced dialogue and weird facial expressions in a classic Groucho Marx film such as *A Day at the Races*.

Mining this wealth of comedy—especially as it applies to film comics— would prove formidable were it not for guidance from film historian and critic Wes Gehring. In this new book, Wes not only defines the major forms of film comedy, he also categorizes the comics and the films that best exemplify these skits, routines, and gags. His encyclopedic mind systematically itemizes the key examples from silent one-reelers to contemporary epics. He knows it, and shares it, often with a dash of his own brand of humor.

Read Wes Gehring's writings and you'll discover that what's new in comedy is actually what's old in comedy. And what's old in comedy remains forever new in comedy. Either way, we can't lose.

—Dennis E. Hensley, Ph.D.

Dr. Dennis E. Hensley is the author of six novels, including *The Gift*, and more than 20 nonfiction books, such as *Write On Target*, and *Positive Workaholism*. His 3,000 freelance short stories and articles appear regularly in *Writer's Digest, Success!, Downbeat, Essence, Reader's Digest* and *People*, among other publications.

PREFACE

W. C. Fields once observed: "I do believe it was Carry Nation or Mrs. Carry Catt who said, 'Take a little wine for thy stomach's sake, but don't get blotto.' "

This work, like all the comedy genre texts I have done, has been influenced by a statement from comedy theorist Jim Leach. With humorous insight he observed, "A genre which encompasses the visions of Jerry Lewis *and* Ernst Lubitsch is already in trouble."[1] Leach went on to suggest a more ambitious examination of multiple comedy genres, noting what many film comedy enthusiasts have long believed: "If a genre is defined too loosely [as in the case of comedy] it ceases to be of any value as a critical tool."[2]

This book examines the most basic type of comedy—the personality comedian as genre, be it Charlie Chaplin and Woody Allen, or teams such as the Marx Brothers and Laurel & Hardy. What components link these and other comedy players?

Chapter 1 addresses this question and provides a historical overview of American film comedy, covering a number of comedians. After this foundation, each chapter examines one or more representative comedians from a different period. Regrettably, not every great figure can be profiled. This was the only down-side to an otherwise wonderful writing experience.

Chapter 2 focuses on America's first (historically) important film comedian, John Bunny, and America's "first" (still the most significant) movie clown, Charlie Chaplin. Chaplin is unique because he moved beyond the silent period (the late 1920s) and continued to do influential work during both the Depression and post-World War II eras.

Chapter 3 scrutinizes the Depression comedians—the Marx Brothers, Laurel & Hardy, and W. C. Fields. The Marxes are cinema's most celebrated team. Laurel & Hardy were the only comedians to successfully (critically and commercially) make the transition from silent to sound films. (Chaplin essentially made the change by making no change—his two 1930s movies kept his Tramp persona silent, save for some delightful gibberish at the close of *Modern Times*, 1936). W. C. Fields is arguably America's greatest native-born comedian.

Chapter 4 studies the pivotal antihero/wiseguy personae of Bob Hope and Woody Allen. Mixing the two traits, the incompetent and the egotistical, took center stage in American film comedy of the 1940s. In that period no one combined them better than Bob Hope, whose career continued well into the 1960s. Appropriately, Hope had a phenomenal influence on Woody Allen, whose film career began in the 1960s. Allen is the modern period's answer to total auteur Chaplin. As did the creator of the Tramp, Allen writes, directs, and stars in his films. Both Allen's and Hope's best works embrace a parody slant, which the chapter examines.

The Epilogue is a brief summing up, a reiteration of some pivotal points and a few closing reflections on a comedy genre—personality comedian—that has fascinated me since childhood.

As in all I write, this book is also a celebration of everything comic. I have never forgotten a graduate school lesson learned from my college mentor, Richard Dyer MacCann. I had entered his office for one of our many discussions, on film and life in general. He had just finished analyzing an essay by one of the department's most gifted students. And in a brief aside MacCann observed, "As insightful as this paper is, . . . [the author] has forgotten he's writing about comedy." Now MacCann did not mean the writer should have punched the essay up with some jokes. He meant the student had neither mentioned his subject was comedy, nor written it in a manner to appreciate the comedy. Always remember the laughter.

NOTES

1. Jim Leach, "The Screwball Comedy," in *Film Genre and Criticism*, ed. Barry K. Grant (Metuchen, N.J.: Scarecrow Press, 1977), p. 75.
2. Ibid.

ACKNOWLEDGMENTS

Old Yiddish proverb: "Man plans, God laughs."

Comedy has always occupied a pivotal position in my family. My dad and both grandfathers loved comic films and playing humorist themselves. It seems only natural that I would continue in this tradition. The twist for me was to be analytical about it. Some would suggest taking humor apart destroys its magic. To me it only helps provide personal insight for the individual. Thus, while I enjoy humorist Robert Benchley's tongue-in-cheek potshot at analysis—"All laughter is a muscular rigidity spasmodically relieved by involuntary twitching"—being a student of humor has not lessened my appreciation of it.

Besides family tradition and encouragement, there are several professional colleagues to thank. My former department chairperson, "Dr. Joe" Misiewicz, assisted with both securing release time for me and facilitating university financial help. I greatly appreciate the ongoing support of Ball State University Provost Warren C. Vander Hill as well as the support of the dean of the College of Sciences and Humanities, Ronald L. Johnstone. Janet Warrner, my local copy editor, was forever available and helpful. The computer preparation of the manuscript was done by Jennifer Ellis and Jean Thurman. And teaching friends Joe Pacino, Dave Smith, and Conrad Lane were often helpful. A final thank you must be given to Chaplin's oldest daughter, actress Geraldine Chaplin. I met her at the 1989 Paris conference celebrating the 100th anniversary of her father's birth. As a featured speaker, I was able to talk with Ms. Chaplin and her encouragement of my work meant a great deal.

Research for this book also involved several important archives and their invariably helpful staffs. These include the New York Public Library System, especially the Billy Rose Theatre Collection at Lincoln Center; the Library of Congress; the Margaret Herrick Library at the Academy of Motion Picture Arts and Sciences (Beverly Hills); the American Film Institute (Beverly Hills); the University of Iowa's main library (Iowa City); and Ball State University's Bracken Library (Muncie, Indiana).

Coming full circle back to family, a special thank you is in order for my parents. They have strongly encouraged my interests through the years and instilled a work ethic that has been more than helpful on book projects such as this.

1

INTRODUCTION

I was the oldest child. We were all very poor, but I was poor first.[1]
> W. C. Fields on his early childhood

Married! I can see you right now in the kitchen, bending over a hot stove, but I can't see the stove.
> "Romantic" Groucho to Marx
> Brothers regular Margaret Dumont
> in *Duck Soup* (1933)

COMEDY HISTORY OVERVIEW

The clown genre is both the most basic and the most obvious of types. Unlike other, more thematic-oriented comedy approaches, the clown model is dependent upon a front-and-center comic figure, or figures, be it W. C. Fields or the Marx Brothers. Around them is fashioned the loosest of storylines. One is reminded of the "Notice" with which Mark Twain opens the adventures of his sometimes literary clown Huckleberry Finn: "Persons attempting to find a motive in this narrative will be prosecuted; persons attempting to find a moral in it will be banished; persons attempting to find a plot in it will be shot." There are clown exceptions to this, such as the generally tight narratives of Buster Keaton, as in his classic *The General* (1927). However, *Variety*'s August 11, 1948, rave review of Red Skelton's greatest film, *A Southern Yankee*, could be applied to the majority of clown films: "an erratic jumble, pulled together only by a funny idea and Skelton's [or fill is the clown(s) of your choice] knack for clowning." Thus, the clown genre should leave no question that ongoing laughter is its goal. In comedy theory this would fall under the category of "release and relief." Without taking anything away from the artist, the viewer has a good idea of what he or she will see. In contrast, the thematic dark comedy of a *Dr. Strangelove or How I Learned to Stop Worrying and Love the Bomb* (1964), or of *Harold and Maude* (1971), keeps the viewer on edge, not always knowing when laughter is appropriate. And even then the laugh is of a nervous nature, easy to recall if the viewer has been mistaken.

The storyline of clown comedy provides a humor hall tree upon which the comedian can "hang" his comic shtick—specific routines and/or variations of them that lend themselves to the establishing of the all-important screen comedy persona. Thus, Charlie Chaplin, of the east-west feet, invariably showcases the underdog Tramp's ability to work a comic metamorphosis on inanimate objects. In *The Pawnshop* (1916), an alarm clock in his examination becomes everything from a medical patient to a can of beans. And there are those fanciful dinner rolls that suddenly become dancing feet in the delightful "Oceana Roll" of *The Gold Rush* (1925). Moreover, Chaplin is equally talented at his own changeovers; he becomes a lamp in *The Adventurer* (1917), a tree in *Shoulder Arms* (1918), and a laughing mechanical figure in *The Circus* (1928). In contrast, the more aggressive comedies of Eddie Murphy often showcase one of his controlled comic tirades, as when in a tight spot he assumes the guise of an authority figure and dresses down his antagonists, such as in the redneck bar scene in *48 Hours* (1982) or the warehouse inventory confrontation in the original *Beverly Hills Cop* (1984).

Other classic material strongly associated with the comic persona includes: Groucho's baiting of Margaret Dumont (see chapter opening quotation); the surrealist sight gags of Harpo, such as the magic coat from which he pulls a blowtorch in *Duck Soup* (1933); the comic piano playing of Chico; Laurel & Hardy having their tit-for-tat exchanges of comic violence with any number of antagonists, such as team regular James Finlayson in *Big Business* (1929), where a house, a car, and a Christmas tree are methodically destroyed.

W. C. Fields, though also a talented physical comedian (he began his career as comic juggler), is best remembered by the nasal drawl of his signature voice. The casually meandering tempo of flowery speech is often also peppered with words that are funny in and of themselves. For instance, in *Poppy* (1936) he describes a cottage as a: "charming little lean-to. Reminds me of my wickiup on the limb-poo-poo."

The comic word games of Danny Kaye, especially his "pellet" from *The Court Jester* (1956), are a key to his shtick. Harold Lloyd's thrill comedy is essential to his persona, hanging from the clock in *Safety Last* (1923) or the skyscraper ledge scenes in *The Sin of Harold Diddlebock* (1947). Bob Hope's ability to fluctuate between the most incompetent of comic antiheroes and the cool, egotistical wiseguy who purrs with satisfaction upon seeing himself in a mirror, is central to his comedy character. Hope's comic duality complements modern humor's frequent fascination with the schizophrenic, especially for Hope disciple Woody Allen. Thus in *Play It Again, Sam* (1972), Allen bounces frenetically between being a Bogart clone and schlemiel of the week.

Lou Costello's inability to understand bullying Bud Abbott's comments, such as in their celebrated "Who's on first?" routine, is the defining component of their teaming. Steve Martin at his best allows a bit of his "wild and crazy guy" stand-up comedy to be legitimately inserted into his screen persona; witness the bar room nose joke scene in *Roxanne* (1987) or the substitute birthday party cowboy segment in *Parenthood* (1989). Robin Williams is even more dependent upon his saturation comedy, improvisational-like stand-up shtick being incorporated into his screen character, such as the machine-gun patter of his comically crazed disc jockey in *Good Morning, Vietnam* (1987).

This is not to suggest that all clown films exist independent of other comedy genres. Indeed, there are few pure examples of any phenomenon. Personality comedians sometimes have an affinity for the thematic comedy genres. Such ties are actually born out of the clown personae themselves. Thus, the comic absurdity of the Marx Brothers sometimes lends itself to black comedy, such as the war scenes of *Duck Soup*. The folksy crackerbarrel axioms of Will Rogers' celebrated populism, especially in *So This Is London* (1930) and *Judge Priest* (1935). And Bob Hope's flip-flops between comic antihero and egotistical wiseguy are nicely attuned to parody, whether in his inspired film noir spoof *My Favorite Brunette* (1947) or his numerous western take-offs, including *The Paleface* (1948).

Thus, clown films frequently work on more than one comedy level, with parody probably being the most frequent comedy sidekick genre. In fact, given that most clowns exhibit some incompetence, there is a degree of parody of the traditionally capable dramatic hero in most clown films. Indeed, for a time Steve Martin closely followed in the Bob Hope spoof tradition with take-offs on film noir (*Dead Men Don't Wear Plaid*, 1982), the horror film (*The Man With Two Brains*, 1983), and the western (*Three Amigos!* 1986).

Clown movies are certainly not dependent on such ties, however, and the majority exist outside all but the broadest of these comedy genre "marriages." And even where parody ties exist, the general public's focus remains on the clown. Consequently, one frequently describes this viewing experience as having seen a Marx Brothers film or a W. C. Fields movie (fill in the clown of your choice), with facts like a storyline or even the production's title superfluous to the conversation. Mere mention of the comedian's name so represents a given shtick that little further explanation is necessary.

The following discussion of the general characteristics of the clown genre—and most specifically the clowns themselves—draws examples from a history divided into four broad periods: the silents, the Depression era, the post-World War II period, and the modern era (1960–   ).

The first, and still most celebrated, category is silent comedy, especially the traditional pantheon of Charlie Chaplin, Buster Keaton, Harold Lloyd, and Harry Langdon. Strong cases can also be made for countless others, from the well-known antiheroic exploits of Laurel & Hardy to the more obscure pioneering work of John Bunny in the early 1910s.

Easily the most central of these early comedians is Chaplin, frequently considered cinema's most celebrated figure, comic or otherwise. It is hard to overestimate the significance of Chaplin to film comedy. Because of both the Everyman universality of his Tramp figure and the range of his mime, he remains *the* standard against which all cinema clowns are measured. Moreover, Chaplin balances an equally celebrated pathos, as at the close of *City Lights* (1931), where the blind girl sees. This balancing act has become an ever-elusive goal for other comedians. Because so many have failed (Langdon and Jerry Lewis are the most famous examples), Abbott & Costello biographer Bob Thomas has labeled the fixation the "Chaplin disease" (for a time, Lou Costello was similarly "afflicted").[2]

Directly related to the "Chaplin disease" was Chaplin's ability to wear all the production hats: He wrote, directed, scored, starred in, and produced his own films. Many film comedians have failed in the attempt to duplicate this accomplishment (again, Langdon and Lewis), but it remains the standard. For example, early in Eddie Murphy's career (1980s) he frequently mentioned this as a goal.[3] But his flawed *Harlem Nights* (1989), which he wrote, directed, starred in, and produced, was a critical disaster; he has yet to attempt to emulate Chaplin since.

Chaplin's greatest artistic rival was—and still is—Buster Keaton, though the latter never had the same contemporary critical and commercial success. In fact, the film now considered his masterpiece and one of the screen's most enduring movies, *The General*, was a decided failure in 1927. Three basic differences separate their work. Chaplin was about socially conscious under-dogs winning. In *The Pilgrim* (1923) Charlie pantomimes the story of David and Goliath; this is a footnote to the sources of all Charlie stories. The Keaton way was a comic battle not with men but with their machines, or with the elements themselves. And his victories were ones of unchanging endurance, as implied by his "great Stone Face" nickname, though his eyes revealed volumes. If one scene encapsulates Keaton, it is his impossibly comic walk leaning into the tornado of *Steamboat Bill, Jr.* (1928). Second, as is suggested by Chaplin's pathos and the unchanging Keaton visage, while the student of Chaplin is invariably first moved by the Tramp emotionally, the Keaton deadpan is more apt to move our minds. Keaton's deadpan is a twentieth-century defense against the absurdities of the modern world. One has only to remember the stoic pessimism in the final scene of *Daydreams* (1922), where Keaton is caught in the whirling boat paddlewheel and climbs ever faster to avoid becoming a comic victim in this metaphor for the treadmill nature of life. The scene also underlines a basic tenet of dark comedy: At best, life is a holding pattern. Third, to maximize the believability of his unique mime, Chaplin the filmmaker shot in long takes and minimized technical special effects. Keaton, equally fascinated by machines in real life, was not adverse to camera trickery for comedy, such as the elaborate masking of the lens for *The Playhouse* (1921), which allowed him to play all the parts.

In Harold Lloyd, Chaplin had his greatest 1920s commercial rival, though Lloyd was a distant second to both Chaplin and Keaton in terms of comic art. Lloyd's character was the proverbial boy-next-door, anxious to succeed. His greatest film, *Safety Last*, with its celebrated thrill-comedy skyscraper-climbing scene, is the perfect metaphor for the Lloyd story: "climbing" to success. Lloyd himself was without the physical grace and skills of Chaplin and Keaton, but he attempted to compensate for this with a nonstop manner consistent with his Puritan work ethic; he was a latter-day Horatio Alger on speed. Still, the Lloyd films are funny because they merge ageless gags (the basted-together suit that begins to come undone in *The Freshman*, 1925) and a central character whose ambitious innocence is still winsome, though without the emotional complexities that make the Tramp so fascinating.

Chaplin's third silent rival, Harry Langdon, came the closest in terms of pathos, but he had nowhere near the comedy range of Chaplin's Tramp. Film critic James Agee appropriately described the Langdon persona as that of "an elderly baby" or "a baby dope fiend" (not unlike the face of Pee Wee Herman), who survived only through the grace of God.[4] But Langdon, whose two-year stay at the top of silent comedy was far shorter than that of other pantheon members (precipitated in part by his break from writer/director Frank Capra), had a comedy persona like Blake Edwards/Peter Sellers' Inspector Clouseau. For instance, though both have guardian angels, neither character is remotely aware such aid is being given. Langdon's character mistakenly believes he has scared away the cyclone in *Tramp, Tramp, Tramp* (1926), and Inspector Clouseau is completely oblivious to the bumbling assassination attempts that become the comic centerpieces of the Pink Panther films. Unfortunately, Langdon was the only pantheon member not fully cognizant of why his persona worked. Though some revisionist historians have recently attempted to disprove this position, his short but brilliant success still seems largely tied to the molding of Capra, with whom he broke in 1927. He had seemingly become afflicted by, and was about to be the victim of, "Chaplin disease." Langdon fan Bob Hope, who found himself on the same vaudeville bill in 1933, was later advised by his comedy hero, "If you ever go out to Hollywood and become a star—and I think you could—don't make my mistake. Don't try to convince yourself that you're a genius."⁵ Coming to the screen at the near height of the silent era, his small but subtle mime was a refreshing variation for the mid-1920s audience, especially one missing a less-productive Chaplin (whose pathos Langdon's persona most resembled). Today's viewer, because he or she is not immersed in the rich silent-comedy mosaic of the 1920s, sometimes misses the subtle greatness of Langdon. As Agee has so poetically stated (see Note 4), "It seemed as if Chaplin could do literally anything, on any instrument in the orchestra. Langdon had one queerly toned, unique little reed. But out of it he could get incredible melodies."

Additional names merit near-pantheon status, especially Laurel & Hardy. Though the duo was not as dependent upon Leo McCarey as Langdon was on Capra, McCarey was as instrumental in their success as he was in the evolution of the comic antihero in American film.

The Depression era provided the impetus for the comedy success of older, more cynical comedy clowns: W.C. Fields, the Marx Brothers (especially Groucho), and Mae West. Two watershed developments marked this transition. First, sound film provided the clown with a voice (except for Chaplin's Tramp and Harpo's trenchcoat-attired Pan). Second, American humor was undergoing a major change, as the childlike comic antihero (the totally frustrated modern individual) took center stage away from the older, more capable crackerbarrel Yankee type—the early 1930s film success of Will Rogers's country philosopher notwithstanding. Earlier antiheroes had existed, of course, but they had not been the dominant norm in American humor. American film comedy had prior antiheroic precedents in the work of John Bunny (1910–15, the country's earliest significant comedy star) and the often neglected silent-film features of W. C. Fields. But the best movie breakthrough example of the antihero should be credited to Leo McCarey who teamed and molded Laurel & Hardy, both because of their unique and timely full-blown articulation of the characters and because of their phenomenal popularity with the public.⁶

While Laurel & Hardy successfully rode this development into the early 1940s, W. C. Fields found great success during the sound era by alternating between antihero and old-fashioned, carnival-style huckster. He played both the milquetoast husband in *It's a Gift* (1934) and the shell-game shakedown artist in *Poppy* (1936, adapted from the 1923 Broadway play that helped popularize Fields as the con man), which opens with Fields successfully selling a talking dog. Both versions of Fields come liberally peppered with examples of the other. In the picnic scene in *It's a Gift*, his wife forces the antiheroic Fields to share a sandwich with a son of whom he is none too fond. But even here a bit of larceny surfaces. Fields cheats when splitting the sandwich—he bends all the meat onto his side before dividing it. Conversely, when the huckster Fields of *An Old Fashioned Way* (1934) courts a wealthy widow, "all dressed up like a well-kept grave," he must antiheroically endure an informal audition by a silly, no-talent singing ninny. She then informs him, "I can act as well as I can sing."

With comic diplomacy befitting his slippery character, Fields answers, "I'm sure of it." Thus, the viewer feels W. C.'s character has more than earned his right to fleece this nincompoop. To paraphrase an old axiom, here is one fool who soon deserves to be parted from her money.

Though not as apparent, there are even antiheroic elements in the Marx Brothers, or more precisely, in Groucho. While best remembered as a modern con artist aggressor in the world at large, whether as president of a country in *Duck Soup* or of a college in *Horse Feathers* (1932), he frequently plays the antiheroic brother within the team. In the standing gag of *Duck Soup*, Harpo and his motorcycle sidecar always leave Groucho behind; in the tutti-frutti ice cream scene in *A Day at the Races* (1937), Chico sells Groucho a library of unnecessary betting books. Moreover, what Marx Brothers author Allen Eyles calls "Harpo's *tour de force* in outsmarting Groucho," the *Duck Soup* "mirror" scene imitation of the mustached one, is arguably the greatest of all Marx Brothers scenes.[7]

As a team, however, the Marxes were not so much victims as victimizers (though this aggression was, unfortunately, toned down in their later, more homogenized, MGM pictures). And that aggression still brings one back to a comic antihero world view. Physically and verbally, especially in their propensity for outrageous puns and malapropisms, the Marx Brothers declared that nothing, including the English language, was what it seemed. Thus, their *verbal* slapstick is not without some antiheroic ties to the tit-for-tat violence of Laurel & Hardy, a comedy of surrealism. For instance, critic Joseph Alsop Jr. contrasts *A Night at the Opera* (1935) with two scenes in Luis Buñuel and Salvador Dali's *Andalusian Dog* (*Un chien andalou* [1929]),which is generally considered the beginning of surrealistic cinema: "You will not find in it a single slit eyeball, or even one ant crawling out of a hole in a . . . hand, but then these are the Marx Brothers, and they are quite sufficient."[8]

Alsop might have added a further surrealistic connection between Dali and the Groucho gang. The manner in which a Dali figure represents several things at the same time can be equated with a Marx Brothers pun—reminding the viewer of the multiple purposes and meanings of words. One is tempted, however, to credit Groucho and company with pushing their often dark humor beyond surrealism. The main difference between black comedy and surrealism, as defined by humor historian Max F. Schultz, is that surrealism plays on "internal disorder" of the subconscious mind; black comedy generally suggests that disorder is the external, real state of things.[9] Certainly a pivotal element in the rediscovery of the Marxes during the chaotic 1960s was the fact that surrealism was more and more becoming the day-to-day norm.

A more apparent influence of the Marxes was their early demonstration of the potential for comic artistry in sound films, despite the often canned-theater nature of their first two movies. To the student of film comedy, their cross-section of an American humor team (con, dialect, mime) made the transition from silents to sound more palatable—especially with the mime of Harpo compensation for the painful loss or decline of so many silent-comedy stars. In fact, as early as 1937, perceptive popular-culture critic Gilbert Seldes observed, "The arrival of the Marx Brothers and the reappearance of W. C. Fields saved screen comedy."[10] And the Marx Brothers' early film success was so great that it paved the way for a series of other zany period comedy teams, such as Wheeler & Woolsey, the Ritz Brothers, Olsen & Johnson, and others. Indeed, MGM's failed attempt in the early 1930s to team Buster Keaton and Jimmy Durante does not seem so unlikely when seen as a variation on a Harpo-Groucho duo.

The third focus era (post–World War II) demonstrates some changes that had begun to take place during the war. Most obvious was the new breed of personality comedians who could fluctuate between the most incompetent of comic antiheroes and the cool, egotistical wiseguy. Bob Hope was the unquestionable master, whether in his "Road" pictures with Bing Crosby or as a Damon Runyon title character like *The Lemon Drop Kid* (1951).

Hope's comic duality complements the modern era's fascination with schizophrenic humor. In fact, Woody Allen, today's greatest and most self-consciously psychiatry-oriented comedy filmmaker, follows the same pattern of antihero to wise guy and back. In *Play It Again, Sam* (1972), Allen even sounds like Hope. Comedy historian Maurice Yacowar notes that Allen's comment to a guard protecting the remains of the evil leader in *Sleeper* (1973)—"We're here to see the nose. We hear it's running"—is pure Hope.[11]

In the 1940s and 1950s the antihero/wiseguy equation was sometimes given to two performers, or what was supposed to be two. For example, Danny Kaye frequently played dual roles in his films and was at his best in *Wonder Man* (1945), playing the most opposite of twins. The phenomenal commercial popularity of Abbott & Costello in the 1940s was also based on the antihero/wiseguy dichotomy. In addition, wiseguy Bud Abbott dished out more comic violence (especially slaps) to antiheroic Lou Costello than any comic this side of the Three Stooges' Moe Howard.

Martin & Lewis, *the* comedy team of the 1950s, often operated on the same antihero/wiseguy formula. Jerry Lewis' screen persona, which he calls the "Idiot," is probably the ultimate antihero. Dean Martin has just as strongly been associated with the wiseguy. Their typical formula had Lewis' character as the "simplest" of adolescents trying in every way to emulate the sharpest of older-brother figures, Martin's persona. Fittingly, in their last year as a team (1956) they made the ironically titled *Pardners*, which showcased the brother-like syndrome to the nth degree. It's interesting that Lewis' greatest solo work, *The Nutty Professor* (1963), finds him playing the antihero/wiseguy quality that is often compared to the makeup of the Martin and Lewis team: Lewis plays both an absent-minded professor and a wise-mouth crooner.[12]

Thus, Lewis' turn as a lounge singer is also a spoof of Martin. This added level is what makes Lewis' original *Nutty Professor* better than Eddie Murphy's entertaining 1996 remake.

The duality has traditionally emphasized the antihero, sometimes to the near neglect of the wiseguy persona, such as the excellent Red Skelton vehicles *The Fuller Brush Man* and *A Southern Yankee* (both 1948). However, some modern film comedy personalities are reversing the emphasis. Both Bill Murray and Eddie Murphy are essentially cool comics who can weather antiheroic situations. While they do this in radically different ways (Murray is the original Mr. Laid-Back; Murphy is the master of comic intensity), they amusingly deny the loss of comic control. Thus, unlike so many of their comedy predecessors, they are able to maintain their outrageousness in establishment positions, whether it is Murphy as policeman (the *Beverly Hills Cop* series), or Murray as a soldier in *Stripes* (1981). Murphy feigns outrage as he cheekily faces down danger with an inimitable comic brashness. In contrast, Murray's Mr. Cool character never seems to be caught off-guard, a pivotal key to the amazing critical and commercial success of *Ghostbusters* (1984).

While Murray and Murphy have been very influential (see especially the Murray-like nature of Michael Keaton and the pre-Forrest Gump Tom Hanks), the emphasis on the antihero in the antihero/wiseguy character still dominates. Examples would include the trials of Chevy Chase in the *Vacation* movies, such Steve Martin tales as 1984's *The Lonely Guy* (whose title underlines the antihero emphasis), *Father of the Bride* (1991) and the sequel *Bride II* (1995); Albert Brooks' attempt to be a yuppy "Easy Rider" (substituting a Winnebago for a motorcycle) in the appropriately named *Lost in America* (1985); and Woody Allen's ongoing anxieties about life and death and other subjects in *Hannah and Her Sisters* (1986), *Crimes and Misdemeanors* (1989), and *Manhattan Murder Mystery* (1993).

However, the modern era is like any other in that reminders of past trends continue to surface, whether they be the funny and poignant Laurel &

Hardy-like film *Planes, Trains and Automobiles* (1987, with Steve Martin and John Candy), or the rebirth of the early 1950s Jerry Lewis with Jim Carrey in *Ace Ventura: Pet Detective, The Mask,* and *Dumb and Dumber* (all in 1994). Lewis himself has called Carrey "the most brilliant physical comedian to come along in decades."[13] In another interview Lewis comically mixed his praise with mock-jealousy: "He's the very thing motion pictures were made for [Carrey's rubber 'mask' of a face and body]. He's wonderful! *The bastard!*"[14]

While Steve Martin's ability as a verbal comedian is topped only by the unique talent of Robin Williams, Martin's skills as a physical comedian (Lewis' praise of Carrey notwithstanding), are in a class by themselves. For instance, when Lily Tomlin's character partially inhabits Martin's persona in *All of Me* (1984), his screwball gyrations in just trying to walk have one scrambling for words like Chaplinesque. Though this role resulted in his winning the New York Film Critics' "Best Actor" award, Martin's physical comedy skills have never been fully appreciated. Robin Williams' warp speed as a verbal comedian is reminiscent of the lightning patter of Groucho Marx. Indeed, both have attributed their saturation comedy ways to tough show-business beginnings in which one had to be funny very quickly or the audience would take you apart. Instead of yesterday's monologist, these two are capable of being comedy Sybils, burying an audience under an avalanche of funny material.

This, then, has been a brief historical overview of some major clowns during a four-part division of cinema history. But despite the many years they represent and their comic personality differences, five common characteristics link them in the clown genre. They are all generally identified with a specific comedy shtick that has lent itself to a winning screen-comedy persona; physical/visual humor is a vital aspect of their delivery; they are perennial underdogs who are often incompetent and/or amusingly unorthodox; they are frequently nomadic; and a "team" situation is commonly pivotal even with the most celebrated of solo comedians.

COMPONENTS OF THE CLOWN GENRE

The first component of the clown genre is the significance of a specific comedy shtick (see the chapter's opening), variations of which are generally brought to each film. It is interesting that just such an example also represents the beginning of cinema in the United States. The earliest whole film on record is the comic *Fred Ott's Sneeze* (1891, from the American father of the movies, Thomas Edison).[15] Ott was an Edison engineer and resident funnyman whose material included a comic sneeze. And while this one-routine "film" lasts only seconds, it holds the double distinction of being the first film and the first film comedy.

The more comically universal the shtick, the more likely it will make a successful transition to movie clown. For instance, Rodney Dangerfield has parlayed the most sweeping of stand-up shticks, "I get no respect" (which could be applied to 99.9 percent of the clown market), into an effective film-comedy persona. In 1994 writer-director Oliver Stone was able to show the comically dark side of Dangerfield's antiheroic persona in the provocative black comedy *Natural Born Killers*. It represents an excellent example of pushing a character envelope while remaining true to a given persona.

Though not taken to the negative extreme of Stone's use of Dangerfield, Woody Allen's antiheroic role in director Martin Ritt's dark comedy about 1950s black listing, *The Front* (1976), also nicely showcased a less than flattering portrait of an antihero.

A second component of the clown genre is that American humor has always placed a high premium on physical and visual comedy, whether in the movies or on the printed page. Thus, even the great literary comedians frequently showcase this phenomenon. Witness the description of bouncing about in a stagecoach in *Roughing It* (1872), by the dean of American humor authors, Mark Twain:

> Every time we avalanched from one end of the stage to the other, the unabridged dictionary would come, too and every time it came it damaged somebody. . . . The pistols and coins soon settled to the bottom, but the ropes, pipe stems, tobacco, and canteens clattered and foundered after the dictionary every time it made an assault on us.[16]

Countless other examples exist. America's celebrated antiheroic author (and creator of Walter Mitty) James Thurber wrote a comic autobiography, *My Life and Hard Times* (1933), which is so full of physical and visual comedy (not to mention his delightful drawings) that even his episode titles create cartoon pictures: "The Night the Bed Fell," "The Day the Dam Broke," "The Dog That Bit People." Today, comic antiheroic authors like Woody Allen continue to provide funny imagery, though it is often of a more surrealistically cerebral kind. For example, Allen's "The Kugelmass Episode," winner of the O. Henry Award for best short story of 1977, is about a machine that can project one into the storyline of any book. Unfortunately, yet apropos for an antihero, the Mitty-like Kugelmass falls victim to a total machine breakdown. Instead of finding himself in sexy *Portnoy's Complaint*, he is permanently thrust into an old remedial Spanish textbook, where he is soon "running for his life over a barren, rocky terrain as the word *tener* ('to have')—a large and hairy irregular verb—races after him on its spindly legs."[17]

Even the term "stand-up comic" is more and more an anachronism. Richard Pryor was the greatest factor in this change. In performance films like *Richard Pryor: Live in Concert* (1979), *Richard Pryor Live on the Sunset Strip* (1982, see Illustration 1), and *Richard Pryor: Here and Now* (1983), he maximizes every inch of the stage, differentiating between a white and a black man walking in the woods or demonstrating his boxing inadequacies in an exhibition match with Muhammed Ali. Part of this departure is necessitated by what critics have sometimes defined as exposing his "naked persona" on stage, a "theater of real life."[18] Thus, one experiences the comic poignancy of Pryor the child running from a whipping by his grandmother, or discussing his heart attack with his body as he collapses on stage. These performances legitimized "the theater of real life," the blue language he brings to his stories, because they are *natural* obscenities.

Much the same can be said of Robin Williams' concert films, particularly *An Evening With Robin Williams*, in which the comic is hypnotic in his seemingly stream-of-consciousness ramblings on myriad subjects, from his drug addiction to Elmer Fudd doing Bruce Springsteen. Williams is not only all over the stage but all over the theatre, interacting with the audience or available props, such as a coat, camera, beverages. At one point a balcony camera captures him in a musical spoof of the trademark Busby Berkeley overhead shot, with Williams lying down on stage making geometric patterns by moving his arms and legs.

Though Pryor and Williams are pivotal in this "movement" away from stand-up, there are precursors in the rope-twirling "poet lariat" of the 1910s, Will Rogers, the skipping steps of the 1930s banjo-eyed Eddie Cantor, or Jonathan Winters' trips into the audiences of the 1950s and 1960s (Winters had an acknowledged influence on Williams).

With America's propensity for comedic physical movement, on the printed page and now from the former stand-up, it is hardly surprising that the big screen should have embraced it so strongly through the years, at least in the clown genre. And for a public so enamored with slapstick, it provides one more reason that the silent period has been on the film-comedy pedestal since critic James Agee's influential essay called it "Comedy's Greatest Era" in 1949.[19]

For the film-genre clown, the visual comedy often begins *before* the story, because clowns look funny. Through costume, make-up, body shape, or fluid contortions of face and body, clowns telegraph the message that this will be a comedy and create the added pressure; this comedy momentum is not to be slowed. Their funny appearance is a key in the clown genre, even when the comic personality might be more linked to verbal humor. For example, while the machine-gun patter of Groucho is famous, it is more than a little dependent upon the visual. Lillian Roth, the young heroine of *Animal Crackers* (1930), best described the total Groucho visual package when she explained why she kept giggling into retakes a scene they had together:

1. *Richard Pryor Live on the Sunset Strip* (1982).

> The line itself wasn't so hilarious, but I knew Groucho was going to say
> it with the big cigar jutting from his clenched teeth, his eyebrows
> palpitating, and that he would be off afterwards in that runaway crouch
> of his; and the thought of what was coming was too much for me.[20]

Groucho himself, once accused of underselling some comedy material on a 1930s MGM road-testing tour for a future film, observed that he could attain a laugh with any line as long as he wiggled his eyebrows. Thus, he was purposely eliminating such actions in order to discover what was intrinsically most amusing. Even then, he had a head start. As the great 1930s film critic Otis Ferguson observed in his *A Night at the Opera* review, Groucho "would be funny in still photographs."[21]

Groucho contemporary Mae West is also famous for her dialogue, invariably full of sexual innuendo. But this ongoing joke was largely made possible by West's exaggerated hourglass figure, seemingly poured into a Gay Nineties dress, and such suggestive physical actions as her provocative strut. Thus, West was already a visual satire before she pursued that same theme verbally. Moreover, her comic crack was invariably visual, such as the X-rated line, "You packin' a rod, or did you just miss me?"

Countless comedians have showcased comic costumes and/or contortions through the years, such as Charlie Chaplin's Little Tramp "uniform" and funny shuffle from the "east-and-west feet"[22]; Harpo's magic-pocketed trenchcoat and the "gookie" grimace of a "Neanderthal idiot"[23]; and the simpler costume of Woody Allen—wrinkled clothing, disheveled hair, and the all-important antiheroic glasses (visually reminiscent of Lloyd's bespectacled character, especially in Allen's *Sleeper*, 1973). Even America's first film star, the short and rotund John Bunny, was affectionately known as "moon [round] face."

After the clown has established a comedy tone through appearance, time is frequently reserved for physical and visual humor. In the 1910s Mack Sennett, creator of the Keystone Kops, emerged as the behind-the-screen father of American film comedy.

Sennett had been a journeyman performer in a cross-section of popular entertainment forms (circus, burlesque, vaudeville, legitimate stage) before finally achieving success in film, originally under the tutelage of the great film pioneer D. W. Griffith. Sennett, a large, naive farm boy, came to New York early in the twentieth century to sing opera but instead found work as the rear end of a horse at the Bowery Burlesque. While not the standard route to the Met, this was an appropriate beginning for a man whose future would be based largely in slapstick irreverence. His later description of why he enjoyed burlesque comics could just as aptly be applied to his film work:

The cops and tramps with their bed slats and bladders [underinflated "slap-sticks"] appealed to me as being funny people. Their approach to life was earthy and understandable. They whaled the daylights out of pretension. They made fun of themselves and the human fate. They reduced convention, dogma, stuffed shirts, and Authority to nonsense, and then blossomed into pandemonium.[24]

For the student of American film comedy, especially physical comedy, this description is appropriate to a great deal of what followed Sennett.

Though the silent 1920s were the golden age of physical comedy, clown films of the early sound era continued to highlight visual comedy. Indeed, Chaplin kept Charlie the Tramp silent until 1936, and Harpo forever maintained the tradition. Close scrutiny of even such distinctly voiced comedy clowns as Laurel & Hardy and W. C. Fields finds much of their work based on the visual gag. This is especially true of the former; witness their Oscar-winning attempt to deliver a piano up a huge flight of stairs in *The Music Box* (1932), or those little habitual gestures that endeared them to audiences, such as Hardy's exasperated look at the camera (the viewer) when Laurel pulled a major boner or Laurel's absentminded scratching at the top of his head when perplexed. Moreover, their body shapes are the classic comedy contrast for clowns: stout and skinny, carrying on the pioneering film contrast of round John Bunny opposite cartoon-thin frequent partner Flora Finch.

Fields, a former vaudeville juggler, invariably included a great deal of physical humor in his work, such as his field goal-like booting of Baby LeRoy in *The Old-Fashioned Way* (1934) or the domestic skirmishes as he tries to shave in the "family" bathroom of his greatest film, *It's a Gift* (1934). The same movie showcased his inspired routine on how not to catch some sleep on the back porch. Like Laurel & Hardy, the Fields persona had numerous patented gestures, such as his ever-present comic difficulty with his hat and cane, or the comic surprise (double-takes) derived from his collection of bent, limp, and otherwise temperamental pool cues and golf clubs. Fields' copyrighted sketches at the Library of Congress document his interest in the visual.[25]

In the 1940s the sight gag of the clown genre was more thoroughly usurped by the verbal, though its decline was greatly exaggerated. For instance, as strong as Agee's aforementioned essay is on the silent clowns, he underestimates the physical abilities of Bob Hope and neglects the unique visual gifts of clowns like Red Skelton, especially in such special outings as *A Southern Yankee*. The film includes Skelton's inspired hike between military lines during battle wearing the "two-piece suit"—a Northern uniform on the Yankee side of his body, a Southern outfit on the Confederate side. Fittingly, he carries a two-sided flag. Thus, for a time he is a hero to be applauded by both armies, *but then the wind changes* (a nice metaphor for the plight of most comedians). Each army suddenly sees the opposing flag, and the battle commences again. This time, however, Skelton is the designated hitt*ee*. Buster Keaton, who wrote film gags for MGM in the 1940s, devised the costume and flag gag, among others, for the Skelton vehicle. Keaton was very close to the material because his greatest film, *The General*, was also a Civil War comedy (though there are few direct parallels between it and *A Southern Yankee*).

One might best measure the significance of physical comedy in the 1940s by the fact that even in the very verbal and commercially popular Abbott & Costello films, slapstick sequences are still very effective. Examples might include Costello's difficulties in learning how to march in *Buck Privates* (1941, which borrows more than a little from a similar scene in Chaplin's World War I comedy *Shoulder Arms*), or the many bits of visual mischief Costello causes as a ghost in *The Tim of Their Lives* (1946). Moreover, even the verbal routines of this duo feature slapstick punctuation, be it the fat man/thin man dichotomy or Costello's exasperated expressions and Abbott's perennial manhandling of his partner.

In more recent years, physical comedy has remained an important part of the clown genre, best showcased in the 1950s and the 1960s work of Jerry Lewis, especially his largely non-dialogue, gag-focused directing debut in *The Bellboy* (1960). The comic contortions of Lewis live on in the 1990s antics of Jim Carrey. And even America's most cerebral clown, Woody Allen, is generous with his visual comedy. Probably his funniest film, *Sleeper* (1973), is dominated by the visual, including the giant chicken and vegetable scene, his attempts to fly with a malfunctioning whirlybird backpack, the *Modern Times*-like conveyor belt scene, and fighting off the huge blob of chocolate pudding while dressed as a twenty-second-century domestic robot with a resemblance to Harold Lloyd. In fact, through the 1970s, much of Allen's most memorable material remained sight gags: *trying to play a cello in a marching band (Take the Money and Run*, 1968); the take-out order for an army (*Bananas*, 1971); the delightfully nervous meeting of a blind date (*Play It Again, Sam*, 1972); basic training problems and flirting at the opera (*Love and Death*, 1975—not to mention being shot from a cannon, which figured prominently in the film's advertising), and trying to catch runaway lobsters and kill spiders (*Annie Hall*, 1977). With all this in mind, it is not so startling to discover that prior to scheduling conflicts, Jerry Lewis had originally been slated to direct *Take the Money and Run*.

Allen's movies since the late 1970s have become increasingly cerebral, but the humor has not been banished. Examples abound, including the monologue about the skeleton in *Manhattan* (1979), the films within the film in *Stardust Memories* (1980), the flying machine from *A Midsummer Night's Sex Comedy*

(1982), and the chase through the warehouse of Macy's Thanksgiving Day Parade figures in *Broadway Danny Rose* (1984). Other examples include characters who come off the screen in *The Purple Rose of Cairo* (1985, borrowing from Buster Keaton's *Sherlock Jr.*, 1924), Woody the hypochondriac facing high-tech medicine in *Hannah and Her Sisters* (1987), a dominating mother who fills the sky in the "Oedipus Wrecks" episode of *New York Stories* (1989), and the Laurel & Hardy-as-detectives actions of Diane Keaton and Allen in *Manhattan Murder Mystery* (1993).

One might add such 1970s and 1980s visual footnotes as the arched eyebrows and fat man grace of John Belushi, so reminiscent of early film's Fatty Arbuckle; Marty Feldman's bulgingly misdirected eyes, in a class with the crossed eyes of silent film's Ben Turpin; the other-worldly appearance and movements of Pee-wee Herman, so like the forgotten silent comedian Larry Semon; the silly pothead antics of Cheech & Chong, who brought a whole new meaning to the term "dopey" comedy team; and the return of Inspector Clouseau, courtesy of the slapstick tradition of director-writer Blake Edwards.

The third characteristic of clowns is that they are underdogs who frequently exhibit comically incompetent behavior. This characteristic is often directly related to the physical humor discussed above. That is, the incompetent clowns' inadequacies are often showcased in some basic physical task, such as Laurel & Hardy trying to put a radio antenna on the roof, with predictable results, in *Hog Wild* (1930); Bob Hope's inability to handle hard liquor in *My Favorite Brunette* (1947); Jack Lemmon trying to maintain his fake breasts in the cross-dressing *Some Like It Hot* (1959); Jerry Lewis' lab-exploding tendencies in *The Nutty Professor* (1963); Woody Allen's bumper car-like attempt to drive an automobile in *Annie Hall* (1977); Steve Martin's difficulties in going to the bathroom while inhabited by Lily Tomlin in *All of Me* (1984); and Bill Murray's adventures with a rodent, among many other things, in *Groundhog Day* (1993).

Teams, even of the merely occasional variety such as Hope & Crosby, often use the capable/incompetent dichotomy for their humor focus. This is the case with Abbott & Costello, Martin & Lewis, and Hope & Crosby. Much of the teams' comedy comes from the capable character taking advantage of "the stooge" (fittingly, also a title of a 1953 Martin & Lewis film). In the "Road" pictures, Bob Hope is frequently the stooge. For instance, Bing Crosby generally wins Dorothy Lamour by the end of each film. Even at the close of *The Road to Utopia* (1946), where it seems Hope's luck has finally changed after we see him and Lamour as an elderly married couple, the ski-nosed comic is a loser. When their now grown child appears, he is the mirror image of (and played by) Bing Crosby.

Conversely, there are teams in which the capable/incompetent framework is established despite the absence of an able character. Humor then arises from one team member's *thinking* he is the more enlightened and taking chaotic charge. This is true of both Laurel & Hardy and the Three Stooges, with the latter team's title nicely demonstrating "stooge equality." Oliver Hardy and Moe Howard play incompetent surrogate fathers to the equally antiheroic and childlike Stan Laurel, Curly and Shemp Howard, and Larry Fine.

While it is tempting to focus entirely on incompetent behavior for this third point, it would be misleading. For instance, much of the motivation behind my 1983 biography of Chaplin was to address the clown's overblown image as a loser. If we examine his Tramp films closely, we more often find a very capable clown, whether in his amazing brick-stacking skills in *Pay Day* (1922) or his balletic grace on skates in *The Rink* (1916) and *Modern Times* (1936).

The Tramp's interaction with mechanical objects is more problematic, but his dexterity almost always wins out. Frustrating moments can occur, such as with the debilitating conveyor belt of *Modern Times*. But for every such stumbling block there are numerous mechanical victories: the Chaplin cop of *Easy Street* (1917), who so adeptly manages to etherize the giant bully (Eric Campbell) with a gas street lamp, or the Chaplin soldier of *Shoulder Arms* (1918), who converts a Victrola horn to a breathing device so he can sleep underwater in his partly submerged bunker.

Consequently, clowns are likely to be as unorthodox as they are incompetent. Besides Chaplin's magic and the magic pockets of Harpo, one might note such diverse examples as the inherently wise and warm crackerbarrel humor of Will Rogers, Eddie Murphy's aggressively comic way of bluffing through any problem, and Buster Keaton's ability to work eccentric, mechanical miracles with large machines. For instance, Keaton manages to transform an ocean liner galley—originally constructed to feed thousands—into a personalized kitchen for one in *The Navigator* (1924).

Unorthodox or incompetent, most clowns qualify as underdogs and outsiders, going against the establishment norm. While few assume the upfront comic attack posture of the Marx Brothers, most would at least qualify as comedy fifth columnists, going against the regimented seriousness of society. This is probably best demonstrated by W. C. Fields' mumbled asides in times of comic frustration.

The fourth characteristic is that film clowns, as comedy outsiders, are frequently nomadic, with direct literary ties to such picaresque heroes as Don Quixote and Huck Finn.[26] Fittingly, cinema's greatest clown, Chaplin's Charlie, is closely linked to the picaresque, through his identity as a wandering Tramp and the celebrated imagery of him literally shuffling down life's highways. Not coincidentally, the inspired teaming of Hope & Crosby is based on a series of "Road" pictures, as the duo comically wander about the globe. In fact, some episodes even chart their helter-skelter movements on a map.

There are four comedy reasons for going on the road. The first is that it gives the clown an endless supply of new settings for his comedy: Witness Harry Langdon's nomadic ways in the cross-country walkathon *Tramp, Tramp, Tramp* and as the touring assistant to *The Strong Man* (both 1926), *National Lampoon's Vacation* (1983) quest for "Wally World," Pee-wee Herman's trip to the Alamo in search of his bike in *Pee Wee Herman's Big Adventure* (1986), and the inspired road humor of the fittingly titled Steve Martin-John Candy movie, *Planes, Trains and Automobiles* (1987).

The picaresque carnival huckster of *Poppy* (1936) established W. C. Fields both on Broadway (1923) and in the movies; Fields starred in D. W. Griffith's original silent adaptation, *Sally of the Sawdust* (1925). Fields' cinema con man continued to focus on the nomadic in his steamboat comedies *Tillie and Gus* (1933) and *Mississippi* (1934), or as another carnival huckster type in *You Can't Cheat an Honest Man* (1939), where he is circus owner Larson E. Whipsnade. Even his more domestic, antiheroic roles sometimes find time for the picaresque, such as his cross-country automobile trip to California in *It's a Gift*.

Will Rogers quickly found critical and commercial success in sound films by playing the American innocent abroad in movies such as *They Had to See Paris* (1929) and *So This is London* (1930). In *City Slickers* (1991) Billy Crystal and his mid-life crisis buddies traveled first to Spain (for a Hemingwayesque run with the bulls) and then out West, all to prove they were still macho.

The mode of transportation can also become an end in itself. Will Rogers took a *Steamboat 'Round the Bend* (1935); the Marx Brothers made use of an ocean liner in *Monkey Business* (1931) and *A Night at the Opera* (1935), of a train in *At the Circus* (1939) and *Go West* (1941), and an airplane in *A Night in Casablanca* (1946). The machine-oriented Keaton had, of course, led the way with his own ocean liner in *The Navigator* and the ultimate nonstop train picture, *The General*. W. C. Fields' *Never Give a Sucker an Even Break* (1941) manages to use a commercial plane to recycle part of an earlier Fields train compartment sketch as well as to justify a bit of comic travel surrealism—he survives jumping out of a plane (without benefit of a parachute) in pursuit of a wayward liquor bottle and lands in the bizarre mountaintop fortress of Mrs. Hemoglobin (Margaret Dumont).

A second comic reason for travel is that placing a clown in some unlikely setting *can be* an ongoing joke itself and is often the starting point for parody. Thus, seeing Chaplin's Klondike-bound Charlie (in full Tramp costume) shuffling around a glacier in *The Gold Rush* (1925) is delightfully incongruous, just as the traditional garb of Laurel & Hardy is comically out of place on their trek into the cowboy country of *Way Out West* (1936). Conversely, seeing the traveling clown in the appropriate garb for some nomadic situation can also make for great comic incongruity. The countless comedy changes Hope &

Crosby go through in their wandering "Road" pictures exemplify this best, but there are innumerable other illustrations. Richard Pryor and Gene Wilder must don chicken costumes at one point in *Stir Crazy* (1980), and Bette Midler and Shelley Long wear male garments to visit a brothel in *Outrageous Fortune* (1987). In *Spies Like Us* (1985) Chevy Chase and Dan Aykroyd provide the viewer with an updated, unofficial "Road" picture, nicely continuing the earlier series' comic-style show tradition, especially in their hilarious *Nanook of the North* parkas, or the equally comic glowing, floor lamp-like UFO alien costumes. (Appropriately, Bob Hope makes a "golfing-through" cameo.)

A third reason for travel is that it justifies introducing a broad cross-section of supporting comedy characters (not to mention the exotic Dorothy Lamour), such as the zany Wiere Brothers of *The Road to Rio* (1947); the laid-back George Carlin of *Outrageous Fortune* (1987); the truckload of on-the-road types in both *National Lampoon's Vacation* (1983) and *Pee-Wee Herman's Big Adventure* (1985, especially the phantom trucker Large Marge); Bronson Pinchot's scene-stealing bit (from Eddie Murphy, no less) in *Beverly Hills Cop* (1984), playing a gay California art gallery worker to Murphy's New York cop; and the Punxsutawney, Pennsylvania, comic types that smug, big-city weatherman Bill Murray turns up in *Groundhog Day* (1993). And these are but a fragment of the examples showcased. Indeed, to better understand the multitude of comedy types encountered, one might quote the original theater poster's description of Midler and Long's plight in *Outrageous Fortune*:

> The CIA is trailing them
> The KGB is tracking them
> The phone company is tracing them
> The police are chasing them
> The cowboys are herding them
> And the Indians are hunting them
> Are they going to fall for all that? [with "fall" a pun on the poster—Midler and Long hanging from a cliff—more visual humor].

This ad copy leads to a fourth fundamental reason for comedy travel: the fourth item "The police are chasing them." From the Keystone Kops to *Smokey* [the highway patrol] *and the Bandit* (1977) and beyond, "picaresque comedian" is often an artsy way of saying "funny person on the run." Besides the obvious reminder that the humorous chase is just what the comedy doctor ordered for *moving* pictures, one can also use the chase as a composite of the three previously mentioned main characteristics of the film comedian: shtick physical humor, and being the underdog; this is in addition to the nomadic given. Comedic shtick often involves movement—Charlie Chaplin's beguiling slide on one foot as he takes a corner too fast; the hurried, mincing walk of Bette Midler; Harpo chasing girls, both on foot and with his trusty bike; the ever speedy, loping walk of Groucho; Lloyd the human fly trying to scale a building, or at least one frightful ledge; Bob Hope's and Woody Allen's wiseguy swagger when they are not feeling antiheroic; and fast cars, whether the surrealistic patrol wagon of the Keystone Kops or a Burt Reynolds speeding car.

In addition to the obvious visual humor such examples represent, they encourage countless other bits of slapstick, such as wrecked cars (from Laurel & Hardy Model-Ts to the used-car lot total of the underrated *Blues Brothers,* 1980). Add to this the broad humor associated with most hide-and-seek chase scenes—Charlie Chaplin successfully pretending to be a floor lamp in *The Adventurer* (1917), the stowaway exploits of the Marxes in *Monkey Business* (1931) or Hope & Crosby in *The Road to Rio* (1947), the encyclopedic survey provided by an army of comics in *It's a Mad, Mad, Mad, Mad World* (1963), Gene Wilder's attempt to pass as Richard Pryor's "brother" in *Silver Streak* (1976), and Bette Midler and Shelley Long's ride down an airport baggage conveyor belt in *Outrageous Fortune* (1987). Finally, what better comic way is there to peddle an underdog-outsider persona than to be a funny fugitive from the law? Film comedy has used the device since the beginning. And even when a clown comedy is not particularly picaresque, there seems to be an unwritten law that a chase, especially as a rousing conclusion (a topper to all that has preceded it), be added.

A fifth common characteristic of these clowns is the often unnoted importance of a team interaction. Even solo clowns frequently need someone off whom to bounce their humor. Their comic interactions with others are what begin to differentiate pure shtick (the concert film) from a clown movie. Little needs to be said about the acknowledged comedy teams, but the unofficial ones merit attention. Many important clowns have been at their comedy best when periodically teamed: Wallace Beery and Marie Dressler, Hope and Crosby, Walter Matthau and Jack Lemmon.

Even some acknowledged teams are better understood when studied as duos. For example, the Marx Brothers are much more likely to appear in twosomes of Groucho and Chico or Harpo and Chico, with the less celebrated Chico actually being most necessary to either maintain comedy lines of communications or to represent the catalyst for the action itself. When all three are together on screen, translator Chico is all the more indispensable. The main exception to this is still another popular Marx Brothers duo—Groucho and Margaret Dumont. (Zeppo Marx's appearances in the team's Paramount films were most often in modest support of Groucho.)

Unofficial teamings are often less apparent because the supporting member is neither a star nor a regular repeater, although the comedy type is. For instance,

W. C. Fields' antiheroic humor was frequently in need of a nagging wife and/or standard comic female busybody, as was Laurel & Hardy's. Through the years a number of women nicely essayed the part opposite Fields, though occasional repeater Kathleen Howard was the best. Moreover, Fields constantly peopled his films with comic physical types who were both visual jokes and fitting targets for Fields' one-liners and/or double-takes. The skinny-as-a-rail American Gothic-type Bill Wolf seemingly was given a number of cameo parts in Fields films just because of his physique. And on more than one occasion an unusually small person was cast so that Fields could utilize the line, "Is he standing in a hole?" As is so often true of this comedian, his cinematic inclinations were duplicated in real life. For example, his real entourage invariably included at least one undersized and/or oddly shaped member.[27] When Fields worked for the famous New York stage producer Flo Ziegfeld he even employed a dwarf known as "Shorty" to be his valet and general Man Friday. Although he originally hired Shorty to spook a superstitious Ziegfeld, Fields later included him in his comedy golf routine. And Fields' professional and personal interest in the diminutive stooge continued during the comedian's Hollywood days.

Other comedy types used more ambitiously by Fields include Franklin Pangborn's patently prissy (shades of another busybody wife) bank examiner J. Pinkerton Snoopington in *The Bank Dick* (1940), or Fields' loyal, deadpan Indian companion Clarence (George Moran) in *My Little Chickadee* (see Illustration 2). (A variation of the Fields-Moran duo occurs in *Texas Across the Rover* (1966), where Joey Bishop does a hilarious turn as another deadpan Indian to Dean Martin's comic cowboy.) *My Little Chickadee* is, of course, best known for Fields' most famous teaming—with Mae West.

Fields sidekick Clarence was probably inspired by a previous, popular teaming of the comedian in the newspaper comic strips of the day. In 1936 Fields was the inspiration for the Great Gusto, a prominent character in the strip *Big Chief Wahoo*, of which Fields was very fond. Wahoo played a stooge to Gusto, who had a medicine show—the classic con-man setting for Fields since his Broadway success as a medicine show huckster in *Poppy* (1923).

An additional period teaming of Fields surfaced in the movies. In 1937 Fields started doing verbal battle with ventriloquist Edgar Bergen's lippy "child" Charlie McCarthy on radio's very popular *Chase & Sanborn Hour*. Though they teamed only once in the movies (*You Can't Cheat an Honest Man*, 1939), the key to their successful comic rivalry was based in Fields' long-established film premise that he hated children. And Charlie McCarthy was just a Baby LeRoy (an earlier Fields nemesis) grown into a smart-aleck kid made of wood.

2. W. C. Fields in *My Little Chickadee* (1940).

The coming of sound films greatly encouraged the team concept, because sound defused the comic centrality of the silent clowns. Dialogue, after all, necessitates interaction between two or more people. But even in the silents, unofficial teams were forever lurking. Fields was like comedy pioneer John Bunny, who was often tied to another shrewish wife (Flora Finch), whose skinniness also comically contrasted with Bunny's roundness. Harry Langdon was frequently paired opposite big men like Vernon Dent, who later often surfaced in the early Three Stooges films. Even Chaplin found numerous ways to create teams. As examined in my 1983 Chaplin biography, Charlie was teamed frequently through dual-focus comic narrative. In certain films, especially the short subjects, this dual-focus meant that his actions repeated or paralleled actions of another central character. This is best exemplified in his work with giant Eric Campbell (his comic rival in the Mutual films, 1916–1917), especially in *Easy Street* (1917). But similar big man-little man pairings occurred earlier, such as with Fatty Arbuckle and Campbell-like Mack Swain for Mack Sennett, and later with Swain in *The Gold Rush* and Jack Oakie in *The Great Dictator* (1940).

The dual focus also surfaced when Chaplin played two parts himself (*A Night in the Show*, 1916; *The Idle Class*, 1921; *The Great Dictator*), and when he became the model for another character's copying instead of portraying the copier himself, as was usually the case in his teaming with big men. The best example of the former occurs in *The Kid* (1921), where Jackie Coogan's title performance "is clearly another presentation of Charlie, so that we have in this film a dual personality, the adult and the child Charlie."[28] Another variation of the dual Charlie occurs in *Modern Times* with Paulette Goddard's gamine, a delightful Tramp-like character who is part love interest and part surrogate Charlie. Indeed, at times she seems to be a cheerleader for the Tramp of old, such as when she encourages him to run from the paddy wagon accident before the police nab both of them.

Film theorists such as Rudolf Arnheim have also made much of a unique dual-focus Chaplin in *The Circus* (1928). This is in reference to the film's fun-house mirror scene exemplifying the surprising and amusing multiplication of man without montage or lens distortion.[29] The scene refers to a house-of-mirrors chase, with Charlie being pursued by a pickpocket, who has planted stolen goods on the Tramp and now wants the goods back, and a cop, who thinks Charlie did the stealing. Although there are several hilarious interactions, Arnheim's reference is to the relationship between Charlie and the pickpocket. When each makes his move, Charlie to escape and the pickpocket to reclaim the stolen goods, there are suddenly innumerable Charlies and pickpockets in the frame, due to the mirrors. A variation of the scene occurs later with the policeman. In both situations, dual-focus Charlie has become a small army.

Consistent with this Charlie "team" concept is the fact that, as with W. C. Fields' 1930s cartoon strip pairing in *Big Chief Wahoo*, during the 1910s the Tramp sometimes emerged as part of a duo in the strip *Charlie Chaplin's Comic Capers*.[30] His occasional partner was an undersized character named Luke, physically not unlike Jiggs of the then very popular cartoon strip *Bringing Up Father*. However, the inspiration for this more normal-sized duo possibly came from Chaplin's occasional teaming with the normal-sized Ben Turpin while both were at the Essanay Company, before Turpin's crossed eyes became the focus of his comedy.

A final common trait of the comic personality is the fascination with a clown's background that has always sustained society. Clowns comically comfort us in our short lives with their resilience, both physical and spiritual.[31] Along the same lines, society seems most fascinated with the clown who reveals tragic roots—the ability to provoke laughter despite personal sadness. For instance, in my 1992 biography of humorist Robert Benchley, I examined the chilling statement inadvertently uttered by his mother in the eight-year-old's presence upon the death of a beloved older brother: "Oh, why couldn't it have been Robert?"

Benchley's later success, despite his mother's numbing plea when her favorite son died, is the stuff of comic legend—humor's version of the phoenix. Interestingly, it has recently been shown that elementary-age children with a marked sense of humor are more likely to have had a lack of early motherly attention.[32] While there are no hard and fast rules in comedy theory, this certainly applies to my writing on Groucho Marx. In an A & E Channel *Biography* segment on the comedian, I joined the Marx family and friends in discussing his mother's preference for older brothers Chico and Harpo. The accepted assumption was that this third-class status undoubtedly contributed both to Groucho's drive to succeed (to impress this woman so taken with show business) and to the often misogynist nature of his comedy.

Charlie Chaplin, cinema's most celebrated icon, did not suffer from the early lack of a mother's love. However, his formative years were like a Dickens tragedy, with his single-parent mother fighting poverty and a descent into madness. Thus, one again sees the resilience that can create laughter regardless of personal pain.

This section examined six major characteristics that link film clowns. Of course, it should go without saying that clowns share one more trait from which all others emanate: they make us laugh—a commonality about which there is nothing common. Comic creativity has obliterated the distinctions of high and low in the history of popular culture. Aristotle's misguided notion that tragedy and the flaws of the upper classes and/or the powerful hold greater significance than the comedy of the common person (a prejudice still held by many, unfortunately) is no longer the norm. If art is to survive the ever-greater technical complexities that loom ahead, clowns must be attached to the realities and redemptions of the ongoing comedy in our lives. If the truth be told, we all live in a comic way. And it should be remembered, entertainment derived from that comic reality still represents a personal outpost of freedom and sanity in a world too often controlled by intimidation (often hooked to the tragedy). Long live irreverent comic stances!

NOTES

1. "Rogue's Progress," *Newsweek*, January 6, 1947, p. 19.

2. Bob Thomas, *Bud & Lou* (Philadelphia: J. B. Lippincott, 1977), p. 130. See also Wes Gehring, *Charlie Chaplin: A Bio-Bibliography* (Westport, Conn.: Greenwood Press, 1983).

3. See especially Gene Lyons and Peter McAlevy, "Crazy Eddie," cover article, *Newsweek*, January 7, 1985, pp. 53, 55; "Interview With Eddie Murphy," cover article, *Ebony*, July 1985, p. 46.

4. James Agee, "Comedy's Greatest Era," in *Agee in Film*, Vol. 1 (New York: Grosset and Dunlap, 1969), p. 8 (originally appeared in *Life*, September 3, 1949).

5. Bob Hope and Bob Thomas, *The Road to Hollywood: My 40-year Love Affair with the Movies* (Garden City, N.Y.: Doubleday, 1977), p. 12.

6. Wes Gehring, *Leo McCarey and the Comic Anti-Hero in American Film* (New York: Arno Press, 1980); and Gehring, *Laurel & Hardy: A Bio-Bibliography* (Westport, Conn.: Greenwood Press, 1990).

7. Allen Eyles, *The Marx Brothers: Their World of Comedy* (1966; reprinted. New York: Paperback Library, 1971), p. 106.

8. Joseph Alsop Jr., "Surrealism Beaten at Its Own Game," *New York Herald Tribune*, December 15, 1935, in *A Night at the Opera* file, Billy Rose Theatre Collection, New York Public Library at Lincoln Center.

9. Max F. Schultz, *Black Humor Fiction of the Sixties* (Athens, Ohio: Ohio University Press, 1973), p. 71.

10. Gilbert Seldes, *The Movies Come from America* (New York: Charles Scribner's Sons, 1937), p. 41.

11. Maurice Yacowar, *Loser Take All: The Comic Art of Woody Allen* (New York: Frederick Ungar, 1979), p. 156.

12. For example, see Andrew Sarris, "Jerry Lewis," in *The American Cinema: Directors and Directions, 1929–1968* (New York: Dutton, 1968), pp. 242–43.

13. Gail Buchalter, "What Failure Taught Me," *Parade*, January 15, 1995, p. 4.

14. David Patrick Stearns, "'Damn Yankees' Has Jerry Lewis on Deck," *USA Today*, p. 1–D.

15. Gerald Mast, *A Short History of the Movies*, 3rd edn. (Indianapolis: Bobbs-Merrill, 1981), p. 15.

16. Mark Twain, *Roughing It* (1872; reprinted. New York: New American Library, 1962), p. 42.

17. Woody Allen, "The Kugelmass Episode," in *Side Effects* (New York: Random House, 1980), p. 55.

18. Jim Haskins, *Richard Pryor: A Man and His Madness* (New York: Beaufort Books, 1984), p. 64.

19. Agee, "Comedy's Greatest Era."

20. Lillian Roth, Mike Connolly, and Gerald Frank, *I'll Cry Tomorrow* (New York: Frederick Fell, 1954), p. 85.

21. Otis Ferguson, *A Night at the Opera* review in *New Republic*, December 11, 1935, p. 130.

22. Carl Sandburg, "Carl Sandburg Says Chaplin Could Play Serious Drama," in *Authors on Film*, ed. Harry M. Geduld (Bloomington, Ind.: Indiana University Press, 1972), p. 264. (Originally in *Chicago Daily News*, April 16, 1921.)

23. Alexander Woollcott, "A Strong Silent Man," *Cosmopolitan*, January 1934, p. 108.

24. Mack Sennett, with Cameron Ship, *King of Comedy* (1954; reprinted New York: Pinnacle Books, 1975), pp. 28–29.

25. Gehring, "W. C. Fields: The Copyright Sketches," *Journal of Popular Film & Television*, Summer 1986, pp. 65–75.

26. Mast, "Comic Climate," in *The Comic Mind: Comedy and the Movies*, 2nd edn. (Chicago: University of Chicago Press, 1979), p. 7.

27. Robert Lewis Taylor, *W. C. Fields: His Follies and Fortunes* (Garden City, N.Y.: Doubleday, 1949), p. 174.

28. Peter Cotes and Thelma Niklaus, *The Little Fellow: The Life and Works of Charles Spencer Chaplin* (1951; reprinted. New York: Citadel, 1965), p. 109.

29. Rudolf Arnheim, *Film as Art* (1933; reprinted. Los Angeles: University of California Press, 1971), pp. 36, 51.

30. See the collection *Charlie Chaplin Up in the Air* (Chicago: M. A. Donohue, 1917).

31. Ernie E. Welsford, *The Fool: His Social and Literary History* (New York: Ferrar & Rinehart, 1935), pp. 314–15.

32. Paul E. McGhee, *Humor: Its Origins and Developments*: (San Francisco: W. H. Freeman, 1978), p. 192.

2

BUNNY AND CHARLIE

Motion pictures, the galloping tintypes—the flicks—ah, now you are yodeling right up my canyon. . . . I directed . . . *Buying an Umbrella* in the old . . . days, you know, [with] John Bunny.
                    Egbert Sousé (W. C. Fields) in the *Bank Dick* (1940)

INTRODUCTION

The previous chapter, which defined the characteristics of the personality comedian as genre, showcased a wealth of special American film clowns. This chapter and the ones to follow examine in more depth what must be a limited number of comedians drawn from the genre periods noted in Chapter 1: the silent era, Depression, post-World War II period, and the modern era. This chapter discusses America's first important film comedian, the neglected John Bunny, and the medium's most celebrated figure, comic or otherwise, Charlie Chaplin. Indeed, Bunny may have been overlooked possibly a result of the still unparalleled meteoric rise of Chaplin shortly before Bunny's premature 1915 death. Conversely, Chaplin's ascent was no doubt assisted by the comedy void created by the latter's death.

Chaplin remains the figure against whom all comedy talent is measured, both in front of and behind the camera, since he also wrote, directed, and scored many of his pictures. And because Chaplin's career was so long and influential, this section does not limit itself to the silent era. In addition to recognizing his huge cinematic impact, this chapter scrutinizes the major slight forever given to the capable nature of Chaplin's screen character. It makes for an excellent contrast with the antiheroic Bunny, a phenomenon further discussed in the following chapter. Moreover, to better facilitate an understanding of Bunny's persona, a brief comparison is done with W. C. Fields' similar (and later) screen character. (For more on Fields, see Chapter 3.)

JOHN BUNNY

It seems most appropriate that the man often considered America's greatest native-born film comedian (W. C. Fields) made reference to the country's first significant movie comic in his classic *Bank Dick*. And the sentiments in the quote that opens this chapter were truly Fields' words, though he wrote the movie under the inspired comedy pseudonym of Mahatma Kane Jeeves.

The *Bank Dick* quote is an indirect documentation of a Bunny comedy shtick item. Fields' character is taking credit for directing the comedian in a film called *Buying an Umbrella*. Bunny never appeared in a movie with that title, but Fields demonstrates an acute sense of the comedian's work, since several Bunny movies involve the obvious antiheroic potential involved in handling an umbrella, such as *Umbrellas to Mend, or Mr. Niceman's Umbrella* (1912) and *Who Stole Bunny's Umbrella?* (1912).

One might say Fields was footnoting the influence of John Bunny (1863–1915) on his own films. When examining the career of such a pivotal though less well-known screen pioneer, it is helpful to sketch the many parallels with a later, more familiar character like Fields (1880–1946). And when studying a groundbreaking historical figure, regardless of medium, the significance of the parallels is further underlined when the impact is easily discernible in Fields' later work.

While researching two books on Fields, I found the Bunny influence never more obvious than in the *Bank Dick*, as well as *It's a Gift* (1934) and *The Man on the Flying Trapeze* (1935), sometimes considered Fields' greatest films.[1] In the *Bank Dick* he plays comic antihero Egbert Sousé (pronounced Su-zay), saddled with a henpecking wife and an equally nasty mother-in-law. As we first meet the family, the latter complains to her daughter about that smoking "souse" of a husband. This is often the same plight of the antiheroic Bunny figure. For example, Bunny's smoking, drinking, and poker-playing in a *Cure for Pokeritus* (1912) always run afoul of his domineering wife (Flora Finch, his frequent screen spouse and/or nemesis). Finch's name also surfaces in the *Bank Dick*.

In contrast to the short, round, 260-pound Bunny (see Illustration 3), with his imposing "moon-faced" head and minimal neck, Finch's tall, angular form resembled the later Olive Oyl of *Popeye* comic strip fame. A period publication said Finch "took up no more room than a long darning needle."[2] Just as Bunny

3. John Bunny—America's first film comedy star—Fat, Funny, and Forgotten (c. 1915).

is considered the first significant American screen comedian, one might credit the Bunny-Finch duo as the first important film comedy team, predating the fat-skinny "couple" Laurel & Hardy by years. Fans referred to their movies as "Bunnyfinchers." Bunny and Finch represent the beginning of the domestic film comedy, a sub-genre that his Brooklyn-based movie company Vitagraph soon seemed to corner when the acting partnership of Mr. and Mrs. Sidney Drew joined the studio in 1912.

A later essay on Bunny likened Flora's appearance to the spinster types in Fields' movies so nicely described by the comedian as "well-kept graveyards."[3] In fact, his *Bank Dick* mother-in-law looks not unlike Finch. Thus, Bunny and Fields are comedy fifth columnists, generally working behind married lines (their own), as they attempt manly things with the "boys." And if it is not the basic carousing, there is always the work of sports, be it Fields sneaking out to a wrestling match in *The Man on the Flying Trapeze* (1935), or Bunny's fascination with baseball in *Hearts and Diamonds* (1914), which featured period stars such as future Hall of Fame pitcher Christy Mathewson, who played for the nearby New York Giants in Manhattan.

Though Fields never quite reached Bunny's weight, both comedians had an amusingly portly shape and a large, bulbous, veined nose. Both showcased their overindulgence in food and drink, whenever this contraband could be consumed, away from their domestic keepers.

Their real-life overindulgence in these areas shortened the lives of both actors. As a later Fields biographer said of the comedian and his friends (though it would also apply to Bunny), "They were their own executioners."[4] One might say their ultimate tragedy was inseparable from their triumph. For Bunny and Fields, this self-destructive tendency fueled the real-life men and their comedy personae. It reminds us how much art can cost and persuades us (not without sadness) that it is worth the price.

Though both performers are amusingly victimized by wives and in-laws, as was the male-dominated norm for early twentieth-century comic antiheroes, their films are also a tongue-in-cheek cry against social and moral pretension. This was frequently personified at that time by women overly concerned with religious, temperance, and upper-class aspirations. For instance, in *Pokeritus*, Finch attempts to reform Bunny's ways with the help of her Sunday school class; the Fields women of the *Bank Dick* are forever harassing him about their low standard of living.

This stereotype of wives was no doubt further fueled by the fact that Bunny's short film career (1910–15) paralleled the growing power of the suffragette movement. In a now very rare 1914 Vitagraph monograph titled *Bunnyisms*, the comedian observes, "A woman must stick to her job of home making. That's enough career for any woman."[5] (As a side note on Bunny's family life, he lived within walking distance of his studio, and his wife and two boys frequently accompanied this Brooklyn born and raised comedian on his stage tours.) Fields's movie heyday (the 1930s) coincided with another male-threatened era, the Great Depression. This was a period when many saw "the husbands' increasing dependence upon their wives to provide additional or even primary income for the family. . . [as] a rapid deterioration of the father's status."6

Bunny was the first in a long line of American screen comedians, both the most basic and the most obvious of comedy genres (see *Handbook of American Film Genres* 1988).7 The clown model is dependent on a front-and-center comic figure, or figures, around whom the loosest of storylines is fashioned. In keeping with this personality focus, Bunny's films frequently featured his name in the title, such as *Bunny and the Dogs* (1912), or *Bunny's Birthday Surprise* (1913). Indeed he later toured with his stage production *Bunny in Funnyland*, which exemplified this lack of story perfectly. For instance, an otherwise rave review described *Bunny in Funnyland* as following "no known rule of dramatic construction but spreads itself like a jellyfish over the evening. It is, like John Bunny, in a class by itself."8

This storyline of comedy convenience provides an anything-goes framework on which the film clown can "hang" his comic shtick. Thus, a John Bunny film stars a chubby, small-eyed antihero (his comically "homely face" was insured for $50,000),9 frustrated by a world over which he has no control, whether a dominating wife or the little individual banalities we all quietly (and sometimes not so quietly) suffer. A Bunny-produced smile of recognition about this seemingly irrational world grants the viewer a minor victory we might not otherwise have known.

When the *Bank Dick* appeared, Bunny was a well-known personality. Today only the clown comedy connoisseur recognizes the name, despite his ongoing significance to American film comedy. Moreover, it is difficult to fully under-line the global popularity of Bunny in the 1910s—a direct result of this new medium called moving pictures. In 1914 London's *Saturday Review* observed, "Not to know Mr. Bunny argues oneself unknown. . . . Mr. Bunny is a universal friend, and the most famous man in the world."10 That year, *American Magazine* reported on his global fame by way of the special names given him in other lands. Typical of the high praise to be found in these nicknames was the affectionate German reference for Bunny—*kintop*.11 This was period slang for the ultimate screen compliment, meaning he was "the movies." The French were more obvious in their similar honoring of Bunny, calling him "cinema." Appropriately, the article was titled "A Man Seen Daily by Millions," while the subtitle of the aforementioned Bunnyism monograph was "The Comedian with a Billion Friends." Because he was a pioneering media star, the *New York*

Morning Telegraph called him a "prisoner" of his frenzy-producing fame: "Mr. Bunny must not be seen in public except on the stage."[12]

At the beginning of movie history, comedy was dominated by the French, particularly performer-director Max Linder and director George Méliès. It was only in the second decade of the century that American film comedy began to take over the world market. In a 1915 interview, however, Bunny graciously acknowledged the unique talents of rival comedian Linder, someone he had now usurped in world popularity. When asked how many real artists there were in motion picture production, Bunny observed, "Well, Max Linder is a great comedian [despite never finding a large American audience]. But outside of him, I'm afraid twenty would be a liberal estimate."[13] Bunny also lent his comic genius to publicity. The *Philadelphia Telegraph* (March 20, 1915) reported the comedian had had his "homely face" insured for $50,000. With tongue firmly in cheek, Bunny expressed concern over the monetary danger of any "sudden beauty."

Comic publicity notwithstanding, Bunny helped elevate what was often considered a second-class medium to critical significance. Indeed, the lengthy 1915 biography article on the comedian in *World's Work*, "The Coquelin of the Movies," equated Bunny with the celebrated French stage actor-comedian Benôit Coquelin (1841–1909).[14] This tribute to Bunny's range was made before the comedian's untimely death at age 52 that year.

His elevation of the medium was most obviously keyed to his understated natural acting style—"the mastery of intricate facial expression and body movement."[15] At the time of his death, no less a publication than the *Times* of London praised this gift by way of his comic minimalism: "A twitch of his mouth provided laughter for the nations of the world."[16] This was no small accomplishment for a comedian who had performed much more broadly during his 23-year stage career, which included minstrel shows and comic opera.

A good example of John Bunny's understatement is best showcased by a closer look at one of his most critically and commercially popular films—*A Cure for Pokeritus*. As previously mentioned, the story pits Bunny's love of poker against a reformer wife, played by Finch. The antiheroic husband never does well at cards as an opening title states—"A game of poker. Loser again." Still one first sees Bunny contentedly immersed in playing and puffing away on his cigarette. As the game continues, he slowly gets up, retying his tie and putting on his suit coat. A black waiter, in what appears to be a men's private club, helps Bunny on with his top coat.

The reason for the early exit, though it is 1 A.M., quickly becomes apparent when Bunny slowly pulls an empty hand out of his topper—he has lost all his money and needs carfare home. With a modicum of hand and eye movement he gets the attention of the nearby club manager, who somewhat reluctantly (Bunny forever the antihero) advances the money.

Arriving home, he slowly lights up another cigarette outside the house. There is a sense of "Why hurry?" (enjoy one last smoke), an upset wife will likely be waiting up anyway. He tiptoes in, but Flora is waiting on the living room couch. Surprisingly, there is no ringing of hands or demonstrative behavior by either party. A defeated Bunny even sits down on the couch before Flora is aware of his return. She points to her watch and John has the hangdog expression of a guilty child caught once again. He reluctantly raises his hand in what seems a well-practiced manner and a title states—"I swear I'll never play again!" Fittingly, however, he has raised his left hand.

A week passes and Bunny's friend offers a solution to his problem. The antihero soon receives a letter written in elegant script—"You are elected to the membership of the 'Sons of the Morning' initiation Wednesday night. Meeting every Wednesday hereafter. Fine for non-appearance—ten dollars." (The organization's title possibly influenced the club name of "Sons of the Desert" used in Laurel & Hardy's 1933 feature of the same name. Appropriately, this film, the duo's best feature, also had them sneaking out on their wives for club activities.)

Bunny's demeanor as he hands the letter to Finch is pleasingly subdued (as befits a selection to a club). With an unaffected rubbing of his chin, he curiously watches Flora read the letter. She accepts the validity of the invitation and with a restrained smile Bunny happily leaves for the "meeting."

When the next club date occurs John casually feigns tiredness, but Flora strongly encourages his attendance. Out of her view he allows himself a chuckle. But Finch becomes suspicious, and the next week she has him followed by her effeminate cousin Freddie. This cousin's demeanor suggests that real men, á la Bunny, played poker and caroused. Flora's suspicions are confirmed and a scheme is hatched whereby Freddie's Sunday school class dons Keystone Kop-like uniforms and raids the next poker game. (Mack Sennett's famous Keystone Kops had first appeared the same year as this Bunny film, 1912.)

The "police" attack is subdued, unlike the speeded-up helter skelter entrance one expects of Sennett's Keystone Kops. Still, the poker players are surprised and Bunny (who has been winning for once!), sadly looks heavenward and mumbles to himself, as if asking the gods of comedy, "Why me?" His only demonstrative action is to make his hands into fists. But this move is inspired, for as a pioneering antihero, he is neither up to hitting anyone nor anything. When Flora then rushes in with a number of women (she has let the wives of the other players in on the raid), Bunny allows himself a modest smile at being rescued from incarceration. However, the shaking head that accompanies that smile would seem to imply he is merely returning to his domestic incarceration. Such is the life of Bunny's underplaying screen persona.

A period critic praised Bunny's understated comic skills, saying that he had shown how a "real actor can make an incredible success before this [film] audience without any of the vulgarity or horseplay which used to be considered essential."[17] Such vulgarity might be exemplified by an unidentified 1914 Mack Sennett-produced Charlie Chaplin picture, which critic James Agee described entertainingly in his Pulitzer prize-winning autobiographical novel, *A Death in the Family*: "Then he [Chaplin's tramp] flicked hold of the straight end of his cane and, with the crooked end, hooked up her [a pretty woman's] skirt to the knee, in exactly the way that disgusted [Agee's] Mama."[18]

This is the type of thing Bunny's screen alter ego might consider, but could never do. For instance, in Bunny's *Stenographer Wanted* (1912), the comedian is anxious to hire a physically attractive secretary, but his wife decides the position's major prerequisite should be ugliness, and applicant Flora Finch is hired. As the later antiheroic Fields might emulate, *Stenographer Wanted*'s last image of Bunny has him finding consolation in a stiff drink.

Bunny's henpecked cinema role represented a conscious toning down by the comedian of his sometimes more provocative stage work. For instance, in turn-of-the-century vaudeville his catch phrase was, "Here's to our wives and sweethearts; may they never meet!"[19]

Needless to say, Chaplin did not take long to find critics singing his artistic praises, too. But Bunny's comic underplaying, and stage ties that included classic works of Shakespeare and Dickens, helped give the fledgling cinema added credibility. Moreover, Bunny encouraged the screen adaptation of such works. In 1915 he noted, "Listen, I went to England [in 1912] and put in some of the hardest work of my life in producing [Dickens'] *Mr. Pickwick*."[20] And though Bunny's literary adaptations were critically and commercially success-ful, the comedian was the first to admit his public still most enjoyed the simple films that totally revolved around his screen character: "They [adaptations] haven't sold at all in comparison with these things I'm turning out every week."[21] Ironically, within a year of Bunny's death (1915), Vitagraph would move towards broad slapstick, especially as personified by the company's next comedy star—Larry Semon. Still, to Vitagraph's credit, they attempted (albeit unsuccessfully) to continue the Bunny tradition by utilizing his brother George and John Bunny's son, billed as junior. But their tries no doubt had more to do with box office profits than underplayed comedy. Yet, they were hardly alone. Such was Bunny's fame that as far away as Russia (a country soon to be torn apart by revolution) there was a failed attempt to find a Bunny replace-ment.

Another way in which Bunny helped elevate the critical recognition of early film was through his strong belief in this young and primitive medium. In a 1914 issue of *Pictures and the Picturegoer*, he commented on his 1910 film beginnings: "It seemed to me that the cinema—in America at least—was to be the great thing of the future."[22] Bunny felt this so passionately that he gave up a stage career in which he had "attained country-wide popularity as an actor" to try the movies.[23] In doing so he risked both his acting reputation and financial security; a publication noted in 1910, "There was still unbounded contempt for the new form of entertainment [film] among the [stage] professionals."[24] After originally offering his Brooklyn (Flatbush) hometown movie company, Vitagraph, a free film performance, he began at $40 a week, one-fifth of his theater salary. But his immediate 1910 critical and commercial screen success resulted in an ever escalating salary. At the time of his death in 1915, his salary matched that of President Woodrow Wilson—$75,000 a year, or nearly $1,500 a week.

An additional manner in which Bunny heightened early cinema's credibility was as the medium's first unofficial world ambassador. Years before the globe-trotting Douglas Fairbanks and Mary Pickford, he was received like royalty abroad: "In Paris, Berlin, and St. Petersburg the cry, 'There goes Bunny!' in as many respective languages, always greeted his appearance in public and was the tune that made of him a modern Pied Piper with a throng clamoring at his heels."[25] Bunny's international film star status was accented further by the shooting of several popular movies in England and Ireland during this 1912 European visit, in addition to *Mr. Pickwick*. Indeed, his work was in such demand that he even made a film while on board ship to the continent, *Bunny All at Sea*.

While abroad, fans were forever praising him for the universality of his appeal. For instance, in London a stranger told him, "I saw you in the movies in South Africa. . . and I tell you those black men over there just love you."[26] At the time of his death the comedian had hoped to take his *Bunny in Funnyland* stage production around the world because he "longed to see the [film] friends he had made in other lands. . . [particularly in Australia], where he had been told, he had friendships as warm and loyal as those in America."[27]

Bunny in Funnyland was a compendium of the comedian's entertainment career. Supported by a cast of 50, from midgets to a chorus of beautiful girls, Bunny was always a prominent feature in this sprawling three-hour musical comedy. It showcased a singing and dancing Bunny little known to his film fans. A key segment of *Funnyland* was a minstrel show that critics said showed "the strength of the entire company."[28] This was a special homage to the comedian's minstrel beginnings decades before, featuring such songs as "I'll Do

It All Over Again" and "All Aboard for Dixie." A Midwestern newspaper observed that "those who went out of curiosity just to see how good or bad a screen actor could be in a speaking part were agreeably surprised in the magnitude and excellence of the entertainment."[29]

But the pivotal segment of *Funnyland* celebrated the movies, and just as appropriately, it was a favorite with audiences. In the production's original late 1914 tour, the show began with a Bunny film in which the screen was positioned so that as the movie ended, the comedian seemed to literally step out of the screen—possibly influencing Buster Keaton's later celebrated *Sherlock Jr.* (1924). As the tour continued in early 1915, the show was streamlined; the entire second part of *Funnyland* focused on film. A stage reproduction of the comedian's Vitagraph studio was used to show how movies were made, with "Bunny in the flesh" (to quote period critics) eventually giving way to the comedian in a film. After Bunny, the movies were clearly the star of *Funnyland*.[30]

Besides these examples of Bunny's ability to help establish the medium's credibility, the comedian's general influence on the arts can be seen in a myriad of cases. For instance, pioneering film historian Terry Ramsaye credits Bunny with being "among the earliest players [who] really starred" in motion pictures.[31] And the comedian's phenomenal sucess in the early 1910s seems to have provided more than a little of the catalyst for George McManus' timing in introducing the famous comic strip *Bringing Up Father*. It featured the short, fat, henpecked Jiggs, always trying to sneak out for a night with the boys and his tall, thin, dominating wife, Maggie. The strip began in 1913, following the late 1912 media blitz generated by Bunny's European visit.

For all of Bunny's worldwide fame and popularity, he seemed to have been most beloved in heartland USA. The year before his death, the *Chicago Tribune* wrote, "His name is, without question, familiar to a far larger number of persons of all ages, lands, races, and tribes than that of any other actor in all the world today."[32] His Midwestern obituaries were more personalized, more prominently featured, and sometimes included the comments of local friends going back to Bunny's stage touring days.[33] The title of his *Indianapolis News* obituary probably demonstrated this poignancy best: "Men, Women and Children Lost Film Friend When John Bunny Died."[34] This truly was America's first important movie comedian.

CHARLIE CHAPLIN

"I am here today." Chaplin's popularity was so great in the teens and twenties that theater owners had only to display a cardboard image of the Tramp with this short statement to draw a large audience. Before examining the long-range impact Chaplin's art has had on film comedy and study, as well as on popular culture in general, it is important to underline the huge initial effect his comedy had on the public. One of the first world media stars, Chaplin enjoyed a popularity that was not limited to any one age group, as is often the case with performers today. While adults celebrated the Tramp in song and dance, the world's children had numerous jingles about their favorite figure. One jingle in Puerto Rico was about "Chali Chaplin" and kitties, and an English version was set to the music of "Gentle Jesus."[35]

His popularity touched off marketing schemes that are still with us. There were Charlie Chaplin lapel pins, hats, socks, ties, complete costumes, spoons, Christmas decorations, statuettes, buttons, paper dolls, games, playing cards, squirt rings, comics, dolls, and anything else on which his likeness could be reproduced. In his autobiography Chaplin also notes having been approached about diverse products such as Charlie toothpaste and Charlie cigarettes.[36]

"Chaplinitis" was fed all the more by countless other entertainers from assorted media who cashed in on Chaplin's popularity. Song writers cranked out such numbers as the "Chaplin Waddle," "Funny Charlie Chaplin," the "Charlie Strut," "Charlie Chaplin: The Funniest of Them All," and the "Chaplin Wiggle." In total there would be at least 20 Chaplin songs, with the most successful efforts being Leslie and Gottler's "Those Charlie Chaplin Feet" and Downs and Barton's "That Charlie Chaplin Walk."[37] Both vaudeville and film suddenly had an overflow of Tramp imitators. Stage versions included no less a figure than Chaplin's one-time Karno understudy, Stan Laurel, long before his teaming with Oliver Hardy. Chaplin's most capable screen copier was Billy West; other prominent film imitators included Billie Ritchie (another former Karno member) and Mexican actor Charles Amador, who even changed his name to Charles Aplin. Chaplin sued and eventually won a judgment against Aplin in 1925 that decreed Chaplin's Tramp suit and shuffle to be his own property.[38]

The world started to take on a certain "trampish" look. The Charlie mustache became the fad. Adults grew them, and children pasted them on or smudged charcoal on their upper lips; "his clothes, his boots, his postures and gait were all imitated by would-be humorists."[39] Always the connoisseur of beautiful women, Chaplin would later express bemused regret that even Ziegfeld Follies girls marred their loveliness with Charlie mustaches and baggy pants.[40] Moreover, theaters everywhere were capitalizing on the craze by having Charlie Chaplin look-alike contests. The winner of one such Cleveland competition was a youngster named Leslie T. Hope; he is better known today as Bob Hope[41] (see Chapter 4). As a lark, Chaplin himself is said to have entered one of these contests—and finished third. The saturation level of 1915–1916

Chaplinitis is nicely articulated in one of several Charlie jokes then making the rounds:

> "You appear worried."
> "Well, you see, I have two invitations to dinner. At one home the young daughter is learning to play the piano, and at the other the son gives imitations of Charlie Chaplin."[42]

While it was not possible to clone Chaplin himself, his early films, which he did not control, underwent a similar fate—they were constantly reissued with new titles to fool the public. This was especially true of his Keystone films, which came first both in chronology and quantity. For example, *The Rounders* (1914) later appeared under six titles: *Revelry, Two of a Kind, Oh What a Night, Going Down, The Love Thief,* and *Tip Tap Toe.* The *Property Man* (1914) knew five additional titles: *Getting His Goat, The Roustabout, Props, Charlie on the Boards,* and *The Vamping Venus.*[43] Additional Charlie films were created "by using a few clips and close-ups from old Chaplin prints and adding scenes done by imitators."[44]

Bunny's Vitagraph studio never grasped the concept of reissuing. Instead, as was the common practice then, the expensive nitrate film prints were often ground up to save money on the manufacturing of new Bunny films. This no doubt greatly contributed to the later obscurity of the comedian. Besides this loss of legacy, Chaplin's unprecedented rise, at approximately the close of Bunny's career, added to the near disappearance of the latter comedian in popular culture.

Chaplinitis enthralled intellectuals as well as the masses, bringing fresh interest to a fairly new art form struggling for recognition. Film critic and historian David Denby suggests, "In a sense, it was Chaplin who created film criticism, perhaps because his combination of slapstick and pathos was a recognizable art form—mime."[45] Historically, the beginning of serious Chaplin analysis is generally attributed to Broadway actress Minnie Maddern Fiske's 1916 article, "The Art of Charles Chaplin."[46]

The Fiske essay is important on two counts. First, she was a prominent member of the legitimate arts (theater, at a time when being in the movies was still often considered theatrical slumming), and her celebration of the comedian's skills helped establish a Chaplin-as-artist precedent. Second, she justified historically the only real complaint (from a group later defined as "middle-class elders"[47]) then still occasionally lodged against his work—that it had vulgar tendencies. Her defense observed quite correctly that broad comedy has always had a certain degree of vulgarity, whether it be a play by Aristophanes or a novel by Fielding.

Through the years a great number of important artists and film scholars have endorsed the Fiske stance. George Bernard Shaw observed that Chaplin was the only genius who had developed in motion pictures; noted historian Gerald Mast likened the comedian to a cinematic Shakespeare. Film critic Richard Schickel was moved to begin an essay on the comedian with a list of Chaplin accolades from the highest level of film comedians and scholars, adding, "One could fill an essay with such quotations and still have plenty left over, . . . [including] nearly every critic and every artist one respects."[48] Chaplin's greatest and most enduring impact has been on screen comedy. Even today he is the standard by which all film comedians are measured. His balancing of a successful comedy with moments of equally successful pathos has been difficult for other comedians to master. Film biographer Bob Thomas goes so far as to call the urge to accomplish this the "Chaplin disease," because so many have failed.[49]

The secret to Chaplin's continuing influence is better understood by examining his work in relation to basic traditions in American humor, an area in which little analysis has been done. A key factor in this neglect is the question: Is the Tramp essentially a capable or an incompetent comedy hero?

"Incompetent" would be the most obvious answer. In thinking of film comedy, one first sees a "little fellow" in baggy pants, derby hat, and floppy shoes shuffling down a dirt road. This image is also probably cinema's most famous icon: Chaplin's defeated Tramp going down still one more road as the film comes to a close. Certainly every student of film has a favorite variation on this theme, whether the dusty road of *The Tramp* (1915) or the abandoned grounds of *The Circus* (1928). Through film compilations and picture book anthologies of memorable screen moments, this image is well-known to the most casual of filmgoers. It is fully chronicled by film scholarship, starting with the dean of American film historians, Lewis Jacobs, for whom the Tramp was "a humble and pathetic figure in search of beauty, the butt of jests, harassed by poverty, the law, and social forces that he can neither understand nor resist."[50] All this is not to say that film scholarship has completely neglected the Tramp's capable side; however, 30 years after Jacobs wrote *The Rise of the American Film*, Raymond Durgnat still felt called upon to note that "so heavily has the stress been laid on Chaplin as waif, as a sentimental clown . . . and so on, that criticism has all but lost sight of the complementary pole of his inspiration."[51]

The bittersweet closing icon of the defeated Tramp has, therefore, become overextended. Defeat does not represent a fair commentary on all of Chaplin's Tramp films and film endings or even a sizable number of them. A close examination of the majority of his films, from the shorts at Keystone, Essanay, Mutual, and First National to the features at United Artists, Attica-archway, and Universal, indicates quite a different situation.[52]

Chaplin's Tramp milieu is much more likely to be upbeat, and despite his English background (and his fascination with Dickens), is heavily immersed in American humor. Chaplin adjusted quite readily to a country he found to be very much like himself, young and ambitious. Chaplin's close friend, writer Max Eastman, remembers the comedian saying quite early, "Of course, I am essentially American. I feel American, and I don't feel British—that's the chief thing."[53] Similar feeling would be repeated over forty years later in Chaplin's autobiography (1964), even after his experiences with McCarthyism. Because of the Tramp's immersion in American humor, if one were to divide American screen comedians into a simple dichotomy of "winners" and "losers," the Tramp would most definitely be in the former category. A film dichotomy of this nature would follow the traditional breakdown already established in American fictional humor, which gravitates toward two types. There is the capable, nineteenth-century "winner," often associated with "the Yankee," the beginning point of American humor; and the incompetent, twentieth-century loser, the comic antihero. The latter category first fully blossomed in the late 1920s in *The New Yorker* magazine, especially in the writings of Robert Benchley, Clarence Day, James Thurber, and S. J. Perelman and in the films of Leo McCarey's Laurel & Hardy.[54] (But John Bunny was playing the antihero in the teens.)

The antihero who tries to create order in a world where order is impossible is not new to American comedy; few comedy types are. This kind of antihero existed in earlier forms of American humor but usually not at center stage, which was reserved for the seemingly rational world of the capable hero.

Chaplin first appeared on screen in 1914, when the capable comedy hero was still dominant in American humor. Though some elements of the anti-heroic are no doubt in his work, the guiding comedy force throughout is that of the capable figure. The key exception would be the frustrations of *Modern Times*. Chaplin himself underlined the unique qualities of that film by the fact that he retired his Tramp character after it.

A thorough study of these two figures, the capable and the antiheroic, indicates that they differ in five essential ways. The capable type is usually employed, whereas the antihero has a great deal of leisure time. The former is involved in political issues; the latter ignores the subject of politics. The first is successful; the other is constantly frustrated. The hero is a father type; the antihero is a child figure. And finally, the capable figure is from the country and the incompetent is from the city.

To erase some of the Tramp's one-sided image as a defeated figure, it would be fruitful to examine him in relation to these five characteristics that differentiate the capable hero from the comic antihero. First, with regard to the Tramp's use of time, the logical choice would be to put him in the leisure class.

The stereotype of the Chaplin character would suggest that he is only a tramp; however, he is more often gainfully employed. Robert Sklar has stated, "No comedian before or after him has spent more energy depicting people in their working lives: his first motion picture was the prophetically titled *Making a Living*."[55] One might also add the title of one of Chaplin's Essanay films, *Work* (1915).

In Chaplin's Mutual films (1916–17), which rate special attention because they were made during "Chaplin's most fertile years, his most sustained creative period, . . . where he made twelve almost perfect comedies," he plays a fireman, a floorwalker, a carpenter, a pawnshop clerk, a waiter, and a police officer.[56] Moreover, *The Immigrant* (1917), another Mutual film, ends just as he and the heroine have acquired jobs. Much of the same occurs in his feature films, from his role as prospector in the *Gold Rush* (1925) to his collection of positions in *Modern Times* (1936): factory worker, maintenance apprentice, night watchman, and waiter-singer.

Even in *City Lights* (1931), where plot demands make more of an issue of his Tramp state in order to juxtapose him with his wealthy friend and with the blind girl's belief that she has a rich benefactor, employment still manages to be a major focus. The Tramp needs money so that the blind girl can have an eye operation. This need results in Charlie becoming first a streetcleaner and then a boxer.

The second manner in which Chaplin follows the characteristics of the capable figure is that his films often center on politics. One might call them a primer of social issues. This is particularly true of the Mutual films, which appeared at the culmination of the Progressive Era in America, 1897–1920, a time of great reform for individual rights.[57]

In 11 of the 12 Mutual films, Chaplin places the Tramp in situations that focus on (and possibly in the case of alcohol, capitalize on) Progressive issues. These films can be divided into five social areas: (1) urban corruption, *The Floorwalker* (1916) and *The Fireman* (1916); (2) the plight of urban poor, *The Pawnshop* (1916), *Easy Street* (1917), and *The Immigrant*; (3) the idle rich (not a specific concern of Progressives but a tangential area to both urban poverty and corruption, especially when contrasted with Chaplin's image of the poor), *The Count* (1916), *The Rink* (1916), and *The Adventurer* (1917); (4) elitism, *Behind the Screen* (1916), which endorses the antistrike stance of the Progressives; and (5) alcoholism, *One A.M.* (1916) and *The Cure* (1917).

Questions might be raised about the inclusion of alcoholism, since comedy and drinking go back to the Greek god of wine Dionysius and to the very origins of comedy. Chaplin also combined drinking with comedy in later films. Yet alcohol was a topical issue at the time the Mutual Films were made: Progressives favored prohibition, and in 1917 Congress passed the whiskey-limiting Lever Act and then the Eighteenth "Prohibition" Amendment, submitting it to the states for ratification. Given Chaplin's "understandable aversion to alcohol, which had brought such tragedy to his family,"[58] the subject of alcohol seems a legitimate final category of the Mutual films.

Not everything Chaplin did at Mutual fit smoothly into the Progressive mold. In *The Immigrant* (see Illustration 4) he plays upon irony in the promise of America and the Statue of Liberty, juxtaposed with the cattle-like treatment the newcomers received on their arrival. In this film Chaplin seemed to take a big-city problem, the plight of the underprivileged immigrant, too far for many Progressives. The typical Progressive was nativist and felt immigration restriction was the answer; legislation along these lines was eventually passed in the early 1920s. It is only fitting that Chaplin, the most famous immigrant of the day, should have expressed the plight of less fortunate immigrants.

Even, here, however, Chaplin appeals to the Progressives' anti-immigration stance, because other than the innocent heroine (Edna Purviance) and her mother, the immigrant passengers are portrayed in a comically negative light, as humor antagonists for Chaplin. Their behavior includes gambling, fighting, the drawing of a pistol, and the robbing of an elderly woman. Moreover, once Chaplin's immigrant character is in New York, he has no job and no money. It is only through the kindness of an artist that he receives employment as a model, a position one assumes can only be temporary. To many Progressives this sympathetic portrayal was an example of why they felt the immigrant was a burden on American society.

Chaplin's Mutual films represent a neglected comic survey of several Progressive issues at the very close of the era. Occurring too late to be called Progressive muckraking in the tradition of Upton Sinclair's *The Jungle* or Ida Tarbell's *History of the Standard Oil Company*, the Mutual films were instead a final summing up of what the Progressive Movement had tried to be.

Chaplin continued to touch on political stances in his later features. This is probably exemplified best by the close of *The Great Dictator*, where his Jewish barber, mistaken for the "great dictator" Hynkel, gives a speech against totalitarianism directly to the viewer. Yet it is only through the "Progressive" Mutual films that some semblance of a political form is brought to the broad-based humanism of Chaplin's films.

The third reason the Tramp is more logically placed in the realm of capable comedy is that he is generally successful at what he does; this also flies in the face of the image of the pathetic little Tramp. To examine his Tramp films closely is to discover a character generally so adept at the task at hand that the "loser" label seems to represent more of a taunt to his larger antagonists than a true description. In *The Rink* Charlie quite literally skates rings around his perpetual Mutual films antagonist, Eric Campbell. In *The Adventurer* even the

4. Charlie Chaplin in *The Immigrant* (1917).

police find him impossible to catch, in part due to his metamorphic abilities; at one point he loses them by imitating a hall lamp. Even in the most basic task, from carrying chairs in *Behind the Screen* to stacking bricks in *Pay Day* (1922), his skills are amazing.

The capable figure's comedy counterpart, the antihero, is most often frustrated by a wife and/or machines, as was John Bunny's character. Such frustration is generally not found in Chaplin films. Indeed, to break one more misconception, the stereotype of the Tramp as a loser at love is largely false. He consistently wins the heroine's hand, from the Mutual films with Edna Purviance to the later feature work with Paulette Goddard. These films also avoid what has become a traditional comedy promise, the battle of the "married" sexes, by seldom going beyond the courtship period.

Chaplin seems to underline this luck at love in the close of the Mutual film *Behind the Screen*, when, after Charlie has defeated the anarchist strikers and won Edna's heart, he steps out of character by facing the camera and winking at the audience, just after kissing Edna. It is as if to ask, "Was there ever any doubt?" Much the same effect is achieved at the close of the last Tramp picture, *Modern Times*, when Charlie goes down one final road, this time accompanied by a lovely gamine (Paulette Goddard). By now no wink is necessary to explain what the student of Chaplin has seen occur repeatedly—the girl usually belongs to the Tramp by the final fade-out. Exceptions, as in the solo close of *The Circus* (1928), are often a result of a deliberate decision by the Tramp to remain alone.

The Tramp's interaction with mechanical objects, the other usual frustration of his antihero counterpart, is more problematic, though his dexterity almost always wins out. Frustrating moments can occur, such as the alarm clock that suffers a fatal operation at the hands of Charlie in *The Pawnshop* or the debilitating conveyor belt of *Modern Times*. But for every such stumbling block there are numerous mechanical victories: the Chaplin cop of *Easy Street*, who so adeptly manages to etherize the giant bully (Eric Campbell) with a gas street lamp. Often when Charlie does not resolve a mechanical mess, such as the dismantled clock in *The Pawnshop*, it is because of a personal whim rather than incompetency; he has fun taking apart a customer's clock but has no particular need or desire to put it back together. In contrast, antiheroes like Laurel & Hardy would not have been able to put a clock together even if they wanted to (see Chapter 3).

With the exception of *Modern Times*, the film world of Chaplin's Tramp has not yet reached the mechanized world of Laurel & Hardy, and Charlie is not as surrounded by gadgets. However, as has been implied, if and when the Tramp desires it, he is quite capable. He flaunts this ability in *Police* (1916), when he breaks into an icebox as if it were a safe.

If the situation demands, Charlie is even capable of inventing mechanical gadgets, which is in the best tradition of Yankee ingenuity. The ability is exemplified by the day care center for one that he constructs in *The Kid* (1921). Anticipating the eccentric inventions Buster Keaton will later feature in some of his 1920s films, the Tramp's "baby machine" replaces the conventional rocker with a baby-sized hammock within easy access to a rope-suspended baby bottle, which is actually a converted coffee pot and rubber glove. Underneath all these contraptions, and under the baby's posterior, is a potty-chair fashioned from an old seat and a spittoon.

Appropriately, Mary Pickford's nickname for Charlie was the "Little Philosopher."[59] And though it might sound overly ponderous, Charlie has a pronounced tendency to philosophize, from the lecture on life he gives the suicidal millionaire in *City Lights* (1931) to the pep talk for the gamine at the close of *Modern Times*. Film titles make short work of both these and other examples (coming, as they do, from silent film), but seen in this manner, Chaplin's later, often controversially verbal, post-Tramp films do not seem so atypical.

Chaplin himself seems to underline his belief in the capable nature of the Tramp by the minor changes he made in the 1942 re-release of *The Gold Rush* (see Illustration 5). For example, where the original 1925 version had the Tramp mistakenly receiving an encouraging note from the heroine (her old boyfriend was playing a joke), in 1942 the editing at no time suggested an error had been made. Thus, the heroine's love for Charlie is established long before the concluding scenes, while in the original version it was uncertain until then.

Charlie as the master of most situations remains a much more defensible position. Celebrated Chaplin biographer Theodore Huff nicely summed up this finesse, as well as the comedian's tendency to place the character in professional settings: "Super-waiter, super-boxer, super-policeman, super-tightrope walker: . . . Chaplin's best efforts have been gained through super expert professional dexterity."[60]

The fourth characteristic, as the baby-oriented mechanics of *The Kid* suggest, is that the capable Tramp is also something of a father figure. Certainly there is a large dose of the child in all comics and in all comedies, and Chaplin's Tramp films represent no exception. Yet in his film interactions with society, the Tramp generally cares for others instead of being cared for himself, as the antihero must be. His relationships with women are constantly as father to daughter, protecting and caring for the waif-like woman, again in direct contrast with the often domineering female "bosses" of the antiheroic world, probably exemplified best in the works of Laurel & Hardy, or John Bunny.

5. Charlie Chaplin in *The Gold Rush* (1925).

This fatherly role is reiterated throughout Chaplin's Tramp career, with the most memorable example (after *The Kid*) probably being his care of the blind girl in *City Lights*. And it is in the celebrated *The Vagabond* (1916), which has been called "a prototype of *The Kid*,"[61] that his parental duties are most thoroughly marked out. The Tramp's fatherly treatment of Edna Purviance in *The Vagabond* also nicely contradicts one more cliché about Chaplin, that the girl in his films was always an idealized object on a pedestal. After all, taking care of a child is quite different from seeing someone on an idealized perch. In a wonderfully thorough scene on personal hygiene, Charlie vigorously washes her face, taking special time to roll a corner of his washcloth into a dipstick of sorts to get at the elusive ears and nostrils. He then proceeds to give her scalp a careful examination for fleas, not calling a halt to this extensive project until he has set her hair with homemade curlers. The film also presents Charlie at such parental tasks as fixing supper and setting the table. *The Vagabond* model anticipates his care of the girl in the often neglected feature *The Circus*, especially the scene in which he lectures her on the dangers of eating too fast. The Chaplin father figure misses few tricks.

The fifth and final characteristic that places Charlie more comfortably in the capable comedian category is that he seemingly is rural in origin. The world of Chaplin's Tramp, which is an outgrowth of pastoral America, depicts the nineteenth- and early twentieth-century view of the city, which as seen by rural America is a dirty, corrupt, and dangerous place. And as the earlier comments on politics and the Progressive Era suggest, Charlie constantly seems to be in the midst of this urban decadence. This focus is kept plausible because the Tramp often seems to be new to either setting, as an apparent stranger in a small rural town or as an immigrant to the city.

Much of the humor in these situations evolves from the quick-witted country Tramp's rapid adjustment to each new urban challenge, from curbing the street fighting of the *Easy Street* slums to passing as upper crust at the society masquerade in *The Idle Class* (1921). In probably his most pointed expression as a stranger in difficult circumstances, Charlie manages in *The Immigrant* to get a free meal in the toughest restaurant in New York (where giant Eric Campbell is the combination waiter-bouncer), to acquire a job, and to marry a beautiful woman, all on his first day in America.

As with the work of Charles Dickens, which always fascinated Chaplin for the parallels he saw between it and his own rags-to-riches story, his scenes in the country are equally significant; yet they are fleeting.[62] In contrast to the lengthy exposés of city problems and ugliness, the country scenes are times of restoration, safety, and female beauty. In *The Tramp* (1915), both the setting and the country girl who cares for Charlie's wound from the foiled robbery very much resemble the setting of *Oliver Twist* and Dickens' young Rose, who cares for Oliver's wound during his sojourn in the country after another bungled robbery.[63] As is to be expected, such juxtaposition favors the country, the place of the capable hero's origins and/or aspirations. And though no setting is without problems, such as the tough farmer in *Sunnyside*, with whom Charlie the hired man must contend, director Chaplin's image of the country is generally one in which the Tramp's "church [is] the sky and his altar the landscape."[64]

In considering Chaplin's use of the country in his films, an interesting coincidence between his real life and his art should be pointed out. In his autobiography he notes that just prior to his entry into film, his goal was to save enough money to buy himself a farm. Over 25 years later, in *The Great Dictator* (1940), Chaplin makes this the goal of Hannah, the girlfriend of the Jewish barber (Chaplin). The farm is to be their sanctuary from the Nazis. And though the film notes that by 1940 not even the country was safe from such dangers (another reason for the permanent exit of the Tramp earlier in *Modern Times*), director Chaplin continues to use the metaphor of the country as a haven.

It is appropriate that late in Chaplin's career he underlined the significance of the country by the title song he composed for the 1959 re-release of *The Pilgrim* (1923). It appeared, along with *A Dog's Life* (1918) and *Shoulder Arms*, in a special film compilation called *The Chaplin Review*. The song, "Bound for Texas" (which is repeated frequently in *The Pilgrim*), referred to being weary of the city and the factory and ready for the wide open spaces.

As a final postscript on the unique position of the country to Chaplin's Tramp, it should be remembered that numerous authors have seen the magic of Charlie in terms of a modern Pan. Nature often plays a key role in his films, whether it is the tree he hides in during *The Vagabond* (1916), or the tree he literally becomes in *Shoulder Arms*, where it is his disguise for reconnaissance.

Charlie as Pan is constantly suggested by the recurring image of a flower, which is almost as much a part of his costume as the derby and cane. Flowers often symbolize love to the Tramp, whether they are for dear Edna in *The Tramp* (1915) or the blind flower girl of *City Lights* (1931). And they also represent freedom, from the wildflower he plucks during his dance of Pan in *Sunnyside* (1919) to the equally wildflowers of the Mexican border close of *The Pilgrim*, when the sheriff releases him by having Charlie pick a bouquet across the border. But in general, like the single flower of Jean Renoir's classic *Grand Illusion* (made in 1937 by the renowned director who was greatly influenced by the comedian), the flower of a Chaplin film symbolized beauty in an otherwise gray world.

Because of the five characteristics enumerated here—the propensity of Chaplin's Tramp to be in a profession and to be political, successful, fatherly, and rural, all characteristics closely associated with America's capable comedy figures—the tendency to see the Tramp as only a defeated figure is misleading. Why, then, has this defeated Tramp image persisted? Herein lies the key to Chaplin's ongoing popularity and influence.

While the central impetus for the eventual ascension of the comic antihero in American humor took place in the 1920s, there were numerous antiheroic foreshadowings, in a host of media, that paralleled Chaplin's 1914 film beginning. These started with John Bunny's movie comedies, as well as the seemingly George McManus influenced comic strip *Bringing Up Father*. Another pertinent strip would be George Herriman's *Krazy Kat* (1913).

Chaplin's prefilm medium, vaudeville, offered its own antiheroic foreshadowing. In fact, in *American Vaudeville as Ritual* Albert F. McLean Jr. notes that again and again after 1900, critics implied that a "new humor" had developed in this country. And though he mentions other media, he gives the biggest nod to vaudeville, because it "was both the major market and the leading innovator in this revolution in popular taste."[65]

The primary manner in which this new vaudeville comedy seemed to anticipate the antiheroic comedy was in its focus on the city. Big industry had come to the cities, and behind it tens of thousands of immigrants, anxious for success (this group also constituted a large part of the early film audience). Yet as in Upton Sinclair's *Jungle*, few of these immigrants succeeded. Thus McLean suggests that urban-based frustrations created a demand for a "new humor": "The task of relieving . . . social tensions had been taken from the . . . dead-pan. . . . A whole new generation of comics, for the most part city-bred, . . . had sensed the utility of humor in oiling the psychic wheels of an industrial democracy."[66]

While Chaplin's comedy was of a capable character, it also embraced the problems of urban living, as demonstrated by its often markedly Progressive stance, portraying a rural and/or immigrant Charlie up against elements of the big city. Chaplin, of course, was more pointed in his look at urban frustration, and also allowed Charlie more room for success, or at least escape (down one more road). In contrast, antiheroic comedy depoliticized urban frustration, making it appear humorously inevitable, or at least more palatable, by packaging the problem in a world of comic absurdity. Examples would include Krazy Kat's love for Ignatz Mouse, who is forever creasing Krazy's head with a brick, only to be arrested by Offissa B. Pupp, the dog in love with Kat, or Laurel & Hardy's never-ending tit-for-tat battle with every aspect of the city, from mechanization to madness. Consequently Chaplin could capitalize on this key comedy element of urban frustration (with Charlie offered more of a chance for success) while still maintaining a screen persona based on the then more familiar and traditional capable comedian. With such a broad base of appeal,

Chaplin's legacy has had a phenomenal impact on film, both in its production and in the critical analysis applied to those productions, as well as on popular culture in general.

William Cahn's biography of Harold Lloyd, done in close collaboration with Chaplin's chief box office rival of the 1920s, observes:

> Chaplin's humor had an amazing effect on almost all the comedians of his era, and after. For many years, there was scarcely a comedian in the United States, and in many other parts of the world, who could operate without showing some of the [Chaplin] influences.[67]

Lloyd himself became established playing a figure named "Lonesome Luke" (1915–17), whom comedy historian Kalton C. Lahue has labeled "a sort of hayseed copy of Chaplin's character."[68] Lloyd did not perform a literal imitation of Chaplin, like Billy West and so many others, but his costume (which attempted to reverse the Tramp's baggy attire with tight clothes) and storylines were often reminiscent of Chaplin's rough-and-tumble comedies at Keystone. And even some of his post-Luke, early Lloyd horn-rimmed glasses films have strong parallels with previous Chaplin shorts. For example, Lloyd's *Fireman Save My Child* (1918) has much in common with Chaplin's *The Fireman* (1916), while Lloyd's *Pipe the Whiskers* (1918) draws from *The Cure* (1917). Lloyd, of course, eventually developed his own distinctive comedy identity, closely tied to the American success story, though today he is best remembered for the "thrill comedy" of such films as *Safety Last* (1923). But it is an excellent gauge of Chaplin's influence that one of silent comedy's pantheon members (Chaplin, Keaton, Langdon, and Lloyd) should have toiled so long in Chaplin's shadow.

Of these celebrated Chaplin contemporaries, however, Harry Langdon owed the most to Chaplin. Although he lacked the physical comedy capabilities of the Tramp, Langdon's mix of pathos and humor was second only to Chaplin's. Moreover, as Mordaunt Hall observed in his *New York Times* review of *Long Pants* (1927): "Mr. Langdon is still Charles Spencer Chaplin's sincerest flatterer. His short coat reminds one of Chaplin, and now and again his footwork is like that of the great screen comedian." [69] Appropriately, Langdon's greatest period of success, both critically and commercially, occurred during one of Chaplin's sustained absences from the screen. Mack Sennett, who gave Langdon his film start in 1924, just as he had Chaplin ten years earlier, has noted, "The two were the same in their universal appeal. They were the little guys coping with a mean universe."[70] The on-screen successes of their comedy persona are dependent, however, on a completely different set of circumstances.

Whereas Charlie's capabilities eventually pull him through, Langdon knows success only through the grace of God.

On occasion even the mature work of Lloyd and Keaton was not immune to Chaplin's influence. The success of *The Gold Rush* (1925) was so great that the next films by both Lloyd (*The Freshman*, 1925) and Keaton (*Go West*, 1925) seem to be consciously striving for Chaplin pathos. Their contemporary reviewer, Edmund Wilson of the *New Republic*, was so struck by this development that he re-evaluated his views of 1920s film comedy.

> And I prophesied [in a September 2, 1925, review of *The Gold Rush* that Chaplin, with his finer comedy [of pathos] and less spectacular farce, would not be able to hold his popularity against [the comedy of Lloyd and Keaton, but]. . . *The Gold Rush* has had a great success; and, so far from playing Chaplin off the screen, Buster Keaton and Harold Lloyd have taken to imitations of him. What is striking in their new films is the reduction of the number of gags and the attempt to fill their place with straight drama. . . . [They] have tried to follow Chaplin's example by allowing their comic characters to become genuine human beings.[71]

If Wilson had saved his overview on the influences of Chaplin's film until May 1926, he could have included the entire silent comedy pantheon, for that was when Langdon's *Gold Rush* derivative feature, *Tramp, Tramp, Tramp*, appeared. Not only its pathos but also the plot itself borrows from or plays on a number of scenes from *The Gold Rush*. Hall's review of *Tramp, Tramp, Tramp* focuses on three of the most obvious parallels: Langdon hanging by a mere nail from a dizzying height is reminiscent of the cabin-over-the-cliff scene in *The Gold Rush*, where Charlie opens the door and nearly strolls into nothingness; Langdon's frequent battles against a high wind occur just as frequently in the Chaplin film; and each film has a comic scene dependent on the flying feathers of a formerly stuffed pillow.[72] Hall might have added several other Chaplin similarities, from the on-the-road central theme (a cross-country foot race), to a heroine very much on a pedestal. Even the title, *Tramp, Tramp, Tramp*, reminds the viewer of Chaplin's most popular nickname (as well as occasionally fooling today's audiences into expecting Charlie).

Chaplin's impact on silent film comedy assumes an almost surrealistic quality when we realize that he was a major influence on the era's most celebrated cartoon figure, Felix the Cat. Anyone who has ever seen a Felix cartoon immediately recognizes the Chaplinesque qualities of the cat, from his ability to metamorphose himself and other items when necessary (his tail would become a cane) to the wickedly pleasing, direct-address grin and wink he periodically gave the viewer. Felix was even called "the Charlie Chaplin of cartoon characters."[73]

The chief animator for the original Felix film cartoons was Otto Messmer, who had previously worked on a cartoon film series of Chaplin. The former project had given Messmer "the opportunity to study Chaplin's pantomime and body movements, which profoundly affected his future work."[74] There is a delightful "in" joke reference to Chaplin in *Felix in Hollywood* (1922), where the cat does an imitation of Charlie, only to run into him and be accused of stealing.[75]

Chaplin's effect on film comedy did not end with sound. His routines have continued to footnote the films of other great comedians, from the Marx Brothers' use of the mirror sequence in *Duck Soup* (1933, employed by Chaplin in *The Floorwalker*, 1916) to recycled variations on the *Modern Times'* (1936) automatic feeder in Bob Hope and Bing Crosby's *Road to Hong Kong* (1962) and Woody Allen's *Bananas* (1971). More important, Chaplin's ability to mix comedy and pathos continues to be the film standard, especially in the later work of Jerry Lewis and Woody Allen.

Chaplin's influence on foreign cinema is equally immense. Nowhere is it more effectively shown than in French film, the second-most significant of all national cinemas, where it is best exemplified by the work of two great French satirists, René Clair and Jean Vigo. The latter died after completing only four films. Because Chaplin was a pivotal hero for both directors, their films are often not only infused with a Chaplinesque quality, but sometimes populated with figures made to look or act like Charlie. For example, in Clair's *The Imaginary Voyage* (1925), a lovesick young bank clerk dreams about a seemingly unattainable heroine (shades of Chaplin's *The Bank*, 1915). But after the fantasy assumes a macabre twist in a wax museum, the endangered hero is rescued when the figures of Charlie Chaplin and Jackie Coogan come to life. Celia McGerr, author of an excellent Clair study, calls the film's dream sequence "almost a homage to Clair's hero Charlie Chaplin."[76]

Chaplin's greatest compliment from Clair came, however, at a time when the French director might have embarrassed him. After *Modern Times* (1936) was released, the producers of Clair's *Liberty for Us* (1931) sued Chaplin for plagiarism. The 1937 suit claimed that Chaplin had borrowed material from the earlier film, especially the conveyor-belt sequence. But Clair refused to join his producers, Films Sonores Tobis, claiming that if there had been any borrowing he was flattered, since he had borrowed so much from Chaplin. Moreover, he stated, "My romance [*Liberty for Us*] is a typical Chaplin romance, only lacking his genius."[77] Films Sonores Tobis later dropped its suit.

How much, if at all, Chaplin was influenced by the sequence will never be known, but there is a most definite Chaplin stamp on numerous other elements of *Liberty for Us*. For example, a Chaplinesque central character, Emile, is comically proficient at kicking tails Charlie-style, yet he knows the pathos of thinking a girl's smile for another was meant for him (shades of *The Gold Rush*). Several other Chaplin touches occur before the stereotypical Charlie-down-the-road exit, this time by two characters (Emile and Louis) assuming the "occupation" of tramp.

While the Chaplinesque elements of various Clair films might be discussed at length (for example, *The Two Timid Souls*, 1928; and *Under the Roofs of Paris*, 1930), the shortness of Vigo's career necessitates focusing on his *Zero for Conduct* (1933). Vigo's film is set in a tyrannically run boy's school, where young exuberance is stifled by a martinet system. The boys revolt against regimentation, like so many young Charlies against the establishment. Appropriately, their joyful destruction of the dormitory, in a feather "snowfall" of broken pillows, seems drawn directly from Chaplin's own joyful feather "snowfall" in *The Gold Rush*. Moreover, the film's narrative makes the iconoclastic Tramp a natural hero for the boys, since the school's only sympathetic teacher manages a delightful imitation of Charlie.

The boys, who are secretly watching their teacher perform his Tramp impersonation, complement this Chaplin footnote by adding their own Chaplinesque response. Each time the teacher turns in their direction (he is shuffling back and forth à la Charlie), the boys duck out of sight, just as the street people responded to both Charlie and Eric in *Easy Street* (1917).

Vigo adds several other Chaplin footnotes, including the rooftop final exit of the boys, reminiscent of Charlie's chimneytop dexterity at the close of *The Kid* (1921). But the most amusing reference to the world of Charlie is Vigo's casting of a three-foot midget as the school's principal, a symbolic undercutting of authority just like the three-foot German commander in *Shoulder Arms* (1918).

Clair and Vigo are but two prominent examples of Chaplin's influence on foreign directors. A number of filmmakers might be mentioned, however, without even leaving France, from comedian-director Jacques Tati (the very name of whose delightful film persona, Mr. Hulot, suggests the French label for Charlie-Charlot), to the country's greatest director, Jean Renoir. In fact, Renoir pays constant tribute to Chaplin, whether in the story of an iconoclastic tramp in *Boudu Saved From Drowning* (1932, which opens with a tribute to Pan) or the *Modern Times*-ish conclusion of *The Lower Depths* (1936). Renoir's greatest film, *The Rules of the Game* (1939), makes direct reference to Chaplin's *The Count* (1916) by the manner in which it replicates that short subject's high society chase and confusion of identities. The French director even credited Chaplin with inspiring the theme of nonviolence in a Renoir film seemingly far removed from the world of the Tramp, *The River* (1950), which focuses on a disabled war veteran of India.[78] Therefore it is not surprising that Renoir states, after a momentous film career originally inspired by the Tramp, that "the master of masters, the film-maker of film-makers, for me is still Charlie Chaplin."[79]

Chaplin's influence on Italian film, the next most significant national cinema after those of the United States and France, has been equally impressive. This is best demonstrated by briefly examining two of Italy's greatest directors, Vittorio De Sica and Federico Fellini, both of whom were profoundly influenced by Chaplin. In fact, De Sica was doubly stirred by the comedian, since he considered his two teachers to be Chaplin and the Chaplin-influenced Clair: "Do you know that I am obsessed by two 'monsters'? They make life completely impossible. They are Charlie Chaplin and René Clair. . . . After them the cinema has become almost impossible! Those two discovered everything."[80] And Clair has gone so far as to return the ultimate compliment to De Sica by calling him "Chaplin's most authentic successor."[81]

While Chaplin often seems to pervade the De Sica world, whether in the folk fantasy of a *Miracle in Milan* (1951) or in the combination slapstick-pathos of an old man and his dog in *Umberto D* (1952—*A Dog's Life* thirty-four years later), the creator of the Tramp is even more strongly felt in Fellini films.

One has only to view *The Road* (*La Strada*, 1954) and the bewitching performance of Giulietta Masina (Fellini's wife) as Gelsomina, the clown-like servant to Anthony Quinn's strongman, to appreciate the depth of Chaplin's influence on Fellini. The film's mix of comedy and pathos, Masina's delightful mimicry, even the title—*The Road*—all suggest the world of Charlie. More specifically, one could define the character of Gelsomina, the lightheartedly loyal but ill-used servant, as a somber variation on the lightheartedly loyal Charlie of *City Lights*. Though Charlie is never so mentally simple as Gelsomina or so defeated (Gelsomina's eventual hurt destroys her will to live), both beautifully portray first the humor of complete devotion, and then the pain of rejection when that love is not returned. Appropriately, Fellini "singles out *City Lights* (1931) as a masterpiece among the silents."[82] The fact that Fellini made the fate of Gelsomina even darker than that of Charlie in *City Lights* might be explained by Fellini's favorite film—Chaplin's black comedy, *Monsieur Verdoux* (1947). Coming just a few years before *The Road*, Fellini considered this comedy of murders to be "the most beautiful film he has ever seen."[83] Yet there is no shortage of other Chaplin-flavored Fellini films, from the *Nights of Cabiria* (1956), with Masina's touchingly comic streetwalker who longs for love, to *The Clowns* (1970), which often evokes individual scenes from Chaplin films, as well as the inclusion of daughter Victoria Chaplin in the cast, as "homage to her father."[84] De Sica and Fellini are the most pivotal examples of Chaplin's followers among Italian directors, yet several other outstanding filmmakers could be examined. They include Pier Paolo Pasolini, especially in the *Hawks and the Sparrows* (1966), which was inspired by the early Chaplin films and features the Chaplin contemporary Toto; Lina Wertmuller, who often focuses on a Chaplinesque underdog fighting the system, such as in *The Seduction of Mimi* (1972); and Franco Brusati, whose *Bread and Chocolate* (1974) is constantly footnoted with Chaplin touches, while still maintaining an identity of its own.

Similar stories of Chaplin's influence are to be found in the histories of nearly all other national cinemas. Japanese film history, once obscure in the West because of cultural and political differences, is now one of the most celebrated of Asian film traditions here and often displays characteristics of the Tramp films. This is best shown in the works of Kiyohiko Ushihara, who studied with Chaplin in the mid-1920s, and Heinosuke Goshu, who was greatly moved by *A Woman of Paris* (1923) and the Chaplin-influenced *Marriage Circle*.[85]

Charlie's popularity also generated a number of Japanese imitations. But whereas this phenomenon had generally occurred elsewhere in the 1910s and early 1920s, *Chaplin! Why Do You Cry?*, a Japanese variation on *City Lights*, had a major impact in Japan as late as 1932. (Director Enjiro Saito generally maintained the Chaplin storyline, though the Charlie figure became a Japanese sandwich man.) Chaplin's popularity in Japan was assisted by the fact that he represented

> the personification of . . . [their] comic ideal. The kind of humor which allows one both to laugh and weep is particularly admired by the Japanese, and when Chaplin visited the country in 1932 the nation overwhelmed him with attention . . . . Even today Chaplin remains something of a national hero. His way of walking is still imitated, usually by sandwich men, appearing complete with cane, derby, and oversize shoes. Packed houses always greet a revival of *The Kid*, one of the early Chaplin films still playing in Japan.[86]

These, then, are some of the major filmmakers influenced by the comedy of Chaplin—filmmakers so moved as to footnote or recreate the mood of the Chaplin films frequently in their own works of art. Yet in addition to the unbelievably high standard he established for film comedy, Chaplin bequeathed to them an even greater heritage. He and Bunny gave the genre a legitimacy it had not had before, and Chaplin established a comedy production precedent of personal control that later film generations would label auteurism. Phrased more succinctly, Chaplin made it easier for the comedy filmmakers who followed him to do what they had to do—make people laugh. The fact that many ambitious comedy projects by bona fide auteurs later failed—for example, Stanley Kramer's *It's A Mad, Mad, Mad, Mad World* (1963) and Steven Spielberg's *1941* (1979)—merely underscores the intuitive comedy genius of Chaplin, who never lost sight, amid all that production power, of the need for a central hero to whom an audience could relate.

The Chaplin model has not been without other snags for prospective disciples. For example, some emulators of his pathos, such as Harry Langdon in *Three's a Crowd* (1927, after his split with Frank Capra) or Jerry Lewis in *Cinderfella* (1960), have mistakenly overplayed the sentimental, while providing no counterbalancing elements of character capability. Thus the viewer was apt merely to feel pity for these clowns, rather than smile the bittersweet smile normally reserved for the pathos of Charlie. It's interesting that the Bob Hope-influenced Woody Allen, whose film comedy persona is diametrically opposed to that of Chaplin's (the frustrated antihero versus capable Charlie), has probably followed Chaplin's behind-the-camera career model more closely than has any other major comedy filmmaker. Each realized early the need for both a consistent, easily identifiable character capable of generating sympathy and the necessity for production control via writing and directing as well as starring. Allen has long admired Chaplin for having the artistic daring to move beyond the security of the Charlie films: "What happens with a more serious artist, like Chaplin, is you try to do other things. You don't go to your strength all the time. And you strike out so people think you're an ass or pretentious, but that's the only thing you can do."[87] (Audiences also resent change in their stars because it represents change in their orderly, oversimplified, idealized past.)

In films like *Manhattan* (1979) and *Stardust Memories* (1980), Allen attempted to move beyond the antihero, just as Chaplin attempted to move beyond Charlie with films like *The Great Dictator* (1940) and *Monsieur Verdoux* (1947). (See my book *Dark Comedy: Beyond Satire* (1996), for the pivotal importance of Chaplin's *The Great Dictator* and *Monsieur Verdoux* on cinematic black humor.) Also, as with Chaplin's production of *A Woman of Paris* (1923), Allen felt a need to prove himself artistically by writing and directing a serious film in which he would not appear. *Interiors* (1978) was the result, a critical success unattended by the American masses, just as *A Woman of Paris* has been. Allen is still an active filmmaker with , it is hoped, many more productions to come. Yet regardless of the direction these productions take, it seems safe to assume that he will continue to look for the artistic challenge, just as Chaplin always did.

Chaplin's influence on cinema has not been limited to filmmakers. He has had an equally significant impact on the history of film theory and critics. In the infancy of the medium his work helped give film the artistic legitimacy to be written about, as well as a standard with which to gauge other performers.

In the years since then, authors from every possible methodology have attempted to include Chaplin's art in their camps, as well as frequently illustrating their systems via the comedian's films. And though this has resulted in many valid insights, the seeming need to utilize Chaplin has also created many provocative twists of their methodologies in order to accommodate the Charlie persona, or the persona has been bent to better match the given "ism."

This theoretical fascination with Chaplin is best demonstrated in film study by probing the work of five pivotal film theorists: Rudolf Arnheim, Sergei Eisenstein, Béla Balázs, Siegfried Kracauer, and André Bazin. In each case Chaplin's unique effect on film has inspired both insights and theoretical gerrymandering.

Arnheim, the traditional standard-bearer for formalist film theory, which accents the media over the subject, was fascinated with Chaplin's comedy, referring to it at length over a dozen times in his *Film As Art* (1933). He justified this fascination from four different perspectives, which I have labeled (1) traditional formalism; (2) forgiven primitivism; (3) forgotten rules; and (4) denial of sound.

First, Arnheim's greatest praise for Chaplin's comedy occurs when the comedian displays formalistic tendencies, for example, whenever Chaplin displays a self-conscious use of the film medium. Arnheim's two primary examples focus on comic surprise though camera placement: the apparently seasick Charlie leaning over the side of the boat (his back to the camera) in *The Immigrant*, and the backside of what appears to be a sobbing husband, whose wife has left him, in *The Idle Class*.[88]

In both cases Charlie soon turns around and completely negates what the viewer has been tricked into assuming by the camera placement. In the first example Charlie has been fishing, and a rather healthy bite has necessitated that he lean over the side to pull it in. When he turns around, you meet a proud fisherman instead of a seasick Tramp. In the second case of the apparently sobbing man who has lost his wife, Charlie's turn reveals that he is preparing some drinks in a cocktail shaker, without a thought to sadness.

Arnheim is impressed with this formalistic filmmaking technique, which he emphasizes by making it the first rule of his "Summary of the Formative Means of Camera and Film Strip," stating that "Every Object Must Be Photographed from One Particular Viewpoint!"[89] Yet in relation to Chaplin's style, Arnheim is misleading. He would seem to suggest that such formalistic techniques as camera placement dominate the comedy situations in Chaplin, when just the opposite is true.

The Chaplin style is essentially that of realist. His mime ability was so great, his interaction with props so versatile, that he generally found it necessary to shoot the majority of his scenes in long take and long shot and direct camera placement to underline the fact that he alone, the performer, was the cause of this veritable comedy magic. To have overindulged in editing and tricky camera placements would have shed doubt on what were indeed real Chaplin skills.

Arnheim indirectly acknowledges this fact by his second justification for embracing the Chaplin milieu, which I have labeled "forgiven primitivism." Chaplin's dominant realistic tendencies are explained away as part of a very early period of cinema history, as "a film style before the 'discovery' of the camera and montage. In these early films, camera and montage serve mainly as technical recording devices for what is acted out on the scene, and are therefore unessential."[90]

Arnheim's phrase for this early film state is "pre-technology." Thus he is in the awkward position of dismissing Chaplin's comedy production know-how as somehow primitive, just after praising the comedian for comedy technique that is formalistic and therefore superior, according to Arnheim.

This qualifying strengthens the misconception that Chaplin, as well as "early American film comedies" in general, were limited in their technical production abilities, that Chaplin was a comedy artist despite this primitivism. Arnheim neglects to explain why Chaplin continued this "pre-technology" approach throughout his lengthy career, long after he should have seen the formalistic light.

Arnheim's third justification goes beyond even the rather tenuous nature of the first two, as I have suggested with the phrase "forgotten rules." Arnheim praises Chaplin's ability to create "unexpected associations. . . between very divergent objects," the prime example being drawn from *The Pawnshop.* Charlie as assistant to a pawnbroker examines the alarm clock brought in by a customer as if he were a doctor examining a patient. "He puts a stethoscope to his ears and listens to the clock ticking (heartbeat-clockwork), then . . . [he] takes off the back with a can opener (food can-alarm clock)."[91]

These "unexpected associations" are one cornerstone of Chaplin's comedy art, his ability to transform any object into something else. In recognizing this phenomenon Arnheim has departed completely from his formalistic shaping process and embraced a realistic subject, complete with minimal editing, long takes, and long shots. Whereas before he seemed to bend his rules for Chaplin, at this point he breaks those rules. His apparent defense of this inconsistent stance is that a Chaplin comedy transformation of an object is comparable to the editing process itself.

It is with Arnheim's fourth Chaplin justification, his position on sound, that he is on his most solid ground, though the theorist does not expand on this greatly. Arnheim opposes the addition of sound to motion pictures, with which Chaplin had concurred by keeping the comedy world of the Tramp silent, although both acquiesce on the use of sound effects. Chaplin had even written more than one defense on the aesthetics of silent cinema (the most well-known being "Pantomime and Comedy," 1931).[92] This Chaplin work no doubt influenced Arnheim's film theory book (it predates *Film as Art* by two years) and might explain Arnheim's reluctance to expand on the point, since Chaplin had dedicated a well-known essay to it.

To defend film as art, as opposed to simple recording, Arnheim underlines the nonrealistic tendencies of film and denies the use of technical innovations of a realistic nature, such as the addition of sound or color, as well as the deployment of realistic techniques such as long takes and long shots: "For Arnheim, every medium, when used for artistic purposes, draws attention away from the object which the medium conveys and focuses it on the characteristics of the medium itself."[93] The film artist must concentrate on the visual and translate any message into this form. If it cannot be translated into the visual, it is not meant to be a film. When it can be translated, the limitations placed upon the medium—in this case, the absence of sound—act almost as a strainer; they create a purified statement. The same formalistic argument could be used to explain why sculpture is not painted.

For Arnheim the silent cinema was just such a purified medium, and with Chaplin, speech is translated into purified pantomime: "He does not say that he is pleased that some pretty girls are coming to see him, but performs the silent dance, in which two bread rolls stuck on forks act as dancing feet on the table (*The Gold Rush*)."[94]

It is only with this last theoretical stance on sound that Arnheim used Chaplin's comedy art as a truly legitimate example in the sense that it was typical of the comedian's work. Otherwise, Arnheim is rather "creative" in his use of a favored artist to showcase his theory.

The second major theorist to consider is Sergei Eisenstein, whose initial writings and film work first appeared in the 1920s, predating Arnheim. I have placed him second, however, because Eisenstein, also a formalist, did not really come to grips with Chaplin theoretically until late in the 1930s, specifically in the essay "Word and Image" written in 1939.[95] Prior to this, Eisenstein's work is most often associated with a montage of collision, his unique approach to film editing.

For Eisenstein the editing process is what makes film an art form. But instead of what was, in the 1920s, the traditional approach to editing—the linking of content-related shots of film to advance a narrative—Eisenstein placed con-flicting shots together—hence, collision—to produce a new meaning. For example, in his film *October* (1927) he shows Kerensky of Russia to be pompous by juxtaposing his image with busts of Napoleon and, later, a peacock.

Such an approach to film as art has little to do with the minimal editing of Chaplin's long-take work. J. Dudley Andrew has noted: "Early in his career [1920s] he [Eisenstein] chided filmmakers who used extensive takes. What could be gained by continuing to gaze at an event once its significance has made its imprint?"[96] Thus there is little of Chaplin in Eisenstein's early theoretical writings. Only later, with Eisenstein's revision of his montage approach in "Word and Image" (also known under the more self-explanatory title of "Montage 1938"),[97] is Chaplin legitimized in Eisenstein's theory.

Eisenstein's revised look at montage, no doubt due in part to the Soviet government's disapproval of his 1920s formalism, negates traditional editing and concentrates on the movements of the film actor. These individual actions of the performer constitute, for Eisenstein, a metaphorical sense of montage. Appropriately enough, at the time that he was turning his traditional approach to montage upside down, his definition of this new montage of acting was based on Chaplin. Eisenstein quoted George Arliss on "restraint" versus "exaggeration" in screen writing, with Arliss using Chaplin as the ideal example of screen acting.

> I had always believed that for the movies, acting must be exaggerated, but I saw in this one flash that restraint was the chief thing that the actor had to learn in transferring his art from the stage to the screen. . . . The art of restraint and suggestion on the screen may any time be studied by watching the inimitable Charlie Chaplin.[98]

Arnheim seems to have anticipated Eisenstein's "Montage 1938" by several years when he cited the fun-house mirror scene in Chaplin's *The Circus* as an example of the comedian's surprising and amusing multiplication of man without montage or lens distortion.[99] The scene refers to a house-of-mirrors chase, with Charlie being pursued by a pickpocket who has planted stolen goods on the tramp and now wants the goods back, and a cop who thinks Charlie did the stealing. Although there are several hilarious interactions, Arnheim's reference is to the relationship between Charlie and the pickpocket. When each makes his move, Charlie to escape and the pickpocket to reclaim the stolen goods, there are suddenly, due to the mirrors, innumerable Charlies and pickpockets in the frame.

A montage of acting, though not without interest, severely stretches the formalistic positions of both Arnheim and Eisenstein by its propensity for the long take. Indeed, when one compares Eisenstein collision montage with his acting montage, there is a temptation to rechristen the latter self-indulgent montage. Both Arnheim and Eisenstein kept Chaplin at the center of their proofs.

The third major theorist, Béla Balázs, whom Andrew (1996) has shown to be the transitional figure between formalism and realism, is more sympathetic toward the comedy art of Chaplin. Balázs' writing has less of a tendency to be bound by iron-clad rules, other than his weakness for the close-up. There are, however, several Chaplin justifications that can be fallen back on if friction occurs between his theory and the art of the comedian.

First, as with Arnheim's pretechnology statements, which I labeled forgiven primitivism, Balázs is not as critical in his demands of early slapstick, in which he includes early Chaplin: "Thus a definite variety of film art [slapstick] with a distinctive style of its own was born before the specific new method of film art and the new form-language of the film was developed."[100]

In speaking of the primitive comedy chase, he approaches the appealing though questionable implications that the chases cannot be critically examined, due to inherent properties not unlike the universal appeal of children and animals in film.

Second, Balázs praises the unique art form of silent cinema, paralleling the sentiments of Arnheim and Chaplin: "A glance from . . . Chaplin spoke volumes—more than the words of many a good writer."[101] Yet Balázs verged from Arnheim's strict path in that he did not deny technological progress in motion pictures, such as sound, as long as it was used in a formalistic manner.[102] Balázs states: "If Chaplin's last [Tramp] films were nevertheless great artistic achievements, they were so not because of their silence but in spite of it. There was nothing in these films which would have justified their silence as an artistic necessity."[103]

But Balázs does not hold Chaplin to this. He fleshes out in detail the reasons for this exception: "Charlie, the little man, would have had to invent some specific manner of speech which would have been as different from the speech of other men as his appearance was different from the appearance of other men."[104] This exception, with regard to Charlie's need for silence, surfaces again in what one might expect to be another factor in Balázs' praise of Chaplin, the close-up.

For Balázs the close-up is a guide to the human soul, to a special humanistic truth—it is the equally special gift of the art of film.

> The language of the face cannot be suppressed or controlled. However disciplined and practisedly hypocritical a face may be in the enlarging close-up we see even that it is concealing something, that it is looking a lie. . . . It is much easier to lie in words than with the face and the film has proved it beyond doubt.[105]

Balázs, who refers most movingly to the human close-up as a "silent soliloquy," has to be called "the poet of the close-up."[106] However, even here

Balázs is willing to make exceptions in the name of Chaplin. Balázs forgives the technical limitations and general lack of close-ups in *Modern Times*; as noted earlier, he felt Chaplin needed to avoid any apparent mechanical problems that the lack of sound would have suggested in dramatic close-ups.

Balázs' final and yet most consistent line of support between his theory and his inclination to praise Chaplin focuses on the comedian as one of the first true personalities of the screen, someone who played himself. The art of film, for Balázs, is closely tied to viewer identification with the performer, and no one better symbolized this for the theorist than Chaplin.

> If Charlie Chaplin came to be the best-loved darling of half the human race, then millions of men and women must have seen in his personality something. . . that lived in all of them as a secret feeling, urge or desire, some unconscious thought, something that far transcends the limits of personal charm or artistic performance.[107]

Siegfried Kracauer, the fourth major theorist we will consider, is a realist, as the title of his work so elegantly phrases it: *Theory of Film: The Redemption of Physical Reality* (1960). Formalistic theory had largely dominated film study until that time, with the result that film realism was often neglected or discredited. Since the comedy art of Chaplin more generally falls in the realist camp, due to such techniques as the long take and the long shot, one would expect many predictable points of agreement from Kracauer. Yet what the theorist writes, though in praise of Chaplin, is often hardly predictable.

The ability to surprise the reader is best exemplified when Kracauer deals with fantasy and Chaplin; for example, the theorist is especially taken with the Tramp's dream of heaven in *The Kid*, which he describes in a quote from Theodore Huff's *Charlie Chaplin*.

> The grimy slum court is transformed into a place of celestial bliss, with its inhabitants posing as white-clad angels; even the little dog grows wings, and the bully plays a harp as he flies about with the others between the flower-decorated facades.[108]

Because this dream is a parody of heaven and Chaplin underlines its staginess, Kracauer praises it in realistic terms: "Their very staginess denotes that they spring from a primary concern for physical reality."[109]

Kracauer, who has little time for editing and is enamored of the long shot (Chaplin realist specialties he does not deal with), truly seems to seek the controversial in the Chaplin scenes he chooses to justify. Thus, in addition to "realistic" fantasy, Kracauer is also capable of interpreting Arnheim's formalistic camera placement as realistic debunking, right down to using the same Chaplin example. That is, Kracauer uses, as Arnheim did, the scene from *The Immigrant* in which Charlie appears to be seasick but is actually fishing. But whereas Arnheim focuses formalistically on the initial ability of the camera placement to fool the viewer, Kracauer keys on the eventual truth (reality) the camera placement shows. For Kracauer it is a realistic task to "make you see."[110]

Kracauer is also a realist hesitant about the use of sound; in a section titled "Speech Undetermined From Within," he praises the opening of Chaplin's *City Lights*, in which the comedian substitutes distorted sound for the speech of a pompous city official.[111] Kracauer is afraid of a "theatrical" situation, in which dialogue would displace the visual. Sound for Kracauer should reinforce the visual, which is just what the Chaplin example does. Yet Kracauer is quite capable of reversing himself to include another favorite comedian, the highly verbal Groucho Marx, in his film theory. He justifies Groucho's dialogue along the same sound-distortion lines as he does Chaplin's speech in the opening of *City Lights*. Kracauer's theory echoes those of the formalists already examined; thus, Andrew writes, "Kracauer's realism was as cautious and conservative as Balázs' formalism was."[112] Indeed, Kracauer is also quick, despite this cautious realism, to support Chaplin's decision to keep Charlie silent. "Realist" Kracauer seems most adept at praising the nonrealist aspects of the comedian.

The fifth and final theorist, André Bazin, is much more a realist in the conventional sense of the word. His praise of Chaplin's comedy is also the most consistent of all the theorists, in relation to the theoretical models each man established. The close of Bazin's 1958 essay, "The Virtues and Limitations of Montage," is also the seminal statement on Chaplin's comedy production techniques:

> If slapstick comedy [early Chaplin] succeeded before the days of Griffith and montage, it is because most of its gags derived from a comedy of space, from the relation of man to things and to the surrounding world. In *The Circus* Chaplin is truly in the lion's cage and both are enclosed within the framework of the screen.[113]

Only with Bazin has Chaplin's comedy of space, his use of long shot and long take, become legitimate in film theory. Chaplin's film world would not exist with traditional editing; it distracts both from the unique ability of his mime and the equally unique setting, such as Bazin's example from *The Circus*, where Chaplin and the lion occupy the same film frame. In either case, the comedy is heightened because we know Chaplin is performing the routine or actually taking the risk, as in entering the lion's cage. Editing would have made us question this. Chaplin's decision to film in long shot and long take was wise technically and represents his production awareness of the most effective form of presentation for his comedy art. Bazin thus reverses a trend that seems to have started with Arnheim: to applaud Chaplin despite what was seen as his technical limitations and/or applaud him for his relatively rare formalistic techniques, such as the "seasick" scene from *The Immigrant.*

Bazin's "reality" is open-ended and clothed in ambiguity. Ambiguity serves as a key term for both the theorist and Chaplin. According to the theorist, everything about Chaplin's Tramp speaks the language of ambiguity. Even his classic kick is open-ended: "It is significant that Charlie never kicks straight ahead."[114] Moreover, Bazin finds any and all objects in Charlie's world ambiguously vulnerable in many ways. Ambiguity in this case is most significant in terms of what Arnheim called "unexpected associations," Chaplin's ability to transform any object into something else. But instead of using questionable parallels with montage in order to include unexpected associations within an Arnheim-like formalistic theory, Bazin merges them quite logically with his ambiguity of realism: Chaplin puts things "to multifarious uses according to his need at the moment": "The street lamp on *Easy Street* serves the function of an anaesthetist's mask to asphyxiate the terror of the neighborhood. . . . In *The Adventurer* a blind [lamp shade] transforms him into a lampstand, invisible to the police."[115]

Bazin closes his examination of the ambiguous nature of Chaplin objects with the "dance of the rolls" from *The Gold Rush,* one of Arnheim's examples in his formalistic explanation of the comedian's ability to "metamorphose" an object.

A major emphasis of Bazin's theory, however, focuses on what could be called the "myth of Charlie": "Charlie is a mythical figure. . . . For hundreds of millions of people on this planet he is a hero like Ulysses or Roland in other civilizations."[116] Bazin even titles one of his essays "The Myth of Monsieur Verdoux."[117] *Monsieur Verdoux* was one of Chaplin's later films and is generally considered outside the Charlie/Tramp milieu.

Bazin's concept of the "Chaplin myth" has much in common, it would seem, with Balázs' interest in the true personalities of the screen, those who consistently played themselves while generating viewer identification. Bazin notes:

> In less than fifteen years [1914–28], the little fellow with the ridiculous cutaway coat, the little trapezoid mustache, the cane, and the bowler hat, had become part of the conscious of mankind. Never since the world began had a myth been so universally accepted.[118]

But whereas Balázs uses this cult of personality as an end in itself, Bazin attempts to expand this cult of myth into less-studied Chaplin territory, what is usually considered the post-Charlie/Tramp films, such as *Monsieur Verdoux* and *Limelight*. By so doing, Bazin is able to produce a greater perspective on these late Chaplin characterizations, as well as to explain audience identification, no small accomplishment when one of the characters, Verdoux, is a very active Bluebeard:

> It is the character [of Charlie in Verdoux] that we love, not his qualities or defects. The audience's sympathy for Verdoux is focused on the myth [of Charlie], not on what he stands for morally. So when Verdoux, with the spectator on his side, is condemned, he is doubly sure of victory because the spectator condemns the condemnation of a man "justly" condemned by society. Society no longer has any emotional claim on the public conscience.[119]

Bazin's use of myth, however, seems to stretch the configuration of his realist theory. This Chaplin myth is, after all, a romantic notion that necessitates prior knowledge of the phenomenon of Charlie when screening any one of the comedian's films. If *Limelight* were the first Chaplin film a viewer had seen, that individual could not draw upon the myth, at least not as fully as could someone who had viewed more. Bazin acknowledges this fact, which he seems to address in two ways.[120]

First, Bazin notes that there is more to *Limelight* than the applied myth. He sketches a corollary more closely tied to realism: Chaplin plays his role of Calvero, an aging former music hall clown, with such intensity that the viewer recognizes the real Chaplin story. Bazin calls this "an example of transposed autobiography."[121]

Second, and rather indirectly, he bolsters the reality aspect of the myth by emphasizing "the unique position of Chaplin, the universality and vitality of his myth."[122] When the myth of Chaplin is seen as that pervasive, everyone could be realistically touched by this comedy icon. Whether everyone is so touched remains open to question.

Bazin's defense of the myth concept points toward one last weakness in the Chaplin segments of his theory: praise to the point of overkill, even beyond Balázs' cult of personality: "Alongside *Limelight*, all other films, even those we most admire, seem cut and dried and conventional."[123] Bazin is even capable of justifying boredom in Chaplin's *Limelight*: "It becomes apparent that even the boredom one might experience enters mysteriously into the harmony of the over-all work."[124]

The five main film theorists on the comedy art of Chaplin embraced parts of the Chaplin milieu, the scholarly "Chaplinitis," even when doing so proved to be inconsistent with the general guidelines of their own theories. Even Bazin, who maintained the most consistency between his praise of Chaplin's comedy and his own theory, had a tendency to overreact.

The theorists examined some viable comedy reasons behind the film production and aesthetics of Chaplin's work, even though a premise for most of these reasons rarely appeared in a Chaplin film. The one major overview to surface is the main thrust of Bazin's theory. With Bazin, and his celebration of realist cinema, Chaplin's comedy of space—so dependent on long shot and long take—finally had a legitimate champion in the realm of film production and aesthetics. Only then was Chaplin's technical awareness of the most effective form of presentation for his comedy art adequately explained in a single film theory.

The varying positions of the five theorists might best be linked by Balázs' statement on the cult of personality, for each theorist seems to have new Chaplin comedy examples and/or new interpretations of the same Chaplin examples, all pointing toward Chaplin's Tramp being cinema's most popular character, regardless of genre. Any further agreement among the theorists would probably be limited to one statement: Everyone makes room for Charlie.

As was the case with the Chaplin-influenced filmmakers, there are just too many similarly moved cinema theorists and critics to attempt to name all of them, or even a sizable percentage. But the five cited, Arnheim, Eisenstein, Balázs, Kracauer and Bazin, have historically had the most sustained impact of film theorists and were the most creative in their ability to utilize Chaplin as an example or a proof of a given axiom.

Chaplin's amazing impact on film comedy and film study is easily matched, if not surpassed, by his influence on a popular culture. The Tramp icon that promoted so many marketing schemes in the teens and twenties remains very much alive today. One can still buy everything from Charlie playing cards to Charlie music box figurines, which twirl to the tune of the Chaplin-written "Smile," from *Modern Times*. Moreover, his image, or its interchangeable coat of arms (various arrangements of Charlie's oversized shoes, cane, and derby) continue to be appropriated for a wide variety of subjects, from a video and print ad campaign for computers to a logo for a chain of comedy nightclubs.

The symbol of Charlie has become what the record industry has long labeled a "hook," a subject that is immediately recognizable and that exerts an equally direct emotional response. And Charlie represents the most effectively complex of symbols. Thus he can be used in the most logical manner, as the emblem of what a comedy nightclub is striving for (laughter), or on a more abstract level, he can bring warmth and humanity to an ad campaign for the most cold and mechanical of products, the computer. And all this takes place decades after the last Charlie film was made and years since the death of his creator.

"Chaplinesque" has become a well-known, and possibly overused, term the world around.

Charlie also continues to be a highly visible figure in the popular arts outside of cinema. Television's two most memorable and durable clowns, Red Skelton and Lucille Ball, owed much to Chaplin's comedy tradition. For Skelton, Chaplin has been a lifelong idol, and there is more than a little of Charlie the Tramp in Skelton's celebrated character, Freddie the Freeloader, who often did skits entirely in pantomime. (Skelton's show, which ran from 1951 to 1971, also featured a silent spot.) As noted earlier, Skelton's popular annual Christmas story, with penniless Freddie ordering and consuming a huge meal so that he might know the warmth of a jail cell, is largely taken from Chaplin's *Modern Times*. And there were other Chaplin-influenced Skelton routines, such as the sketch in which he played a starving tramp who is mistaken for an actor in costume. Forced to play out a scene with an actress, hunger eventually causes Skelton's Tramp to mistake the heroine's hand for a scrap of chicken, from which he then takes imaginary morsels in the most delicate mime. The routine beautifully salutes *The Gold Rush* Thanksgiving scene, bringing to mind the Tramp's methodical eating of his stewed boot and Mack Swain's hunger-induced hallucination of Charlie as a chicken.

Chaplin's importance to Skelton might best be summed up by Skelton's key reason for buying Chaplin's former studio (which was by then quite antiquated).

> It had once belonged to the Master pantomimist of all time. . . . The aura of Chaplin still hung over every . . . sound stage and dressing room. And once Red became its owner, he would be able to sit in the very same office He used, and at the same desk He ruled from, and control his own destiny much in the way He did.[125]

Lucille Ball's slapstick comedy in the famous *Lucy* shows, which ran between 1951 and 1974, also seems to have been greatly influenced by Chaplin, from an occasional television storyline that allowed her to do a costumed impersonation of the Tramp to the physical sight gags with which she became frequently involved. Like Skelton, she tended to utilize the less capable components of the Tramp for her humor. And again like Skelton, possibly her greatest skit seems to have been drawn directly from *Modern Times*. This sketch finds Lucy and close friend Ethel Mertz (Vivian Vance) working on a candy shop conveyor belt wrapping chocolates. Like Charlie's *Modern Times* factory job, where he finally cannot keep up with his own conveyor belt, Lucy and Ethel soon suffer the same comic fate. Besides being a delightful Chaplin footnote, it remains one of Ball's favorite *I Love Lucy* episodes.[126]

The most celebrated of the more traditionally oriented contemporary mimes, such as Marcel Marceau, owe a huge debt to the artistry of Chaplin. In fact, the award-winning Marceau largely credits his idol Chaplin for his decision to study pantomime. It's interesting that Chaplin's daughter Victoria is a former circus clown and tightrope walker, as if she were specifically stirred by her father's film *The Circus.*

Chaplin's influence on theater has been equally impressive. For example, the comedian had a profound effect on German playwright Bertolt Brecht, "whose dramas are said to have done more to shape the modern theatre than any playwright since Ibsen."[127] The Chaplin touch can be seen in such Brecht productions as *Herr Puntilla* and *His Knight Matti*, which features a *City Lights*-like millionaire who is humane to a poor man only when he (the moneyed individual) is drunk. Brecht's *Caucasian Chalk Circle* has thematic parallels to *The Kid*, and the physical comedy of the playwright's *In the Jungle of Cities* is often seen as a general tribute to Chaplin. An even more impressive yet frequently overlooked Chaplin influence can be seen in the sequel-like nature to *The Gold Rush* of Brecht's *The Rise and Fall of the City of Mahogany.*[128]

During Brecht's "American exile" (1941–47, after fleeing Nazi Europe), biographer Frederic Ewer notes:

> he met and became friendly with Charlie Chaplin, whom he had admired since his boyhood, and who inspired so many of his own ways of thinking [both as a playwright and in his writing on stage theory and epic theater method]. Now a closer association only served to strengthen that admiration.[129]

Brecht's plays, however, often come to rest upon a helpless irony that is neither derivative of nor applicable to Chaplin's work, despite film historian Gerald Mast's comparison of *Easy Street*'s conclusion with those of Brecht's *Threepenny Opera* and *The Good Woman of Setzuan.*[130] This is not to deny Chaplin any sense of irony in his productions but rather to draw attention to the indestructible underdog persistence of the Tramp, as well as the genre expectations of the comedy. The Chaplin-Brecht relationship was not a two-way street in terms of influence, at least during the Charlie years.

Chaplin's impact on theater can also be demonstrated in a number of other ways, from a Broadway show on his life and times to his effect on Nobel Prize-winning author Samuel Beckett. Beckett's writing, particularly his most celebrated work, *Waiting for Godot*, often shows signs of Charlie. For example, *Observer* theater critic Kenneth Tynan noted that the tramps of Godot "converse in the double-talk of vaudeville: one of them has the ragged aplomb of Buster Keaton, while the other is Chaplin at his airiest and fairiest."[131] Beckett later attempted to cast Chaplin in his avant-garde movie *Film* (1965), in a part that eventually went to Keaton. Beckett biographer Deirdre Bair observed that as a child, the playwright "never missed a film starring Charlie Chaplin."[132]

Chaplin's continued influence on writers outside film also includes fiction and poetry. Fiction showcases an especially diverse Chaplin panorama, from James Agee's use of Charlie as one of the special ties between a 1915 father and son in his Pulitzer Prize-winning *A Death in the Family*, to the sometimes Chaplinesque nature of James Joyce's celebrated Leopold Bloom (see especially Mary Parr's *James Joyce: The Poetry of Conscience*, Inland Press, 1961). And Chaplin's life has even become a source for popular "fiction," such as John Baxter's rather bald use of Chaplin's biography as the basis for his "novel" *The Kid* (Viking Press, 1981). Baxter, who has also written several film texts, tells the story of Tommy Timpson, a former Dickensian waif in turn-of-the-century London who becomes the film comedian of all time. The "coincidences" with Chaplin's life are endless and include everything from Tommy Timpson having a Japanese "Man Friday" named Kito (Chaplin's long-time Japanese assistant was named Kono) to Timpson being knighted by the queen of England. This left-handed salute to Chaplin is topped off with the book's dust jacket caricature of Charlie (Tommy's comedy costume matches the Tramp's exactly, right down to the toothbrush mustache) and a title that does not exactly distract from the comparison.

Countless poets have been inspired by Chaplin's artistry (including myself), and the comedian himself acknowledges the phenomenon by the inclusion in his autobiography of Hart Crane's "Chaplinesque," which the poet personally dedicated to Chaplin in appreciation of *The Kid*. Poet and painter e. e. cummings was moved to create a delightful abstract pencil drawing of Charlie as Pan, which Parker Tyler used as the frontispiece in his book *Chaplin: Last of the Clowns*.

As with all great artists, Chaplin's work has had the poignancy to be seen and enjoyed at many levels, from intellectual stimulation to the sheer joy of laughter. But unlike many great artists whose unique gifts are dulled by time and popular culture's absorption of their innovations, Chaplin's gift of comedy remains as bright today as it was back in 1914 at the birth of Charlie.

The preceding examples that helped document Chaplin's ongoing heritage represent merely a surface scratching of the comedian's impact on film and popular culture. As important as this influence has been, it says little about the given factor behind all of it—Chaplin's awesome ability to make millions upon millions of people laugh, generation after generation. As René Clair observed as early as 1929, "the masses do not know that Chaplin is the greatest author, the greatest creator of fiction, living today."[133] The masses merely know that he is funny, and from this all else continues to evolve.

NOTES

1. Wes D. Gehring, *W. C. Fields: A Bio-Bibliography* (Westport, Conn.: Greenwood Press, 1984); and Gehring, *Groucho and W. C. Fields: Huckster Comedians* (Jackson, Miss.: University Press of Mississippi, 1994).

2. Harold Dunham, "John Bunny," in *Silent Picture*, Winter 1968–69, p. 12.

3. Sam Gill, "John Bunny," in *The Silent Comedians*, ed. Richard Dyer MacCann (Metuchen, N.J.: Scarecrow Press, 1993), p. 29.

4. Gene Fowler, *Minutes of the Last Meeting* (New York: Viking Press, 1954), p. 104.

5. John Bunny, *Bunnyisms* (New York: Vitagraph, 1914), p. 7, in the John Bunny File, Billy Rose Theatre Collection, New York Public Library at Lincoln Center, New York.

6. Henry Jenkins, *What Made Pistachio Nuts? Early Sound Comedy and the Vaudeville Aesthetic* (New York: Columbia University Press, 1992), p. 255.

7. Gehring, *Handbook of American Film Genres* (Westport, Conn.: Greenwood Press, 1988).

8. "John Bunny in the Flesh," *Indianapolis News*, November 10, 1914, p. 4.

9. Bunny article, citation incomplete, *Philadelphia Telegraph*, March 20, 1915, in the John Bunny File, Billy Rose Theatre Collection.

10. John Palmer, "Mr. Bunny," *Saturday Review*, April 11, 1914, p. 466.

11. Ralph Brock Pemberton, "A Man Seen Daily by Millions," *American Magazine*, August 1914, p. 60.

12. Bunny article, citation incomplete, *New York Morning Telegraph*, September 30, 1914, in the John Bunny File, Billy Rose Theatre Collection.

13. Henry Wysham Lanier, "The Coquelin of the Movies," *World's Work*, March 1915, p. 576.

14. Ibid., pp. 566–77.

15. Gill, "John Bunny," p. 29.

16. "Death of Mr. John Bunny," *Times* (London), April 29, 1915, p. 5-d.

17. Lanier, "The Coquelin," p. 577.

18. James Agee, *A Death in the Family* (1957; reprinted New York: Bantam Books, 1972), p. 20.

19. Leslie Halliwell, *Double Take and Fade Away* (London: Gragton Books, 1987), p. 305.

20. Lanier, "The Coquelin," p. 577.

21. Ibid.

22. Quoted from Harold Dunham's "John Bunny," *Silent Picture*, Winter 1968–69, p. 11.

23. "John Bunny, Famous 'Movie' Comedian Dies in Brooklyn," *Indianapolis Star*, April 27, 1915, p. 6.

24. Lanier, "The Coquelin," p. 569.

25. Pemberton, "A Man Seen," p. 60.

26. "John Bunny Dies; Movie Funmaker," *New York Times*, April 27, 1915, p. 13.

27. "Men, Women and Children Lost Film Friend When John Bunny Dies," *Indianapolis News*, April 27, 1915, p. 3.

28. For example, see "Lyceum [Theatre]—John Bunny," *Indianapolis Star*, January 15, 1915, p. 15.

29. Mique O'Brien, "Stage Jottings," *Terre Haute Tribune*, November 9, 1914, p. 7.

30. For more background on *Bunny in Funnyland*, see "Lyceum—'John Bunny—Himself,'"*Indianapolis Star*, November 10, 1914, p. 15; "John Bunny Again," *Indianapolis Star*, January 10, 1915, p. 12.

31. Terry Ramsaye, *A Million and One Nights*, (New York: Simon and Schuster, 1926), p. 547.

32. *Bunny in Funnyland* review, *Chicago Tribune*, October 11, 1914, Section 8, p. 2.

33. For example, see front-page articles in the *Des Moines Tribune* (Iowa, April 26, 1915) and the *Muncie Star* (Indiana, April 27, 1915). Bunny's *Indianapolis Star* obituary (see Note 23) is the best example of a piece including comments of local friends.

34. "Men, Women and Children Lost Film Friend," *Indianapolis News*.

35. Gerald D. McDonald, Michael Conway, and Mark Ricci, eds., *The Films of Charlie Chaplin* (New York: Bonanza Books, 1965), p. 13.

36. Charlie Chaplin, *My Autobiography* (1964; reprinted New York: Pocket Books, 1966), p. 183.

37. Gerald D. McDonald, *The Picture History of Charlie Chaplin* (New York: Nostalgia Press, 1965), p. 25.

38. Theodore Huff, *Charlie Chaplin* (1951; reprinted New York: Arno Press, and the *New York Times*, 1972), p. 65.

39. William Dodgson Bowman, *Charlie Chaplin: His Life and Art* (1931; reprinted New York: Haskell House, 1974), p. 70.

40. Chaplin, *My Autobiography*, p. 183.

41. Charles Thompson, *Bob Hope* (New York: St. Martin's Press, 1981), p. 8.

42. McDonald, *The Picture History of Charlie Chaplin*, p. 16.

43. Raoul Sobel and David Francis, *Chaplin: Genesis of a Clown* (London: Quartet Books, 1977), pp. 233, 234.

44. Huff, *Charlie Chaplin*, p. 64.

45. David Denby, "Introduction," in *Awake in the Dark: An Anthology of American Film Criticism, 1915 to the Present*, ed. David Denby (New York: Vintage Books, 1977), p. xxi.

46. Minnie Maddern Fiske, "The Art of Charles Chaplin," *Harper's Weekly*, February 6, 1916, p. 494.

47. Huff, *Charlie Chaplin*, p. 6.

48. Richard Schickel, "Hail Chaplin: The Early Chaplin," *New York Times Magazine*, April 2, 1971, p. 13. (Ironically, after Schickel opens with these quotations of praise, he assumes a rather critical position on Chaplin.)

49. Bob Thomas, *Bud & Lou* (Philadelphia: J. B. Lippincott, 1977), p. 130.

50. Lewis Jacobs, *The Rise of the American Film* (1939; reprinted New York: Teachers College Press, 1971), p. 247.

51. Raymond Durgnat, *The Crazy Mirror: Hollywood Comedy and the American Image* (1969; reprinted New York: Dell, 1972), p. 80.

52. There were also single Chaplin features at Keystone (*Tillie's Punctured Romance*, 1914), First National (*The Kid*, 1921), Attica-Archway (*A King in New York*, 1957), and Universal (*A Countess from Hong Kong*, 1966).

53. Max Eastman, *Heroes I Have Known: Twelve Who Lived Great Lives* (New York: Simon and Schuster, 1942), p. 200.

54. For more information on this area, see especially Walter Blair, *Native American Humor* (1937; reprinted San Francisco: Chandler, 1960; Gehring, *Leo McCarey and the Comic Anti-Hero* (New York: Arno Press, 1980); Jennette Tandy, *Crackerbarrel Philosophers in American Humor and Satire* (New York: Columbia University Press, 1925); and Constance Rourke, *American Humor: A Study of the National Character* (1931; reprinted New York: Harcourt Brace Jovanovich, 1959).

55. Robert Sklar, *Movie-Made America* (New York: Vintage Books, 1976, p. 100.

56. Huff, *Charlie Chaplin*, p. 65.

57. A paper on this subject, "Charlie Chaplin and the Progressive Era: The Neglected Politics of a Clown," was presented by the author at the Second International Conference on Humor, Los Angeles, August 25, 1979. It was published in the Autumn 1981 issue of *Indiana Social Studies Quarterly*, pp. 10–18.

58. Huff, *Charlie Chaplin*, p. 18.

59. Charlie Chaplin Jr., *My Father, Charlie Chaplin* (New York: Random House, 1960), p. 242.

60. Huff, *Charlie Chaplin*, p. 296.

61. Huff, *Charlie Chaplin*, p. 70.

62. For this fascination with Dickens, see especially Charles Chaplin, *Charlie Chaplin's Own Story* (Indianapolis: Bobbs-Merrill, 1916), and to a lesser extent his *My Autobiography*. The first text reads very much as if Chaplin were transcribing from a copy of *Oliver Twist*. In fact, it has been noted that "critics in 1916 found this autobiography a mixture of fact and fiction. Because of embarrassment, the comedian eventually had the book withdrawn from the market." See Donald W. McCaffrey, ed., *Focus on Chaplin* (Englewood Cliffs, N.J.: Prentice-Hall, 1971), p. 27 (footnote). More recent criticism suggests that *Charlie Chaplin's Own Story* was ghostwritten. See John McCabe, *Charlie Chaplin* (Garden City, N.Y.: Doubleday, 1978), p. 90.

63. Charles Dickens, *Oliver Twist* (1841; reprinted New York: Times Mirror, 1961), pp. 281–89.

64. A film title in Chaplin's *Sunnyside* (1919).

65. Albert F. McLean Jr., *American Vaudeville as Ritual* (Lexington, Ky.: University of Kentucky Press, 1965), p. 106.

66. McLean, *American Vaudeville as Ritual*, p. 110.

67. William Cahn, *Harold Lloyd's World of Comedy* (London: George Allen and Unwin, 1966), p. 61.

68. Kalton C. Lahue, *World of Laughter: The Motion Picture Comedy Short, 1910–1930* (1966; reprinted Norman, Okla.: University of Oklahoma Press, 1972), p. 90.

69. Mordaunt Hall, March 29, 1927, review of *Long Pants* [the influence of Chaplin on Langdon], in *New York Times Film Review, 1913–1931*, project manager Abraham Abramson (New York: New York Times and Arno Press, 1970), pp. 356–57. See also Donald W. McCaffrey, *Four Great Comedians: Chaplin, Lloyd, Keaton, Langdon* (New York: A. S. Barnes, 1968), p. 105.

70. Mack Sennett with Cameron Shipp, *King of Comedy* (1954; reprint New York: Pinnacle Books, 1975), p. 141.

71. Edmund Wilson, "Some Recent Film" [the impact of *The Gold Rush* on Lloyd and Keaton], *New Republic*, December 16, 1925, p. 109. See also Edmund Wilson, "The New Chaplin Comedy," *New Republic*, September 2, 1925, pp. 45–46.

72. Mordaunt Hall, May 24, 1926, review of *Tramp, Tramp, Tramp* [the influence of *The Gold Rush*], in *New York Times Film Review, 1913–1931*, p. 313.

73. Leonard Maltin, *Of Mice and Magic: A History of American Animated Cartoons* (New York: New American Library, 1980), p. 24.

74. Ibid., p. 22.

75. I frequently use Felix cartoons in my film history class, and *Felix in Hollywood* always receives the best response, no doubt assisted by the caricatures of other Hollywood personalities besides Chaplin. See also Maltin, *Of Mice and Magic*, p.24.

76. Celia McGerr, *Rene Clair* (Boston: Twayne, 1980), p. 44.

77. Ibid., p. 104.

78. Jean Renoir, *My Life and My Films*, trans. Norman Denny (New York: Atheneum, 1974), p. 205.

79. Ibid.

80. Roy Armes, *Patterns of Realism: A Study of Italian Neo-Realist Cinema* (New York: A. S. Barnes, 1971), p. 144.

81. Ibid.

82. Edward Murray, *Fellini the Artist* (New York: Frederick Ungar, 1976), p. 32.

83. Ibid., p. 32.

84. Ibid., p. 197.

85. Joseph L. Anderson and Donald Richie, *The Japanese Film: Art and Industry* (1959; reprinted New York: Grove Press, 1960), pp. 51, 357.

86. Ibid., p. 99.

87. Eric Lax, *On Being Funny: Woody Allen and Comedy* (1975; reprinted New York: Manor Books, 1977), p. 172.

88. Rudolf Arnheim, *Film as Art* (1933; reprinted Los Angeles: University of California Press, 1971), pp. 36, 51.

89. Ibid., p. 127.

90. Ibid., p. 151.

91. Ibid., p. 148.

92. Charles Chaplin, "Pantomime and Comedy," *New York Times*, January 25, 1931, Sec. 8, p. 6.

93. J. Dudley Andrew, *The Major Film Theories* (New York: Oxford University Press, 1976), p. 33.

94. Arnheim, *Film as Art*, p. 106.

95. Sergei Eisenstein, "Word and Image," *The Film Sense*, trans. and ed. Jay Leyda (1942; reprinted New York: Harcourt, Brace and World, 1947), pp. 3–69.

96. Andrew, *The Major Film Theories*, p. 48.

97. Andrew Tudor, *Theories of Film* (New York: Viking Press, 1974), p. 38.

98. Eisenstein, *The Film Sense*, p. 23.

99. Arnheim, *Film as Art*, pp. 123–24.

100. Béla Balázs, *Theory of the Film*, trans. Edith Bone (1952; reprinted New York: Dover, 1970), p. 26.

101. Ibid., p. 225.

102. Andrew, *The Major Film Theories*, p. 89.

103. Balázs, *Theory of the Film*, p. 237.

104. Ibid.

105. Ibid., p. 63.

106. Andrew, *The Major Film Theories*, p. 99.

107. Balázs, *Theory of the Film*, p. 285.

108. Siegfried Kracauer, *Theory of Film: The Redemption of Physical Reality* (New York: Oxford University Press, 1960), p. 86.

109. Ibid.

110. Ibid., p. 307.

111. Ibid., pp. 107–108.

112. Andrew, *The Major Film Theories*, p. 119.

113. André Bazin, "The Virtues and Limitations of Montage," in *What Is Cinema?* Vol. 1, trans. Hugh Gray (1958; reprinted Los Angeles: University of California Press, 1967), p. 52.

114. André Bazin, "Charlie Chaplin," in *What Is Cinema?* Vol. 1, p. 150.

115. Ibid., p. 146.

116. Ibid., p. 144.

117. André Bazin, "The Myth of Monsieur Verdoux," in *What Is Cinema?* Vol. 2, trans. Hugh Gray (1958; reprinted Los Angeles: University of California Press, 1971), pp. 102–103.

118. Ibid., p. 105.

119. Ibid., pp. 112.

120. Bazin, "The Grandeur of Limelight," in *What Is Cinema?* Vol. 2, p. 136.

121. Ibid.

122. Ibid., p. 138.

123. Ibid., p. 139.

124. Ibid., p. 132.

125. Arthur Marx, *Red Skelton* (New York: E. P. Dutton, 1979), p. 245.

126. Bart Andrews, *The Story of I Love Lucy* (1976; reprinted New York: Popular Library, 1977), p. 248.

127. James K. Lyon, *Bertolt Brecht in America* (Princeton, N.J.: Princeton University Press, 1980), p. 3.

128. Jennifer E. Michaels, "Chaplin and Brecht: *The Gold Rush* and *The Rise and Fall of the City of Mahogany*," *Literature/Film Quarterly* 8, No. 3 (1980), pp. 170–79.

129. Frederick Ewer, *Bertolt Brecht: His Life, His Art and His Times* (1967; reprinted New York: Citadel Press, 1969), p. 386.

130. Gerald Mast, *The Comic Mind: Comedy and the Movies* (Indianapolis: Bobbs-Merrill, 1973), pp. 83–84.

131. Kenneth Tynan, August 1955 *Observer* review of *Waiting for Godot*, in *Samuel Beckett: The Critical Heritage*, eds. Lawrence Graver and Raymond Federman (Boston: Routledge and Kegan Paul, 1979), p. 969.

132. Deirdre Bair, *Samuel Beckett* (New York: Harcourt Brace Jovanovich, 1978), p. 4.

133. René Clair, *Cinema Yesterday and Today*, trans. Stanley Appelbaum, ed. R. C. Dale (New York: Dover, 1972), p. 86.

3

THE MARXES, LAUREL & HARDY, and W. C. FIELDS

The only tradition in our family was our lack of tradition.[1]
Harpo on the childhood of the Marx Brothers

Opening title for Laurel & Hardy's *Big Business* (1929): "The story of a man who turned the other cheek—and got punched in the nose."

When once asked if he had ever had DT's, Fields replied: "I don't know. It's hard to tell where Hollywood ends and the DT's begin."

INTRODUCTION

This chapter examines three acts from the American film comedy period that follows the silent era: the Marx Brothers, Laurel & Hardy, and W. C. Fields. This studio era (1929–1945 and World War II), like any period, draws upon hallmarks of the preceding age. For example, the evolution of the comic antihero continued during this period (especially with the added catalyst of the Great Depression). Avant-garde film work of the late 1920s, such as the surrealism of Luis Buñuel and Salvador Dali's *Andalusian Dog* (*Un chien andalou* [1929]), found mainstream commercial outlets in the work of all three acts noted here, particularly the Marxes'. This dovetailed nicely into the then-establishment comedy of this period's clowns. This age was well prepared for comedy that rocks the boat. All in all, the Marx Brothers, Laurel & Hardy, and W. C. Fields are major comedy players.

MARX BROTHERS

How does one describe the influence of the Marx Brothers? Their impact on American humor and on American popular culture in general has been immense; one should mention in particular their significance as cultural icons, their richly ambitious influence on schools of comedy, their impact on modern entertainment, and their easing of the transition from silent to sound comedy. Moreover, their comedy has made a distinct imprint on Western culture itself—lofty accomplishments for a comedy team that struggled for years in the lower levels of vaudeville. This cultural metamorphosis was also ironic, since the most distinctive characteristic of their comedy has always been its iconoclastic nature. Thus, while in *Horse Feathers* (1932) the brothers comically dismantle university life, today's university dissects *Horse Feathers* for educational purposes. But before examining the more philosophical ramifications of their work, permit me to relate a personal story that showcases the continuing impact of the Marx Brothers on our culture.

In doing research on a Marx Brothers book (Greenwood Press, 1987), one must, of course, visit archives across the country. Away from one's family and after long hours in a special collections library, one naturally searches for a diversion. For the student of film, as for many others, this often means going to a movie. Thus, on one Marx Brothers research trip I managed to take in two then current commercial theater releases: the highly praised Woody Allen film *Hannah and Her Sisters* (1986) and Terry Gilliam's *Brazil* (1985). Though both are comedies in the broadest sense of the word, they are radically different. The former film, like much of Allen's work, fluctuates between humor based on the problems of a strongly defined personality comedian (Allen) and a romantic comedy that frequently parodies love itself. But unlike the guarded optimism that frequently closes Allen films, *Hannah and Her Sisters* ends on a decidedly upbeat note. The film even manages to include the two most archetypal elements of comedy's classic formula for a happy ending—the new beginnings symbolized by both a marriage and a child's birth. In contrast, *Brazil* is the blackest of comedies. Gilliam, best known as the only American member of the British comedy troupe Monty Python, fashioned a film without hope—a nightmare comedy of the future. Like a slapstick *1984*, *Brazil* offers the standard black comedy message: Not only is the individual insignificant, he is forever fated to contribute to his own demise.

Both of these very different films, however, utilized the Marx Brothers as cultural symbols of equally different things. In *Brazil* the anti-establishment heroine watched *The Cocoanuts* (1929) on television. In this case the Marxes represent two things: an iconoclastic ideal for a radical, and comic prophets who recognized early the inherent pointlessness of the modern world. The "saturation" comedy style of *Brazil* (à la Monty Python) has indirect roots in the Marxes' own comically complex presentation. In *Hannah and Her Sisters* a suicidal Allen wanders into a screening of *Duck Soup* (1933). Prior to this he had been asking himself: If the world is without reason, why go on living? But slowly the comedy magic of the Marxes envelops him. Here the Marxes symbolize pure comedy, those random moments of joy that make life worth living. Allen leaves the theater completely revitalized, once again a believer in hope and in the modest milestones (marriages, births) of the modern human.

Here, then, was a Marx Brothers researcher who tried and failed, on two successive nights, to find a simple momentary escape from this focus of study. That failure would seem to say a lot about the ongoing significance of the Marxes.

Allen's recognition of the unique qualities of the Marxes is important because he has evolved into one of America's greatest creative artists. His accomplishments range from an Oscar for best motion picture to the O. Henry Award for best short story. And in 1986 the nominating theater critics for the Pulitzer Prize in drama recommended that his screenplays be eligible for the competition. This is especially relevant here, for besides calling Allen "America's Ingmar Bergman," the critics' action was prompted by the fact that the only narrative script they had agreed on in their 1986 nominating capacity was *Hannah and Her Sisters*, with its pivotal reference to the Marxes.[2]

Besides Bob Hope, one might say the spirit of the Marxes brings out the best in Allen. This influence is most apparent in such early Allen films as *Take the Money and Run* (1969) and *Bananas* (1971). For example, Allen's disguised return from San Marcos (where he, like *Duck Soup's* Groucho, has become president!) is straight out of the *A Night at the Opera* (1935) scene in which the similarly costumed Marxes also attempt to re-enter the country. And though the most integrated Marx Brothers' influence on Allen (such as gag usage and overall comic framework) occurs early, his most pointed previous highlighting of the Marxes, or more specifically, Groucho, came at the opening of his most acclaimed film, the Academy Award-winning *Annie Hall* (1977). At that time he had quoted Groucho's famous real-life putdown: "I would never want to belong to any club that would have someone like me for a member." But not before *Hannah and Her Sisters* had Allen so baldly showcased the importance of the Marxes' comedy art. Moreover, he offered no verbal or printed lead-in (such as even a "now showing" movie poster) as to whom or what the *Hannah* viewer was about to see in this movie-within-a-movie. The *Duck Soup* excerpt, from "The Country's Going to War" number (where the Marxes brilliantly satirize the unthinking jingoism that welcomes war), is simply presented without fanfare as the comic masterpiece it is. While it would be an overstatement to call the Marxes, or *Duck Soup*, the motivating spark behind *Hannah*, one must remember that Allen's narrative goal in the scene is to present a symbol of comedy at its greatest. High praise for these former low-level vaudevillians.

With the world's ever-increasing marketing, the importance of the Marx Brothers as cultural icons can be neither denied nor avoided. Caricatures of them appear on nearly anything which can be purchased. Their much-hawked images rank with such diverse characters as Chaplin's Tramp figure, Monroe's sex goddess, and Bogart's tough guy, possibly the most universally recognized of American films icons. But the Marxes' significance as images goes beyond mere sales.

As with the others, caricatures of Groucho, Chico, and Harpo have become an enduringly popular logo for Americans, even for those who have not seen a complete Marx Brothers film. This is possible because it has become a common cultural heritage to know what they represent. The Marx Brothers as icons symbolize two things: pure comedy and an anti-establishment spirit. The Marxes are not only funny, they look funny, whether you are watching them in a film or studying a caricature. As noted in Chapter 1, Groucho "would be funny in still photographs," with his greasepaint mustache and eyebrows. The quote might only have been improved by stating the obvious: *All three* Marxes would be funny in still photographs. Thus, as is true of the most traditional clowns, one would be prone to laugh at their appearance without prior knowledge of who, or what, they were.

Their significance as comedy symbols is underlined by the frequency with which stage shows appear that include impersonations of one or more of the brothers. An excellent overview of this phenomenon can be found in recent issues of another Marx Brothers fascination—*The Freedonia Gazette*, which bills itself as "The Magazine Devoted to the Marx Brothers" (New Hope, Pennsylvania).[3] Along these same lines one should note today's stage revival productions of two Marx Brothers celebrations that originally played on Broadway: *Minnie's Boys* and *A Day in Hollywood/A Night in the Ukraine* (two independent one-act shows, with the second showcasing the Marxes). *Minnie's Boys* is a musical comedy biography of sorts, while *A Night in the Ukraine*, loosely drawn from Chekov's "The Bear," captures the spirit of the Marxes better. Moreover, the play *Animal Crackers* is also frequently revived. That the team should still be generating so much interest today is a tribute to their continuing influence.

Besides being symbols of pure comedy, they also represent the ultimate in anti-establishment icons. As Martin A. Gardner thoroughly discussed in his 1970 doctoral dissertation, their talent for satirizing society can be divided into three broad categories. They comically undercut history, politics, and the economy; manners and customs; and literature and popular entertainment.[4] While one most frequently associates them with the comic usurpation of high society (manners and customs, especially as personified by Margaret Dumont), their satire seems to touch nearly every aspect of American culture. Thus, *Duck*

Soup is a satirical send-up of politics that makes comic inroads into govern-
mental policy on everything from the economy to diplomacy, managing to
scramble American history along the way, from Harpo's rendition of Paul
Revere's ride to the then current state of world depression. *Horse Feathers*' (see
Illustration 6) satire of university life manages to skew a range of literature and
popular entertainment from Theodore Dreiser's *An American Tragedy* to college
football.

The Marx Brothers analogy can be expanded more broadly. That is, part of
the modern fascination with football is its multifaceted execution, which
reflects the complexities of today's world, as opposed to the simpler one-thing-
at-a-time progression of the more nineteenth-century sport of baseball. The
Marx Brothers represent that same principle of entertainment diversity in
comedy, both in terms of the humor types exhibited in their team, as well as
their tendency to be entirely unpredictable in what they do for a laugh. This
broadness of type and target also brings us full circle back to their importance
as satirical and establishment icons. This is because their work seldom takes
aim one subject at a time. It is a complex, multilayered use of satire and parody
that invariably draws one in, even if not every comedy jab connects. The viewer
is simply mesmerized by the amount and the diversity of the comedy.

The second broad influence of the Marxes, after their significance as
comedy/anti-establishment icons, is in their impact on schools of comedy.
Most specifically, this means their involvement in the zany world of the comic
antihero in American humor, best typified by *The New Yorker* writing of
authors like Robert Benchley and James Thurber. The Marxes did not invent
this character type, but their memorable period successes with it (from vaudeville and Broadway to the movies) helped to disseminate widely the phenomenon. However, unlike so many of their contemporary screen comedians, such
as Leo McCarey's Laurel & Hardy and W. C. Fields, they did not impersonate
the frustration of the individual in the comic, antiheroic, and absurd modern
world. Instead, the Marxes donned the mantle of comic absurdity as a defense,
and beat the world gone mad at its own game. In fact, they were cocky enough
to "take what order there is in life and impose chaos on it."[5] The daydream
victories of Thurber's Walter Mitty were business as usual for the Marxes.[6]
Groucho is, however, often victimized by his brothers, and in these encounters
Groucho becomes the more traditional antiheroic male. Moreover, Groucho's
solo writing for print more fully embraced the antihero's frustrations, be it
essays like the 1929 *The New Yorker* piece, "Press Agents I Have Known," or
books like *Memoirs of a Mangy Lover* (1963).[7]

The Marxes acknowledged this tie to what they call "lunatic" comedy in a
1939 article in *Theatre Arts* magazine, correctly observing that they were
"followers" of such pioneering antiheroic writers as Stephen Leacock, Donald

6. The Marx Brothers in a wrongfully discarded scene from *Horse Feathers* (1932).

Ogden Stewart, and Robert Benchley.[8] The label "lunatic" is merely a characteristic of a comedy movement that generally focuses on the comic frustrations
of an antiheroic male, or what American humor historian Norris W. Yates
frequently refers to as the "little man."[9] The authors noted by the Marxes all
belong to this school of comedy, though today a more representative grouping
would be Benchley, Thurber, Clarence Day, and S. J. Perelman.[10] It's not
surprising that Benchley was a close friend of the Marxes, Perelman was a Marx
scriptwriter, and Thurber was a major Marx fan (see especially his comic
mini-review of *A Day at the Races—Der Tag Aux Courses*—in the March 1937
Stage magazine.)[11] And as early as 1931 John Grierson, in his perceptive
criticism of the Marxes, likened their work to Benchley's.[12] Even the nonsense
literary example that film comedy historian and critic Gerald Weales notes as
being most similar to the world of the Marxes, Donald Ogden Stewart's *Mr.
and Mrs. Heddock Abroad* (1924), finds the zany Groucho-like verbal patter
belonging to a supporting character who, to a great extent, is victimizing an
antiheroic or "little man," Mr. Heddock.[13]

Although the Marxes fittingly labeled themselves "followers," their initial
Broadway triumph in *I'll Say She Is!* (1924; essentially a zany anthology of their
"greatest hits" from years of vaudeville) was enough for Gerald Weales to justify
placing the team in the vanguard of the movement. Their 1920s centerstage
ascension as Broadway's resident crazies, on and off stage (including participation in the Algonquin Round Table), does make them early participants in this
comedy evolution. Thus, Weales has suggested that "it is more useful to think
in terms of a shared intellectual and social climate [in 1920s New York, the
center for the ultimate literary articulation of the movement] in which lunacy,
verbal and physical, could flourish."[14] Although it is tempting to follow Weale's
suggestion, especially since the Marxes' material is forever preserved on film,
they are still best described as important early disciples of antiheroic comedy
but not as founding fathers.

Purists still distracted by the presence of Marx Brothers playwrights and
screenwriters should keep in mind that while the brothers did not control their
film productions in the unquestioned auteur manner of Chaplin, they were,
like W. C. Fields, largely undirectable. And while one must acknowledge that
the team needed writers, it is frequently forgotten that Groucho was often
involved, though uncredited, with the writing and was a successful author
himself. Harpo, though not as concerned with the overall scope of the play or
film as Groucho, was generally the key "author" for his own visual material. In
addition, much of the team's classic material for both stage and screen was first
tinkered with daily as the brothers either toured or tested it on the back roads
of America. And finally, the Marxes exerted their influence even when they
were involved with a pivotal antiheroic "lunatic" writer like S. J. Perelman in

Monkey Business (1931), and *Horse Feathers*.[15] In fact, Perelman's own article, "Week End with Groucho Marx,"[16] has the satirist coming off as a Marx Brothers groupie, whose writing on *Monkey Business* would seem to borrow from Perelman's boyhood memories of the vaudeville Marxes. Still, one can hardly say that every Marx Brothers scriptwriter was under their spell; people like George Kaufman and Morrie Ryskind obviously had an impact on the team. But it is important to credit the Marxes with more of a collaborative status than they have been given.

Weales credits William Troy's negative review of *Duck Soup* with making an important connection between the Marxes and the lunatic comedy movement.[17] Troy observed: "Like the whole 'crazy-fool' humor of the post-war epoch, it [Marxian humor] consists in a dissociation of the faculties rather than a concentrated direction of them towards any particular object in the body social or politic."[18] Troy might have provided an example of his "dissociation of the faculties" analysis with the following *Duck Soup* conversation between the president of Freedonia (Groucho) and a peanut vendor (Chico):

> *Groucho:* Now listen here. I've got a swell job for you, but first I'll have to ask you a couple of . . . important questions. Now, what is it that has four pairs of pants, lives in Philadelphia, and it never rains but it pours?
>
> *Chico:* 'At'sa good one, I give you three guesses.
>
> *Groucho:* Now, lemme see. Has four pair of pants, lives in Philadelphia. Is it male or female?
>
> *Chico:* No, I no think so.
>
> *Groucho:* Is he dead?
>
> *Chico:* Who?
>
> *Groucho:* I don't know. I give up.
>
> *Chico:* I give up, too . . . [Chico insults Groucho]
>
> *Groucho:* Just for that you don't get the job I was going to give you.
>
> *Chico:* What job?
>
> *Groucho:* Secretary of war.
>
> *Chico:* All right, I take it.
>
> *Groucho:* Sold!

The Groucho-Chico conversation nicely showcases their ability to personify the absurdity of the antiheroic modern world without also playing its comic victim, though Chico slightly gets the better of the argument. More often than most of their comic contemporaries, the Marxes vaccinated themselves against a zany work by assuming part of that zaniness themselves. It's interesting to note that this crazy comedy antidote is more apt to appear in the women who populate the comic antiheroic world, from the Looney Tunes Gracie Allen of (George) Burns & Allen, to the Thurber grandmother who thought electricity would leak from sockets without light bulbs.[19] But as eccentric as these women were, they made decisions (Thurber's grandmother was always screwing in the bulbs), and then got on with living. Meanwhile, the comic antihero male generally attempts to make sense of it all (women and the world) and goes near crazy trying. In the film genre of screwball comedy, this type of antihero male/eccentric female dichotomy exists, but merely represents a more sophisticated, feature-length variation, which broadened the audience for the antiheroic misfit.[20] Thurber more fully articulates this antiheroic male-female difference later in the story "Destructive Forces in Life," concluding:

> [T]he undisciplined mind [that of the woman] runs far less chance of having its purpose thwarted, its plans distorted, its whole scheme and system wrenched out of line. The undisciplined mind, in short, is far better adapted to the confused world in which we live today then the streamlined mind [the disciplined mind of the man]. I am afraid, there's no place for the streamlined mind.[21]

While the Marxes were much more likely to assume the "undisciplined" mind normally attributed to the female in this comedy movement, it should again be noted that interactions within the team often had Groucho playing the more traditional antihero male. This is best exemplified by the close of the long comedy dialogue between Groucho and Chico in the 1930 *Animal Crackers*. This conversation includes Chico's classic, irrational crime-solving suggestion to build a house next door in order to question the people who would then live there. Thus the "undisciplined mind" of Chico has so fractured both reason and the language that Groucho's "disciplined mind" is reduced to incoherency in trying to make sense of Chico. The mustachioed one stumbles out of the scene mumbling, "Ahh, ahh . . ." Although this victimization of Groucho to antihero status is not nearly as common as Groucho 's own comic attacks on an absurd world, they do occur regularly. Examples include the standing gag in *Duck Soup* that Harpo and his motorcycle sidecar will always leave Groucho behind, and the tootsie fruitsie ice cream scene in *A Day at the Races* (1937) in which Chico sells Groucho a library of unnecessary betting books. Moreover, what Marx author Allen Eyles call "Harpo's tour de force in out-smarting Groucho," the *Duck Soup* "mirror scene" imitation of Groucho, is arguably the greatest of all Marx Brothers scenes.[22] Although variations of the mirror skit occurred earlier, as in Chaplin's *The Floorwalker*, (1916) the

Marxes' version is so comically inspired that it is the one to which film historians most often refer.

Added detail has been given to this examination of the Marxes' second broad influence, their involvement in the evolution of antiheroic comedy in American humor, for three reasons. First, unlike their high visibility as icons of comedy and the anti-establishment, their links to the world of the comic antihero are not always immediately apparent. Moreover, they are made more complex by Groucho's dual status as comic aggressor outside the family (the stance that most readily comes to mind, especially when it involves his baiting of Margaret Dumont), and as the sometimes antiheroic male within the team. It is not unlike the duality managed by his 1930s contemporary, W. C. Fields, who fluctuated between his comic antiheroic male and that of carnival huckster, sometimes combining them in the same role.[23] Second, understanding the Marxes' ties to antiheroic comedy makes Groucho's much more pronounced use of comic frustration in his solo writing considerably less jarring. Students of the Marxes frequently have expressed surprise over this apparent disparity, but the seeds of the antiheroic male were always in the Groucho persona, and comic interaction with his brothers made them surface, on occasion, in the team films.

Third, joining the Marxes' often aggressive use of absurdity to the world of antiheroic comedy makes all the more understandable the pervasive influence of their comedy today. The same qualities that attracted surrealist Salvador Dali in the 1930s[24] moved Eugene Ionesco to declare that the three biggest influences on his work were Groucho, Chico, and Harpo Marx.[25] Martin Esslin agrees on the significance of the team to the Theater of the Absurd—a theater that has also been called black comedy.

Black comedy is not in itself new, but its increased pervasiveness is.[26] Thus, in a modern world that appears more and more unhinged, the Marxes seem even more contemporary. Moreover, their humor was often black to begin with. This is especially true in *Duck Soup*, where the foolishness of war is so effectively dramatized by Groucho's accidental machine-gunning of his own men. Indeed, Groucho's comic paranoia about the intentions of Ambassador Trentino, which satirizes the paranoia often connected with the decisions of American government,[27] has direct ties with the even darker comic paranoia of *Dr. Strangelove*'s Sterling Hayden. Playing General Jack Ripper, he believes fluoridated water is a Soviet plot to assist in the takeover of America. Thus, one frequently thinks of the Marxes when dealing with the ironic absurdity of the modern world. This would include dark comedy film director Billy Wilder's plan in the early 1960s to use the Marxes in a *Dr. Strangelove*-type satire; the more recent view of playwright Dario Fo's darkly comic *Accidental Death of an Anarchist* as a "left-wing *Duck Soup*," and the Marxes' ties to *Brazil* mentioned earlier.[28] More visible popular culture footnotes to the Marxes' influence on today's dark comedy are countless. They range from the obvious debt Alan Alda owes Groucho for the anti-establishment, womanizing Hawkeye Pierce of *M.A.S.H.* to the frequent tendency among political cartoonists to comment on the escalating absurdity of today by including the Marxes in their drawings. For example, *The Freedonia Gazette*, which regularly includes such cartoons in its pages, has a devastatingly comic one in its November 1980 issue. A reprint of a *Washington Star* syndicated Marx Brothers caricature, it has the team as Pentagon heads preparing for a second mission after their involvement in the failed hostage rescue by the Carter administration. Its black comedy detail might be summed up by the fact that Chico is reading a booklet on "Helicopter Maintenance."[29]

The Marxes', third broad influence has been on the complex, multifaceted phenomenon that is modern entertainment. The team might be called a cross-section of American humor, from the fast-talking Groucho and the dialect comedy of Chico to the mime of Harpo, which was forever supplemented by cartoonish sound effects. One might even count Zeppo as an example of the romantic light comedian for which sound comedy increased the need. When the Marxes' comic diversity was married to the brothers' propensity for a scatter-shot range of satire topics, the entertainment possibilities were almost overpowering. In fact, Irving Thalberg's MGM softening of the Marxes' screen characters and his addition of more traditional story elements were in part attempts to make them more palatable to a general audience by making them less irrational. Numerous critics have commented on the danger of this homogenization. For example, Patricia Mellencamp says: "To be classically narrativized [as the Marx Brothers were] is to be sanitized [robbed of your humor]."[30] However, in fairness to Thalberg, his two productions, *A Night at the Opera* and *A Day at the Races*, are still funny films; it is just that total anarchy no longer rules. (Though Thalberg died during the production of *A Day at the Races*, the extensive on-the-road testing of the script had been completed and was finished according to Thalberg blueprint.)

After the disappointing reception given *Duck Soup*, their last Paramount film and typical of their works for that studio, Thalberg thought the diversity of their comedy was too much for the 1930s audiences. Not surprisingly, today's more demanding viewer prefers the comically complex actions of the Marxes' Paramount films, especially *Duck Soup*, to their later work. This was the position Groucho himself later came to endorse.[31] Marx author Thomas H. Jordan quite logically observes:

> They were without question the most prominent forerunners of the rapidly paced situation comedy reintroduced to modern audiences through

such television programs as *Laugh-In*, *The Ernie Kovacs Show*, *That Was the Week That Was*, and in Britain, *The Goon Show* and *Monty Python's Flying Circus*. Few modern film comedies have been able to recreate the headlong rush of humor which characterized the Marxes.[32]

Jordan goes on to note what has always been a popular refrain about the team and a key reason for their ongoing popularity: "Their films can be seen many times without losing their appeal, for there are so many gags and jokes that no one can possibly remember more than a small number."[33] However, it should be underlined that they monopolize the comedy roles. Unlike *Laugh-In*, which most people have forgotten was titled *Rowan & Martin's Laugh-In*, there has never been a danger of forgetting the title characters in a Marx Brothers film.

It's surprising that the influence of one Marx Brother has also been credited with just the opposite model (from saturation comedy) for television. Groucho Marx's casual conversations while sitting on a stool for the static camera *You Bet Your Life* was, according to television historian Max Wilk, instrumental in the similarly casual nature of many television programs that followed, especially the variety show.[34]

The Marxes' fourth broad influence was their early demonstration of the comic artistry potential of sound films, despite the often canned nature of their first two movies. To the student of film comedy, their cross-section of American humor eased the transition from silents to sound, especially with the mime of Harpo acting as a salve on the painful loss and/or decline of so many silent comedy stars. In fact, as early as 1937, Gilbert Seldes observed: "The arrival of the Marx Brothers and the reappearance of W. C. Fields saved screen comedy."[35] While Seldes goes on to credit Disney with being the ultimate sound replacement for the silent slapstick short, the live-action team diversity of the Marxes (especially when sound was decentralizing the formerly single comedy character focus of the silent films), demonstrated that film comedy's future could still be bright. More recently, theorists like Mellencamp have demonstrated the comic brilliance the Marxes brought to sound comedy. Their assault on the language produced a verbal slapstick every bit as iconoclastic as their attack on the establishment. Verbally as well as visually, their comic message remained the same: Things are not what they seem! Moreover, the brothers' early film success was so great that they paved the movie way for a series of other zany comedy teams. For example, even the earlier madcap team of Wheeler & Woolsey can be categorized as under the indirect assistance of the Marxes. While Wheeler & Woolsey entered film the same year as the Marxes (1929), the duo's initial Broadway teaming (1928) came at the height of the Marx Brothers' influential reign on America's premier theatrical street.

Thus, one cannot disregard the influence of the Marxes as unique icons of both comedy and the anti-establishment, as major contributors to new developments in American humor, as pivotal early examples of what might best be called saturation comedy, and as a pioneer measuring stick for the great potential of sound film comedy. One must never, however, lose sight of their greatest and continuing impact: They make people laugh. There is no greater gift.

LAUREL & HARDY

What is there about Laurel & Hardy's personae that even makes their mere caricatures so popular? First, and most basic beyond their obvious ties to comedy, the team quite literally looks funny. Theirs is the most fundamental of comic contrasts—the interaction between a fat person and a skinny one. And they further accent the difference in various comic ways. For instance, Stan's scarecrow dry hair is forever combed straight up, as if he had just had an electrical shock, while Ollie's hair is invariably slicked down close to his head. More subtly, when Stan is confused or frightened, he goes into his elongated, vacuous facial expression (tears optional), vertically culminated by his reaching up and scratching the top of his head (like a comic El Greco, if the master of lengthened figures had done clowns). In equally subtle contrast, Ollie's most memorable comic "mask" (expression) occurs when he broadens his face in disgruntlement over another boner by Stan, tilting his head slightly downward and allowing his many chins to pile up onto his chest. And unlike Stan's elongating hand motion to the top of the head, Ollie's corresponding trademark gesture happens during times of shyness, when he plays with his tie, thus breaking its perpendicular lines.

Of course, instead of inferring humor, one might also translate the meaning of these fat-skinny contrasts into metaphor, such as unconventional symbols for feast and famine. Granted this is a rather outlandish suggestion. But in the spirit of "Ripley's Believe It or Not," such a correlation occurred at a remote shrine in 1930s China, where their picture was used on an altar for just that reason. This is not an invitation to dust off one's knees and begin worshipping the duo. It does, however, underline the worldwide pervasiveness of the team as well as the almost primal contrast in their body shapes.

The second factor behind the universality of their personae as icons (after simply looking funny) is that they represent the ultimate symbol of comic frustration. Of course, rare is the humor figure that does not know some degree of comic frustration. But Laurel & Hardy established new highs for comic incompetence as they participated in the evolution of America's comic antihero (to be expanded upon later in the chapter). While the last section examined the Marx Brothers' part in the evolution of the antihero, Laurel & Hardy is *the* team when comic frustration is discussed. Even W. C. Fields (see below), whose screen roles vacillated between hucksters and antiheroes, is most often seen today in the former guise, as the high-hatted, gloved con man making a comic pitch out of the side of his mouth. For example, the fraudulent Fields is the model for the crooked lawyer Larsen E. Pettifogger in Johnny Hart and Brant Parker's newspaper comic strip, "The Wizard of Id" (since 1964). And advertisers invariably latch onto the huckster image of Fields, such as the very successful potato chip ad campaign with cartoon spokesman "W. C. Frito." In contrast, Stan & Ollie as icons symbolize complete comic frustration—the forefathers of today's Charlie Brown. Instead of representing envied actions, one either equates Laurel & Hardy's problems with exaggerations of personal problems or feels comically superior to two such lame-brained characters. But even when the duo is at its chuckleheaded best, such as its opening title description from *The Hoose-Gow* (1929)—"Neither Mr. Laurel nor Mr. Hardy had any thoughts of doing wrong. As a matter of fact they had no thoughts of any kind"—one still feels an empathy for two such warm and decent characters. *The Times* of London probably said it best when it praised the team as "an expression of well-intentioned muddle-headedness in a harsh and practical world."[36]

A second major influence of Laurel & Hardy, after their two-pronged significance as icons, was their contribution (with Leo McCarey) to a change in silent comedy pacing. As opposed to silent comedy's typically fast motion, Laurel & Hardy came to represent an innovatively slowed pace. This inspired slower-comedy rhythm (such as their methodical take-your-turn, tit-for-tat violence) had four supporting factors. First and foremost, it was fresh and funny—the requirement that makes the other points possible. The duo's only significant slower-paced silent competitor was Harry Langdon, and his career self-destructed just as Laurel & Hardy's were taking off (1927). Second, the slower pacing anticipated the more realistic needs of sound film production, allowing Laurel & Hardy to make the smoothest transition to "talkies" of all silent comedians. Third, this reduced speed enabled the team to display a comic tendency best defined as anticipation. As critic and historian Walter Kerr suggested, while the typical silent comedian hid the gag in the setup, the team "showed everyone the joke, explained it most carefully, anatomized it."[37] For instance, the insert of a misplaced roller skate just before the oblivious Oliver steps on it comically telegraphs the impending pratfall. Thus, while their material might seem hoary with age (even for the late 1920s), this was perfectly consistent with a methodical comedy style that embraced viewer anticipation instead of the more traditional comic surprise. (Unfortunately, it is this ritualistic nature that sometimes turns off the contemporary viewer, who finds the duo's films too drawn-out.) The fourth factor concerning their slower pacing was its appropriateness for screen personae who were equally slow-witted.

Their silent comedy gift of slower pacing and its aid in their transition to sound film also had another important dimension—the team's continued use of visual comedy. Despite the duo's early grasp of the comic potential of the new sound technology, Laurel & Hardy were an ongoing demonstration that one need not jettison a silent comedy shtick to succeed in sound films. After Chaplin, who made even less of a concession to sound (the Tramp spoke only once, and then not until 1936), visual comedy remained alive and well in the sound world of Stan & Ollie. I am particularly reminded of the simple but comically deliberate hand gestures Ollie frequently uses in the award-winning *The Music Box*. Like a silent comedy conductor, he frequently makes words seem superfluous.

For a period contrast, one might counter Laurel & Hardy's visual slapstick with the verbal slapstick of the Marx Brothers. That is, despite the often canned nature of the Marxes' first two movies (*The Cocoanuts*, 1929, and *Animal Crackers*, 1930, both screen adaptations of two earlier Marx Brothers plays), they were first and foremost pioneers of comic sound potential during the early "talkie" years. While this is most obviously linked to the machine-gun delivery of Groucho or ethnic Chico, even the comic silence of Harpo was closely tied to sound, from his ever-present bicycle horn to the fractured English transla-tions of his mime by dialect comedian Chico. Moreover, Harpo's best sight gags were invariably set up by a verbal comment, such as the *Duck Soup* call for a cigarette lighter that results in Harpo pulling a blowtorch from under-neath his magic coat.

No such necessary link between sound and comedy existed for Laurel & Hardy, though their voices (which nicely matched their physical personae) came to be famous, too.

Despite Laurel & Hardy's emphasis on visual comedy, their third important influence—following their significance as icons and comedy pacing innova-tors—was their creative use of early sound, such as comic off-screen noise and the addition of cartoon-like sound effects. The more sound-dependent Marx Brothers notwithstanding, Laurel & Hardy did have two central traits that lent themselves nicely to sound film-bumbling incompetency and comic tit-for-tat violence. As critic and documentary pioneer John Grierson observed in 1935: "They are clumsy, they are destructive . . . [T]he world of sound is theirs to crash and tumble over [making this] a first creative use of [film] sound."[38]

In the 1930s, celebrated realist filmmaker Alberto Cavalcanti also graded the team high in this category: "They were the pioneers of sound comedy."[39] But whereas Grierson felt Laurel & Hardy's sound innovations were most assisted by the duo's lack of dependence on (and thus freedom from the distraction by) verbal comedy, Cavalcanti more generally credited the team's wisdom in minimizing change during the coming of sound. Indeed, between the slower pacing and modest need of dialogue, a critic would be tempted to label Laurel & Hardy "soundproof."

A fourth and final significant influence is McCarey's orchestrated participation in the evolution of the comic antihero in mainstream American humor. While McCarey's Laurel & Hardy did not invent the comic antihero, their phenomenal late-1920s rise to prominence in that comic guise paralleled the centerstage emergence of the character on the national scene. Five distinctive characteristics of the comic antihero emerge from extensive study of the subject: his constant frustration, his childlike naivete, his abundant leisure time, his apolitical nature, and his life in the city.[40] Each characteristic also constitutes a break with what had formerly been the dominant character type in American humor—the capable, crackerbarrel Yankee (see Chapter 2).

The core characteristic here, of course, is frustration. Stan & Ollie succeed at very little. Any attempts to deal with an irrational world in a rational matter are generally doomed from the beginning. Their only parallel with the capable Yankee is that they do manage, as the Benchley comic antihero does, to be persistent (which they complement with slow thinking). A famous illustration is their piano-moving exploits in *The Music Box* (1932). The following brief Laurel & Hardy overview demonstrates the comic richness of their antiheroic appeal. The examples are drawn from their early films in order to parallel the time when the comic misfit was moving to the centerstage of American humor.

First, Stan & Ollie's frustration is centered around conflict with both wives and machines. Their wives dominate them, though Ollie generally finds himself to be the most comically misused (as was the case with Thurber's "battle of the sexes"). Still, even when the story seems to overlook the woman, there exists a foreboding tension just beyond the screen. For example, the opening title of *Should Married Men Go Home?* (1928) asks the question: "What is the surest way to keep a husband home? Answer: Break both his legs."

The domestic "front" provides the team with one of its most popular settings for a pivotal Laurel & Hardy theme—escape. They are often trying to sneak away from the restrictions of marriage, if only for an evening. These matrimonial "jail breaks" also provide a more logical understanding of what might first seem an illogical Stan & Ollie setting—their propensity also to turn up in prison, with the expectation that a comic escape will be attempted. Yet for this team, marriage and prison are two comic extremes of what the boys symbolically are always trying to escape—the debilitating restrictiveness of modern life itself.

The subjugation, real or imagined, also includes an irony befitting an antiheroic world view. An extended escape by Stan & Ollie is not only rare, it is probably not in their best interests. Domination by prison guards and wives might be viewed as supervision for truly childlike antiheroes. Regardless, the price of their security is suppression, especially when we see their increased incompetency on their own. A comic analogy could be made between Stan & Ollie's suppression for security tendencies (at the risk of comic chaos of their own) and the still-provocative hypothesis of film theorist Siegfried Kracauer toward the German Expressionism film movement of the 1920s, paralleling the early Laurel & Hardy career.[41] Kracauer felt the limited narrative choices provided by fatalist German Expressionism—tyrants or chaos—aided the rise of Hitler, the tyrant who rose from the chaos of Germany's post-World War I Weimar Republic. While no comparably sweeping generalizations seem to relate to Laurel & Hardy, the growth of antiheroic humor was not hindered by the 1930s Depression, which made many people feel antiheroic.

The other primary source of frustration for the antihero is his dealings with the mechanical. For Stan & Ollie (especially Ollie), mastering a mechanical device is another way to assert manhood. But unlike the escape attempts, this attempt at technological dexterity represents not so much proving manhood (necessitating secrecy from one's wife) but rather playing it out before her and for her benefit.

In *Hog Wild* (1930) Stan & Ollie systematically destroy a house in order to get a radio antenna on the roof. Granted, Ollie's wife has set him to the task, but it is a matter of male pride for him to accomplish it. Thus, when he comes crashing down the chimney, like some out-of-season Santa in civvies (after several other unplanned exits off the roof), his wife tells him maybe he ought to call it off. Ollie refuses, however, with a resounding, "I'll put it on the roof if it's the last thing I do!" (Had the film been produced in today's black comedy world, Ollie just might have received his wish.)

The second commonality between the antihero and Stan & Ollie is their childlike nature. Several of their films begin with Stan just dropping in at Ollie's home, as if to say, "Can you come out and play?" Comedy film historian Gerald Mast goes so far as to say: "The starting point of every Laurel and Hardy film is that they are overgrown children."[42] Certainly the relationships with their wives are more that of parent and child than of husband and wife. There is seemingly no sexual bond and the mothers/wives make the decisions. Moreover, the periodic escape attempts by the "boys" might best be equated with that nearly universal childhood dream (invariably pondered if not always acted upon) of running away from home, even for only a short adventure. And such pivotal comedy components as Stan's crying routine and Ollie bashfully playing with his tie are direct links to childhood.

In *Brats* (1930) they literally double as both fathers and sons. The dual-focus narrative convincingly illustrates that the Stan & Ollie adults are no different from children. While the twosomes play at separate games (checkers and pool or blocks and boxing), both pairs tend to fight and to be comically destructive. Appropriately, while the earlier activities of the fathers and sons were usually reciprocal, the finale is something of a shared experience. Their children have left water running in the bathtub from the beginning of the film, and when little Ollie asks for a bedtime drink, his father unleashes a tidal wave by merely opening the door.

Playing on the title of this film, Mast observes that the world of Stan & Ollie "is populated solely with brats. The childish spite of the central pair runs up against the equally childish spite of their opponents [the celebrated tit-for-tat encounters]."[43] Though one might question whether Stan & Ollie's realm is solely composed of brats (see this chapter's later examination of Tiny Sandford's cop role in *Big Business*, 1929), Mast does point up the centrality of the childlike characteristic to the team's comedy.

A third shared trait between the team and the comic antihero is their quantity of leisure time. While there are exceptions to this, Stan & Ollie still seem to have a preponderance of free or play time, which also reinforces one's image of them as children. Historically, this reflects a period (1920s) when increased leisure time for the masses was first becoming a reality. And it also demonstrates, as noted by author Hamlin Hill, a retreat from the ever-more complex and dangerous modern world. That is, the antihero deals with this frightening outside realm by not dealing with it at all. Instead, he focuses "microscopically up on the individual unit . . . that interior reality—or hysteria. . . . In consequence, modern humor deals significantly with frustrating trivia."[44] An excellent example of Stan & Ollie leisure-time activity occurs in *A Perfect Day* (1929), a film that also complements some of the antiheroic points examined thus far. As the title indicates, it was just the right sort of day for a picnic. Stan & Ollie, their wives, Uncle Edgar (Edgar Kennedy, with a bandaged gouty foot), and the family dog prepare for a carefree day.

Stan & Ollie make the sandwiches while their wives attend to other details. Just when the sandwiches have been arranged on a tray being held by Ollie, the kitchen's swinging door shoots Stan into Ollie and the sandwiches are broadcast all over the room. The two fight, make up, and eventually rearrange the sandwiches, But all the mayhem has encouraged the dog to attack Uncle Edgar's bad foot. When Hardy tries to tear the family pet off Edgar's foot, he again scatters the sandwiches.

Eventually all is ready and the car is packed. Neighbors yell goodbye and the trip begins, almost. A tire hits a nail in the driveway and now there is a flat to fix. As Ollie fixes the tire, Stan accidently assumes the dog's role of attacking poor Edgar Kennedy's foot. He manages to sit on the foot, step on it, slam it in the car door, and, in the grand finale, drops a tire jack on it. Eventually the tire is fixed, but numerous other comic frustrations deny the bunch their picnic. So much for the fate of antiheroes, even on a "perfect day."

There is more to Stan & Ollie's free time, however, than just the domestic scene. They play golf in *Should Married Men Go Home?* (1928), while their original plan in *We Faw Down* (1928) was a night of poker with the boys. But their nondomestic leisure time more often found them in a nightclub, such as with unplanned dates in *Their Purple Moment* (1928), their adventure at the Pink Pup Club in *That's My Wife* (1929, with Stan in drag as Ollie's wife), and *Blotto* (1930), where they manage to get drunk on a nonalcoholic beverage.

The fourth common characteristic linking Stan & Ollie to the comic antihero is a nonpolitical nature. The closest they come is probably one of their prison or police films. Still, there are no real issues at stake. The comic interactions are more a game of hide-and-go-seek between overgrown kids. Gerald Mast, while comparing law enforcement characterizations in the films of Charlie Chaplin and Mack Sennett, makes a comment pertinent to the world of Stan & Ollie: "The prison cops in [Chaplin's] *The Adventurer* [1917] . . . shoot rifles at the escaping Charlie, and their bullets, unlike the bullets in Sennett comedies, look as though they could kill."[45] Like Sennett's cops, Laurel & Hardy's men in uniform are harmless. Indeed, the Laurel & Hardy cop is often given enough personality (something generally lacking in Sennett films) to make him likable. For instance, Laurel & Hardy stock player Tiny Sandford has a small but endearingly memorable cop role at the close of *Big Business*. He runs through a roller coaster of comic emotions as he first incredulously observes a classic tit-for-tat confrontation, and later tearfully commiserates with the boys as they momentarily feel remorse for their violent actions.

The utter incompetency of the comic antihero encourages the nonpolitical stance. He is constantly buffeted by the day-to-day frustrations of an irrational world. This figure is hardly capable of planning his leisure time, let alone becoming political. Crucial issues for Laurel & Hardy included things like keeping their derbies on or safely lighting a gas stove.

Just to play a comic devil's advocate, one might still wonder: If a political event were thrust upon an antihero, would he respond? No. Even then he would probably miss it because of vacuity reminiscent of Laurel & Hardy, which fittingly might be called the "derby disease." That is, pioneer antiheroic writer Robert Benchley, in a well-documented study of news photographs taken of "cataclysmic events," found that:

> If you want to get a good perspective on history in the making, just skim through a collection of news-photographs which have been snapped at those very moments when cataclysmic events were taking place throughout the world. In almost every picture you can discover one [antihero] guy in a derby hat who is looking in exactly the opposite direction from the excitement, totally oblivious to the fact that the world is shaking beneath his feet. That would be me, or at any rate, my agent [such as Stan & Ollie] in that particular part of the world in which the event is taking place.[46]

Noncontroversial comedy has long been a major selling point for Stan & Ollie audiences, just as it has no doubt contributed to the fact that many critics now take the duo seriously. Appropriately, one period critic who did recognize the team's significance, novelist Graham Greene, also praised the importance of their nonpolitical stance. His 1940 review of the team's *A Chump at Oxford* ranked it

> with their best pictures—which to one heretic [Greene] are more agreeable than [the often political] Chaplin's; their clowning is purer; they aren't out to better an unbetterable world [later that year Chaplin released his black comedy on Hitler, *The Great Dictator*]: they've never wanted to play Hamlet [an unrealized Chaplin project, as well as a frequently cited serious role when a comedian starts to go somberly self-reflective].[47]

The fifth and final connection between Stan & Ollie and the comic antihero is that they are citizens (read: victims) of the city. Born of a period that for the first time found America's urban population outnumbering rural residents, Laurel & Hardy's classic films often presented the masses comically running amok, be it the epic pie fight of *The Battle of the Century* (1927) or the cartoon-like traffic jam/demolition derby called *Two Tars* (1928). Even in the seemingly more subdued California suburbs, those rows upon rows of identical white bungalows represent a bottled humanity just waiting for an excuse to explode comically, such as the team's greatest tit-for-tat encounter with stock company regular James Finlayson in *Big Business*.

Laurel & Hardy soon experienced in real life (1932) the violent chaos of massed humanity, in their first joint visit to Europe, where huge admiring crowds became dangerously out of control. For a darker view of the people, one is also reminded of novelist and scriptwriter Nathanael West, especially the uncontrollable crowd in his *The Day of the Locust* (1939). (In the novel the central character's fate is left ambiguous. The excellent 1975 film adaptation strongly suggests the mob quite literally tears him apart.)

The city is synonymous with all the frustrations of the antiheroic modern world, from America's fundamental Jeffersonian democracy fear of cities (the unnatural mixing of too many people) to the anti-individualism of an ever-escalating mechanization of society. Of course, the Laurel & Hardy film (see Illustration 7) turns such frustrations into fun. The large urban pool of people becomes a reservoir of comedy types, and the machines forever give the boys comic fits. Indeed, the antiheroic car of cars—the Model-T Ford—is often associated with them. It need not be a focus of a film, such as the problematic automobile of *A Perfect Day*. For instance, the streetcar demolition of Stan's Model-T at the close of *Hog Wild* was a most fitting close to the team's (especially Ollie's) urban nightmare. This includes the antenna excursions that kept Ollie falling off the roof, and later being nearly flattened in traffic after falling off a ladder—from the back of the Model-T.

Thanks also to the tit-for-tat encounters, one sees just how thin modern urban man's veneer of civilization is. Despite the cleansing effect of comedy violence, Stan & Ollie and their comic combatants still take turns while wreaking havoc. This telling residue of politeness—even during violence— nicely demonstrates the artificial facade of graciousness with which modern urban society frequently covers its stress fractures.

Naturally, this does not say Stan & Ollie are any more capable when in the country, as their comic problems in *Them Thar Hills* (1934) witnessed. But it does suggest that there are more potential conflicts in the city, as well as temptations—which often means the same thing, since antiheroes like Stan & Ollie are constantly frustrated. Thus, a boy's night out might be more inviting if there are nightclubs nearby, especially as in the early Laurel & Hardy films made prior to the repeal of Prohibition in 1933.

For the antihero, the often-harried urban setting can be emasculating, which is hardly something this comedy victim needs, since his dominating wife already wears the pants in the family. But whereas this last reference to pants was metaphorical, there is something just off-center enough about the anti- heroic city that its comic male victims sometimes literally appear in drag.

For Stan & Ollie, this most often means the former plays the girl. Without getting too Freudian in interpretation, this is perfectly in keeping with a modern (antiheroic) comedy movement in which gender roles are often topsy-turvy to begin with. Such sexual inversions are even more obvious in screwball comedy, which, beginning in the mid-1930s, builds on antiheroic comedy. This new genre dressed up the urban surroundings and added beautiful people, but this was more of a reflection of the need to mass-market feature films than of a substantive difference. The outcome was essentially the same: an eccentrically comic battle of the sexes, with the male generally losing.

7. Laurel & Hardy's garage door problems in *Blockheads* (1938).

Besides the emasculating appropriateness of periodically seeing one of the team in drag (in *Twice Two*, 1933, they both don women's clothing to play each other's wife), it is altogether fitting that Stan & Ollie's special friendship is occasionally portrayed as that of an actual couple, comic as that may be. Their friendship is clearly more important than anything else, including their screen marriages.

For instance, in *That's My Wife* (1929), where Stan convincingly plays Ollie's wife (an ongoing gag has a drunk flirting with Stan), the thin one has definitely supplanted his stout friend's spouse. Stan had dropped in on Ollie and his wife for two years! She had demanded a choice of her husband: Stan or her. When Ollie proved indecisive, she left. One should hasten to add, of course, that Stan's new identity as Mrs. Ollie was only a temporary ploy to suggest the fat one was happily married and therefore qualified to meet an eccentric inheritance requirement.

Consistent with their antiheroic world, a comic couple dichotomy of Ollie as male and Stan as female (whether in drag or not) still finds the "woman" as the ultimate winner (or, more precisely, Ollie as the primary sufferer). This occurs despite the fact that Stan is hardly the physically or verbally abusive wife with whom Ollie usually has to cope.

These are the five core characteristics of the comic antihero, the twentieth-century humor evolution in which Laurel & Hardy played such an important part. This chapter also examined three other significant influences of Laurel & Hardy: as comedy icons, developers of a pivotal change in American film comedy pacing, and as movie pioneers in the innovative early use of comic sound.

While these have been the key thrusts of Laurel & Hardy's impact on American humor and popular culture, other items could no doubt be mentioned, for instance, their influence on comedians. This is best exemplified by the parallels between the team and early television's classic *Honeymooners* duo of Jackie Gleason and Art Carney as Ralph Kramden and Ed Norton.

As with Stan & Ollie, Ralph & Ed are in the age-old comedy contrast tradition of fat man/skinny man. Like Ollie, Ralph thinks he has all the answers, only to suffer constantly comic frustrations. His companion in these misadventures is the dumb but amazingly loyal Stan-like Ed. While Ralph & Ed bring a more blue-collar backdrop to the *Honeymooners*, it is still a program fundamentally wrapped around their leisure time, especially their bungled attempts to obtain permanent leisure time through their ever-changing get-rich-quick schemes. And though Ralph is much more verbally combative with wife Alice (Audrey Meadows) than Ollie ever was with a spouse, the wife also controls things in the *Honeymooners*. Finally, with Ralph & Ed, as with Stan

& Ollie, there is no designated straight man. Both team members share the laughter.

The ties are so many that one is tempted to read more into Gleason's popular 1950s catchline using a Laurel & Hardy stock company figure—"the ever popular Mae Busch." Regardless, Gleason was an acknowledged fan of early film comedy, and on at least one *Honeymooners* episode Ralph & Ed consciously played at being Stan & Ollie. These roots to an earlier team seemed to come out in truly diverse ways.

There are countless other examples of Laurel & Hardy's influence. These would include their international fan club, the "Sons of the Desert," or Lou Costello's appropriation of the famous Stan cry and blink of the eyes when problems became a bit too much for his childlike screen character. Costello also did a variation with his fingers of Ollie's tie twiddling. Laurel bitterly resented these liberties, no doubt in part because Abbott & Costello usurped Laurel & Hardy as the film public's favorite comedy team in the early 1940s. In contrast, Dick Van Dyke's persona draws more broadly from the inspired physical comedy presence of Stan. They became close friends and Van Dyke has been active in past celebrations of Laurel's career. Laurel & Hardy also had a strong influence on the British comedy team of Morecambe & Wise and on Johnny Carson—such as his Ollie-like direct address to the camera in moments of comic frustration or his occasional fond aping of both Stan's and Ollie's mannerisms and their celebrated comic anthem, "Here's another fine mess."

Countless artists in other media (and with radically different target audiences) have been influenced by the team. Two of the most diverse examples are Nobel Prize-winning playwright Samuel Beckett's existential *Waiting for Godot* (1957), and award-winning children's author/illustrator Maurice Sendak's *In The Night Kitchen* (1970).

Beckett, sometimes considered the most important of the post-World War II playwrights, draws strongly (according to some) on Stan & Ollie for the derby-wearing characters Vladimir and Estragon in *Waiting for Godot*. (For a breakdown of their ties, see Jordan Young's fascinating essay "Popularity Grows on Borrowed Roots."[48]) But critic Kenneth McLeish provides a more manageable encapsulization: "The shifting, double-act, busy-doing-nothing relationship of Vladimir and Estragon . . . is based on that of Laurel and Hardy."[49] In contrast, the three cooks of Sendak's *In the Night Kitchen* are identical clones of Ollie. (For a Chaplin slant on Beckett see p. 70.)

While it is hardly recommended procedure to compare existential plays and children's literature, if a general connection (besides Laurel & Hardy) were made between the two works, it would be in their dark comedy. Granted, there is a world of difference between examples, especially with a play sometimes unofficially referred to as *Waiting for God*. Still, a key point here is how the continuing relevance of Laurel & Hardy is maintained, at least in part, by the team's anticipation of today's ever-popular dark humor. In fact, pivotal black-comedy novelist Kurt Vonnegut dedicated his book *Slapstick* (1976) "to the memory of Arthur Stanley Jefferson and Norvell Hardy, two angels of my time."[50]

For Vonnegut, this very loosely autobiographical novel has Stan & Ollie ties because their slapstick films are "what life feels like to me. There are all these tests of my limited agility and intelligence. They go on and on." And for Vonnegut, Stan & Ollie's "fundamental joke" is that they try their hardest at every test, always in "good faith" that this time will be different. Even though this is why Vonnegut, and viewers in general, find Laurel & Hardy funny, there is also a certain "common decency" about their patient, methodical persistence in the face of life's constant frustrations.

If anything, the continuing impact of Laurel & Hardy has begun to escalate in recent years. For instance, film writer/director John Hughes' inspired 1987 *Planes, Trains and Automobiles* has Steve Martin and John Candy in a classic Stan & Ollie love-hate relationship of continuous comic disaster, including the mandatory destruction of a car. (And in the true spirit of a wrecked Stan & Ollie Model-T, Martin & Candy's totaled automobile produces one final laugh when it manages to work even after its comic Armageddon.) For the discerning viewer, it was hard to miss the comic inspiration for Hughes' film, or as *Variety* observed: "Steve Martin and John Candy repeatedly recall a contemporary Laurel & Hardy."[51]

In late 1987 the most direct and moving homage to the duo appeared in Ray Bradbury's affectionately poignant short story, "The Laurel and Hardy Love Affair."[52] This bittersweet tale chronicles a romance built on a special fondness for Stan & Ollie. As sentimentally one-dimensional as that may sound, Bradbury is very effective in his intermingling of a real-life relationship with a host of Stan & Ollie basics (including tie twiddling and frequent picnicking by the celebrated 131 steps the team endlessly carry the piano up in *The Music Box*, 1932). Indeed, the ultimate severing of the couple's relationship is made all the more moving because just as they defined their love in Laurel & Hardy terms (right down to calling themselves "Stan" and "Ollie"), their breakup makes one feel as if Laurel & Hardy—the ultimate bonded couple—had broken up as well. Moreover, Bradbury's application of Stan & Ollie traits to a romance reminds the reader that one of the greatest yet most forgotten influences of any phenomenon is how it resurfaces in the little events of day-to-day existence, little things that slowly mold one over a lifetime. Such has been the case with Laurel & Hardy.

These Laurel & Hardy influences have surfaced often, with 1988 being a special benchmark. Film director/producer Martin Brest's critical and commercial hit *Midnight Run* had direct links to Laurel & Hardy. The film stars Robert De Niro and Charles Grodin as a bantering male couple in another love-hate relationship of nonstop fighting and making up, with soft-spoken Grodin a delightful contrast to loud, domineering De Niro (one plays Stan to the other's Ollie). And, like *Planes, Trains and Automobiles*, *Midnight Run* also comically features a constant change in types of transportation.

Brest-directed films often feature such male teams; see the comic coupling of Judge Reinhold with John Ashton in *Beverly Hills Cop* (1984). And Brest has observed:

> I think it all has to do with the fact that when I was growing up, the things I used to watch on TV that I enjoyed were Laurel & Hardy movies and "The Honeymooners." Those are the things that entertain me more than anything. Having them as sort of role models.[53]

On Bob Newhart's second hit television show, "Newhart," there is more than a little of Stan & Ollie in the comic interaction of Newhart's Dick Loudon character (a Vermont country inn owner) and Tom Poston's George Utley (the inn handyman). Newhart's persona plays off the simpleton nature of Poston's character. In a 1988 article, Newhart observed: "There's a lot of Laurel & Hardy in the relationship, with me being Hardy and him being Stan Laurel. I do everything but look at the camera and say, 'Did you see what he just did? Can you believe it?'"[54]

Newhart might also have added that, as in the antiheroic interaction of Stan & Ollie, the dominant Loudon is more likely to play the final fool, because unlike Utley, he tries to make rational sense (after all, this is crackerbarrel Yankee Vermont) of an irrational world.

Other 1988 Laurel & Hardy surfacings start with the limited-run critical and commercial success of *Waiting for Godot* at Lincoln Center's Mitzi E. Newhouse Theatre. Steve Martin and Robin Williams starred, reminding at least one reviewing critic of Laurel & Hardy.

Casting Martin and Williams, whose fame first came from their individual standup comic work, would certainly have met with Laurel & Hardy's approval. But one cannot help thinking: What if the veteran team had been able to appear in the play they helped inspire, especially since Beckett's fascination with silent film comedians would seem to be heightened by the ambiguity of their old age? Witness his use of Keaton in the movie *Film* (1965) two years before the comedian's death. Though the part was originally offered to Chaplin, Keaton (like Laurel & Hardy) seems much more appropriate for Beckett's tragicomic world. While Chaplin's Charlie is generally in control, if he so desires, Keaton's screen persona could beautifully suggest fatalist defeat even in victory, such as the close of his *Cops* (1922) or *College* (1927).

Additional 1988 links to Laurel & Hardy are as eclectic as a rambling storyline for Stan & Ollie. They range from notable actor Jack Gilford's funny/sad imitation of both comedians in *Cocoon II* (with old age, naturally, being the factor for both the scene and the movie), to renowned black-comedy cartoonist Gary Larson "starring" Stan & Ollie in one of his "The Far Side" cartoon strips. The boys are seen running down a long highway (toward the viewer), with an atomic mushroom cloud rising in the background. The Ollie caption simply reads: "Now you've done it!" Larson has merely served up an amusingly pessimistic modern version of "Here's another fine mess." One safe bet is that Laurel & Hardy will remain "contemporary" for some time to come.

W. C. FIELDS

Shortly after Field's death some of his friends ran the following full-page ad in the *Hollywood Reporter*:

> The most prejudiced and honest and beloved figure of our so-called "colony" went away on a day he pretended to abhor—"Christmas." We loved him, and—peculiarly enough—he loved us. To the most authentic humorist since Mark Twain, to the greatest heart that has beaten since the Middle Ages—W. C. Fields, our friend.
>
>
>
> Dave Chasen
>
> Billy Grady
>
> Eddie Sutherland
>
> Ben Hecht
>
> Grantland Rice
>
> Greg LaCava
>
> Gene Fowler
>
>

Requiescat in Peace[55]

Though this tribute displayed some of the exaggerations known to any circle of friends who has lost a fellow reveler—it is hard to compare heartbeats between the Middle Ages and 1964—the salute seems to have become more apt with the passing years. Fields was "authentic" because while the man could fluctuate between prejudice and honesty, just as his persona could fluctuate between con man and antihero, the message remained the same: Laughter can make survivors of everyone.

Why does Fields as an icon, particularly a con man icon, continue to have such a strong impact on America, from commercials to comics to the sale of countless products on which his likeness is reproduced? There are two key reasons.

First, his is a genuinely funny image, as demonstrated by its propensity to turn up in newspaper comic strips. The rounded body, the flamboyant costume, the tomato nose produce an immediate comic environment. Moreover, the exaggeration that makes the Fields icon amusing also reinforces the frequently tall-tale nature of his comedy. In addition, it is very difficult to view an image of Fields without hearing his nasal drawl, probably the most imitated vocalism in America. Consequently, while a commercial is more effective if it can get the viewer to finish a product jingle, the Fields icon can go beyond this by producing an auditory response from a purely visual stimulus. (It can be especially challenging to re-evaluate Fields' silent films without mentally adding his voice.)

The second reason Fields as an icon has an ongoing comic love affair with the American public is the well-defined nature of his persona and the uniformly high quality of his surviving works. Despite a gift for ad-libbing, he finely honed a number of now-celebrated routines over a fifty-plus-year career. His work was further polished by adapting the same or similar situations for a number of different media: stage, screen, radio, and print. And in the late 1930s he even talked of "a career in television."[56] (His 1933 film *International House* had, of course, an early television device at the center of its wacky plot.)

His most complete gift to the world of entertainment was his sound motion pictures, with film being the medium that best combined his unique visual and auditory gifts in the most sustained presentation of his routines. While he did not control his film productions in the unquestioned auteur manner of Chaplin, he was, like the Marx Brothers, largely undirectable. As a result, there have been minimal references to his directors in this text, because their primary act of creativity was to contain Fields in some way. The comedian's view of the position's overrated nature is articulated beautifully in *Never Give a Sucker an Even Break* (1941): Fields' character takes over the film within a film from the constantly inebriated director, A. Pismo Clam (Jack Norton), and is pompously carried aloft on a ceremonial litter by four strongmen.

Unlike the Marx Brothers, Fields was much more responsible for authorship of his persona and general comedy surroundings. While there is no denying the genius of the Marx Brothers, particularly that of Groucho, their best films were shaped by some of the age's most gifted comedy minds, such as George S. Kaufman, S. J. Perelman, and Morrie Ryskind. But without the right material, even the Marx Brothers could be unfunny, as was frequently the case in their RKO picture *Room Service* (1938) and the MGM films that followed.

Fields owed an unquestionable debt to writers Dorothy Donnelly and J. P. McEvoy. But Donnelly's *Poppy* opened comic con-man possibilities more than it provided the comedy itself. Fields seems to have done much of the fleshing out over the years as he performed comic variations on the huckster. And the *New York Times* review of the original Broadway production of *Poppy* stated the Dorothy Donnelly book was not intrinsically funny.[57] The play's own debt to the world of Dickens no doubt encouraged Fields to utilize better his own great appreciation of the novelist.

McEvoy's antiheroic *The Comic Supplement* (1924) was, on the other hand, funny to begin with, and the revised *Supplement* of 1925 seems to display a strong Fields influence. Moreover, as Fields' copyrighted comedy material (generally of an antiheroic vein) demonstrates, the McEvoy-Fields union was much more a meeting of similar minds than merely a contact of author and gifted performer. Fields' copyrighted sketches, in fact, are the ultimate evidence that separates him from most 1930s comedians of personality. The Marx Brothers, for example, seem to have left no copyrighted comedy plans of their own, though Groucho eventually authorized several loosely autobiographical humor books.

Because Fields seldom ventured far from his own material and liberally peppered anything new with patented, established bits of his own, his films maintain—at least when he is on screen—a consistently high level of comedy. This is something censorship, after 1934, kept even from the highly original Mae West, often her own chief author.

All in all, the success of Fields as icon points toward three primary influences on American film and popular culture. The first is that he has become a universal symbol as important in today's mass communication age as the celebrated literary characters of the past. The other two key influences are that he was a pioneer in both the development of the American antihero and in "the revolt from the village."[58] Fields has been equated with many important literary characters. But as if to justify the appropriateness of singling out Fields as equally unique, it should be noted that he has most frequently been compared with Charles Dickens' Micawber and Shakespeare's Falstaff, two of the most significant literary comedians in the English language. And without trying to be sacrilegious in the halls of literature, Fields is now unquestionably more universally accessible to the general public, and he has been for some time.

Fields and the world of Dickens' Micawber have already been compared closely as an outgrowth of the examination of the 1935 film adaptation of *David Copperfield* in which Fields plays the character of Micawber. Fields' personae (and the comedian himself) also encompass key comedy characteristics of Falstaff and the comic peculiarities of players who are satellites of Falstaff.

This comparison does not imply that the character of Falstaff directly affected Fields, as seems to have been the case with Micawber. Instead, it puts into perspective the significance of Fields as a modern-day Falstaff, for when critics linked the film comedian with the Shakespeare character, they were using a literary comedian ranked above even Micawber. In fact, according to honored literary critic and historian J. B. Priestley, "With the exception of Hamlet, no character in literature has been more discussed than this Falstaff, who is, like Hamlet, a genius, fastening immediately upon the reader's imagination, living richly in his memory."[59]

Unfortunately, a detailed comparison of Falstaff and Fields (personae and individual) never seems to have been done. Therefore, I will examine them according to the criteria of: (1) celebration of alcohol; (2) bragging and telling tall tales; (3) quickness of wit and gift for language; (4) physical incongruity of their being men of action; (5) performance of the cowardly act; and (6) characteristics and general ties between Falstaff's circle of supporting players and Fields'.

Falstaff's and Fields' personae frequently are tall-tale-telling revelers who like nothing better than the camaraderie of male drinking companions, just as Gene Fowler chronicled the real Fields inner circle in *Minutes of the Last Meeting*.[60] Fascination with drink would seem the best starting point for comparison. After all, a beer was even named for Falstaff. And in the Act IV of Shakespeare's *Henry IV, Part II*, Falstaff expands at length on the merits of alcohol:

> A good sherris sack [wine] hath a twofold operation in it. It ascends me into the brain; dries me there all the foolish and dull and crudy vapors which environs it; makes it . . . delectable shapes, which, delivered o'er to the voice, the tongue, which is the birth, becomes excellent wit. The second property of your excellent sherris is the warming of the blood.[61]

Fields' films represent a nonstop celebration of drinking, but he best articulates the importance of imbibing (in preference to man's best friend, the dog) in the essay "Alcohol & Me." Probably his most comic exultation of alcohol, however, is "The Temperance Lecture," the title notwithstanding. Easily the most anthologized of all his radio recordings, it provides a Fieldsian version of the past that makes him a much closer historical neighbor to Falstaff: "Throughout the Middle Ages the use of liquor was universal. Drunkenness was so common it was unnoticed. They called it the middle ages because no one was able to walk home unless they were between two other fellows. I was the middle guy."[62]

Alcohol was just as important in Fields' private life as in his professional one, though he always claimed his red nose was a product of numerous childhood beatings, because his runaway freedom was a source of envy to some boys. Serious drinking came later as a way of coping with the stress of nearly nonstop juggling practice and performing. And while there were few drinks he had not tried, eventually the martini became his staple. His martini intake was massive; during the California years most sources suggest nearly two quarts daily.[63]

Fields claimed martinis were best for him because "they work fast, and the sensations are lasting. They prick my mind like the cut of a razor blade. I work better with them inside me."[64] And they seemed to have had this positive effect, for he drank continuously, even during film productions, and did not become drunk. (In fact, he strongly disliked drunks.) During film work Fields' only cover-up for his martini cocktail shaker was to claim that it was full of pineapple juice—a hoax generously accepted by all, though pranksters once filled it with real pineapple juice, causing him to boom, "Somebody's been putting pineapple juice in my pineapple juice."[65]

And while Falstaff takes a symbol of the tavern onto the battlefield in Act V of *Henry IV, Part I* (Prince Hal discovered Falstaff is carrying a bottle of wine in his pistol case),[66] Fields' excursions on the estate or in his Cadillac were complete with a portable bar. (His in-house stock could have doubled for a commercial outlet store.)

In the second comparison, both Falstaff and Fields are also excellent at bragging and telling tall tales. Possibly the most comic example involving Falstaff occurs in the second act of *Henry IV, Part I*, just after Prince Hal and Poins have robbed Falstaff and several companions, only moments after the latter gang has done some robbing of its own. Falstaff's initial response is to claim the gang was beset by a hundred robbers, though the prankster prince keeps Falstaff on a braggart's defensive: "If I fought not with fifty of them, I am a bunch of radish! If there were not two or three and fifty upon poor old Jack, then am I no two-legged creature."[67]

Fields, of course, is never far from the tall tale. The antiheroic Ambrose Wolfinger of *The Man on the Flying Trapeze* (1935) claims to have a wrestling hold so unique "there isn't a man or boy born in the United States or Canada that could get out of [it]"; the con man Commodore of *Mississippi* (1935), relating his Indian-fighter career, is forever describing how he "cut a path through this wall of human flesh."

In real life Fields was also forever spinning tales, which, as he admitted in a 1934 article, were starting to catch up with him.[68] That is, he had been creative with so many facts that when friends and associates requested rehashes of specific stories, he was frequently at a loss. However, there is no denying the ties between Fields' public and private yarns. For example, his mistress Carlotta Monti observed:

> At dinners Woody [Fields] sometimes grew verbose knowing he had a captive audience, and would grossly exaggerate happenings that supposedly occurred to him in far-off and generally unheard-of spots in the world. The "Rattlesnake" story [about the close friendships of a particular man and his snake] from *You Can't Cheat an Honest Man* [the mere word "snake" always made the film's stuffy Mrs. Bel-goodie wail and faint] is a good example.[69]

Third, while the tales of Falstaff and Fields sometimes got both in trouble, their quick wit and gift for language often came to the rescue. For instance, Prince Hal eventually calls out Falstaff's yarn about bravely fighting a veritable army of robbers on the highway—an army only of the disguised prince and Poins—by stating, "Falstaff, you carried your guts away as nimbly, with as quick dexterity, and roared for mercy, and still run and roared, as ever I heard bullcalf. . . . What trick . . . canst thou now find out to hide thee from this open and apparent shame?"[70]

Falstaff smoothly replies, "By the Lord, I knew ye as well as he that made ye. . . . Was it for me to kill the heir apparent? . . . Why, thou knowest I am as valiant as Hercules, but . . . I was now a coward on instinct."[71] In a similar manner, the bravery of Fields' former Indian-fighting Commodore is called into question on the point of his character having pulled out a revolver during a battle years before. Revolvers had not been invented at that time, interjected some skeptic, to which Fields' Commodore coolly replied, "I know that but the Indians didn't know it." (Regarding the verbal magic of Fields' persona, one should not, of course, fail to mention his ability to sell someone a talking dog in *Poppy*, 1936.)

The private Fields was, if anything, even more determined not to lose a point of debate on any issues. A typical example can be drawn from the comedian's earlier tendency during touring years to open bank accounts all over the world as a reflection of both his poor beginnings and the hazards of being stranded on the road. Thus during a World War II gathering of friends, Fields revealed he had approximately $10,000 in a Berlin bank. David Chasen thought he must be kidding, while Gene Fowler volunteered, "Or else you're nuts. With the war on, and the inflation in Germany, how do you expect to get your dough from Hitler?"[72] (A motionless toothpick meant he was disgruntled. Fowler compared it to a "readied stinger.")

The comedian then replied, "Suppose the little bastard wins?"[73]

It should also be noted that the real world frequently echoed (and continues to echo) the words of this performer—words that also frequently represented a clever skirting of difficult situations, such as Fields' use of "Godfrey Daniel" as a substitute for "god damn" in the censorship era, or his often blanket endorsement to both the pretty and the not-so-pretty with endearments such as "my little chickadee," "my glowworm," and "my dove." Of course, many of Fields' nationally acclaimed statements or catchwords merely turn a traditional observation on its ear, such as his widely quoted *Bank Dick* (1940) comment on bathing. Fields, as Egbert Sousé is having a scotch and water at a bar. He downs the alcohol, dips his fingers in the small water chaser, and methodically wipes them on a napkin. Sousé then requests of the bartender, "Make it another one, and another chaser. I don't like to bathe in the same water twice."[74]

Fourth, while Falstaff and Fields look and feel most natural in taverns and other venues of leisurely debauchery, they often are called on to be men of action—obviously, a visual source of much of their humor. To see the big-bellied, uncourageous Falstaff on the battlefield—despite his position as a soldier—is the most delightful of comic incongruities, probably best captured by Orson Welles (in the title role) in his own outstanding film production *Falstaff* (1967, sometimes titled *Chimes at Midnight*).

Comedian Fields is not unknown to military settings. In *Janice Meredith* (1924) he plays a drunken British sergeant during the American Revolution; in the 1928 remake of *Tillie's Punctured Romance* Fields' circus assists the World War I Allied cause by a slapstick involvement with the German Army. One might say the comedian even improves on Falstaff's military incongruity, because in both cases Fields' greatest involvement is with the losing side. (Fields also co-wrote and copyrighted, with coauthor Mortimer M. Newfield, a three-act army farce set on an American base at the time of the U.S. entry into World War I. The farce was titled *Just Before the Dawn*.)

Despite these comedic army scenes, Fields is much better known for his civilian skirmishes, all showcasing admirably the comic incongruity of him in battle. In *The Man on the Flying Trapeze* (1935), the gun-toting, pajama-clad Ambrose Wolfinger falls down the cellar steps (in the best tradition of the antihero) as he hunts for burglars. Professor McGargle goes on the lam in *Poppy* when a posse materializes. In *My Little Chickadee*, Cuthbert J. Twillie attempts to fight Indians with a slingshot. And in *The Bank Dick*, Egbert Sousé is at his uniformed-guard best when he attempts to strangle a cowboy-clad child toting a toy pistol.

The real Fields maintained his own private war with the world, a war that sounds as if he were direct from the antihero pages of James Thurber. For instance, like Thurber's eccentric collection of relatives in "The Night the Bed Fell," Fields had his own established routine when he was especially aroused by fears of burglars.[75] He would prowl the grounds of his estate, gun in hand, frequently adding a monologue suggesting someone was with him—no doubt intended to further intimidate any crooks in the area, yet also lessening the chances of a direct confrontation.[76] During another period his fears of being kidnapped caused him to multiply his fictitious bodyguards. And in the middle of the night he would give his crew, who answered to names like Joe, Bull, and Muggsy, directions such as: "I know you boys are former prize fighters and gunmen but I'd rather you didn't shoot to kill. Try to get them in the spinal cord or the pelvis. Ha ha ha ha ha."[77]

There was also a comic military air in the manner in which Fields frequently surveyed his estate from the house with a large pair of binoculars. Gene Fowler likened Fields to "an admiral on the bridge of a flagship."[78] The comedian also had a loudspeaker over the main door, and thanks to his binoculars, he was more than prepared for unwanted visitors. For Fields, just about the whole world was the enemy. Thus, he once scared away two nuns collecting for a charity by impersonating

> the violent quarrel of lovers—snarled in his own voice, then answered in falsetto. There were threats by the male voice, piteous entreaties by the artificial voice, such as, "I'll murder you with this baseball bat, you double-crossing tart!" "Don't! Please don't beat me again, Murgatroyd! Think of poor little Chauncey, our idiot child!"[79]

Fields also played spy, having all his rooms wired so that he could monitor conversations of his servants, whom he rarely trusted.

Real war did, however, touch Fields' private life. During World War II (at sixty-plus years of age), he and several drinking companions, all of whom were suffering from various physical ailments, appeared at an army center prepared to register for home defense. While they were given forms to fill in (Fields is said to have requested a commando assignment), the woman on duty caught the comic absurdity of the event quite nicely when she inquired: "Gentlemen, who sent you? The enemy?"[80]

Fifth, not only are Falstaff's and Fields' personae comically incongruous with battle, they are very capable of performing cowardly deeds, if it serves their purposes. Thus, in Act IV of *Henry IV, Part I*, Falstaff first plays dead during battle and later stabs an already deceased Hotspur, claiming credit for his death.[81] Fields' entertainment alter egos are just as apt to do such deeds, from booting Baby LeRoy in *The Old-Fashioned Way* (1934) to pushing his rival (Leon Errol) for Margaret Dumont off a mountain in *Never Give a Sucker an Even Break* (1941). But probably the best example of this, and certainly the one in which the onscreen Fields projects the most pride, occurs in *My Little Chickadee* (1940).

Twillie, tending bar, tells a customer how he knocked down Chicago Molly. When someone else claims credit, Fields replies yes—but he was the one who started kicking her. Then he tops this proud admission by going into depth on the kicking experience: "So I starts to kick her in the midriff. Did you ever kick a woman in the midriff that had a pair of corsets on?"

The customer replies, "No, I just can't recall any such incident right now."

Twillie continues, "Why, I almost broke my great toe. I never had such a painful experience." (Later, however, it is revealed that Twillie and another man were eventually beaten up by the victim and an elderly gray-haired woman with her.)

One would not say the real Fields performed cowardly acts, but his methods could be dangerously eccentric. Probably the most famous case in point is the night he was doing his pool routine in the Ziegfeld Follies and found the laughs were not coming at the right times. Eventually he discovered a mugging Ed Wynn under the table. Fields was not amused, and he promised fatal consequences if it happened again.

It happened again. This time Fields brained Wynn with his pool stick during the routine, knocking him unconscious. The audience thought it was a set piece and loved it. Fields continued his popular pool routine, which received additional laughs when Wynn uttered unconscious moans. Fields later offered to incorporate the episode into his act, but Wynn declined.[82]

In later Hollywood years, Fields had a muscle-bound butler who worked out on still rings in the garage. The comedian was intimidated by him and eventually sensed disrespect. Thus Fields acted—perhaps. That is, the next time this live-in Charles Atlas took a swing on his rings, they gave way at the most inopportune time: "As he lost consciousness, he said later, he heard a kind of hoarse, maniacal laughter from a darkened corner of the building."[83] The two parted company.

These are the obvious parallels between Falstaff and Fields. But the comparison does not stop there. Several of Falstaff's supporting players also seem to have similarities or ties to Fields. Most obvious is Bardolph, attendant to Falstaff and possessor of an impressive red nose that invites witty comment. When Bardolph suggests Falstaff is too heavy, the latter directs an attack against the attendant's nose: "Do thou amend thy face, and I'll amend my life. Thou are tour admiral [flagship], thou bearest the lantern in the poop—but 'tis in the nose of thee: thou art the Knight of the Burning Lamp."[84]

Fields, of course, owned quite a "burning lamp" too, and references to it are frequent in his comedy, from the radio rivalry with Charlie McCarthy to numerous films. Except for Jimmy "Schnozzola" Durante, no major comedian probably ever better utilized his proboscis (the term Fields preferred to "nose"). Strangely enough, however, he was unusually sensitive about his nose in private life and could easily become offended, even when the cracks were from close friends. One such offending comment was reminiscent of Falstaff's aforementioned jab at Bardolph's nose. After John Barrymore's death, his friends had difficulty convincing Fields to serve as a pallbearer, because he felt the time to help friends was when they were alive. But when Fields continued to demur, painter-friend John Decker replied, "Well, in case it gets dark, your nose would make an excellent tail light."[85]

Prince Hal's companion Poins, who devises the comic robbing of the robbers (Falstaff and company), suggests Fields' con man persona. Pistol, the tavern warrior whose overblown speeches mask a coward, can be like a boastful Fields. Silence, the truly "silent" partner-stooge to country justice Shallow, is like any number of stooges Fields had on stage and in films, as well as in real life. And Dame Quickly, hostess of Bora's-Head Tavern and lender of money to Falstaff, rather anticipates those gullible women whom a conning Fields could manipulate.

This extended comparison to Falstaff is intended to dramatize the most significant legacy of Fields today—a universal symbol in American film and popular culture, on an equal footing with the greatest figures of literature.

Fields' second-greatest influence also has literary ties—his nearly ground-floor participation in the popularization of the comic antihero in American humor. Fields' natural writing inclinations were toward the antihero character, as best demonstrated in his copyrighted sketches. The antihero's attempt to find sanity where only insanity reigns describes most domestic situations in which Fields' antihero persona found himself.

It should also be noted that Fields, though a world-famous comic juggler since the turn of the century, had been showcasing his antiheroic talents annually, since 1915, in all-important New York City—the eventual center for the ultimate literary articulation of the movement. Moreover, Fields was doing this in probably the city's most visible entertainment marketplace, the Ziegfeld Follies.

As noted earlier in the chapter, the antihero is nonpolitical, urban, childlike, leisure-oriented, and frustrated—often at the hands of a domineering wife and machines in general. This is practically a blueprint for Fields' copyrighted sketches, which generally embrace all these characteristics. For example, "Off to the Country" (1921) is a frustrating attempt to leave the city by subway for a rural holiday, with man/child Fields saddled with a henpecking wife, a troublesome family, and an irritating ticket taker.

Leisure activity, which America was discovering in a big way during the 1920s, has a key two-pronged part in Fields' sketches. First, there are leisure athletics—his comic frustrations in playing golf and tennis, as in the 1918 copyrighted routines "An Episode on the Links" and "An Episode of Lawn Tennis." People also had more time to follow major sporting events; thus golfer Bobby Jones and tennis player Bill Tilden were major athletic stars of the decade. Second, leisure travel, especially by car, becamemore common during the 1920s, and Fields was there with "The Sport Model" (1922) and three versions of "The Family Ford" (1919–20). Still another, "The Midget Car," was copyrighted in 1930. Routines like these also provided an important source of comic aggravation based on mechanical breakdowns.

The defeat of leisure at home occurs in "The Sleeping Porch" (1925), where the central character is just trying to get some rest, and "10,000 People Killed" (1922), a saga of the family disruptions caused by the mass communication marvel of the 1920s—the radio. (The latter also adds more humor from mechanical frustrations.)

These and other copyrighted sketches by Fields also had a generous sprinkling of irritating women and children and a comic frustration with more of an undercurrent of anger than is present in his sound films of the 1930s. The stage routines are discussed here, despite his equally antiheroic and more famous late films (frequently drawn from the same routines), because of their timeliness—the beginning of the national transition to a comic antihero. However, such later, classic Fields renderings of the antiheroic as *It's a Gift* (1934) and *The Bank Dick* deserve equal billing with the most acclaimed literary works of such pivotal antiheroic authors as Clarence Day, Robert Benchley, James Thurber, and S. J. Perelman.

Fields' interest in the antihero spilled into the comedy world of his con men, who, though generally having more in common with the nineteenth century's capable comedy figures of American humor (particularly of the old Southwest), still frequently exhibited antiheroic characteristics, such as even the Great McGonigle's inability to get away from Cleopatra Pepperday's unending warbling of a sea shell song in *The Old-Fashioned Way*. (The setting for most of Fields' con man roles was also the nineteenth century.)

Fields' third-greatest influence was his unrecognized involvement in what literature terms "the revolt from the village," a movement of the late 1910s and 1920s that focused on small-town hypocrisy and emptiness but "was in actuality an over-all attack on middle-class American civilization."[86] The new wave was precipitated by Edgar Lee Masters' *Spoon River Anthology* (1915), "though it required five years for the influence of that book to pass thoroughly over from poetry to prose."[87] There were earlier precedents in American literature, such as Mark Twain's complex, biting short story "The Man That Corrupted Hadleyburg" (apparently, Twain was Fields' favorite author after Dickens).[88] Masters' haunting collection of free-verse poems—each one spoken from the grave by a different individual whose life had often been wasted—found the early twentieth century a much more receptive environment. And while *Spoon River Anthology* might not sound like vintage Fields, the general metaphor of Masters' examination of wasted—that is, buried— lives is a cornerstone of any artist's work that (like Fields') attacks hypocrisy and its frequent companion, smugness. There are however, black-comic moments in Masters' work that sound quite Fieldsian. One such is prohibitionist Deacon Taylor admitting his death was not watermelon related (as reported) but rather cirrhosis of the liver—the result of a 30-year passion for a drug store bottle labeled "'spiritus frumenti.'"[89]

Carl Van Doren's watershed article, "The Revolt From the Village," begins with a brief overview, stating: "For nearly half a century [prior to 1915] native literature has been faithful to the cult of the village, celebrating its delicate merits with sentimental affections."[90] And Anthony Channell Hilfer's *The Revolt From the Village: 1915-1930* examines even more deeply the roots of America's affection for the village.[91] Understandably, this reinterpretation of a basic American institution created a storm of controversy. But while other important works followed *Spoon River Anthology* (especially Sherwood Anderson's *Winesburg, Ohio*, 1919), it took Sinclair Lewis' *Main Street* (1920) "to bring to hundreds of thousands the protest against the village which these [earlier revolt] books brought to thousands."[92] Lewis followed *Main Street* with his equally significant *Babbitt* (1922).

Lewis is of central importance to both the antiheroic movement and a better understanding of Fields' ties with it. As noted in Chapter 1, there are a number of parallels between Fields' antiheroic persona and Lewis' Babbitt, with the possibility that the novelist influenced Fields' "Sleeping Porch" routine. Moreover, one could argue that the comic antihero movement had direct ties with "the revolt from the village," because *The New Yorker* (so important in the birth of the antihero) was founded with a pledge that stated, in part: "*The New Yorker* will be the magazine which is not edited for the old lady in [small-town] Dubuque. It . . . is a magazine avowedly published for a metropolitan audience."[93] Regardless of how closely related these two movements are, Lewis' entry into the revolt group is dependent on his use of a more direct and broad comic attack, precisely Fields' style during the same period (1920s), as well as later. Both Fields and Lewis are caricaturists who produce cartoon-like portraits of a frequently proud shallow-mindedness that anticipates by years painter Grant Wood's real portraits of the same subject (see especially Wood's *American Gothic*, 1930, and *Daughters of Revolution*, 1932).

Lewis' *Main Street* characters are also said to be "indistinguishable because, though some are kinder or better-natured, they all think in the same clichés. . . . [T]he group mind thinks in stock formulas and . . . group conven-

tions."94 Lewis underlines a key point of this and other 1920s revolt texts—
the inherent dullness of these tunnel-minded burgs. This is certainly true of
the characters who inhabit Fields' sketches and films of the decade, from the
comedian's own Fliverton tribe to the Jones family of *The Comic Supplement* (1924
and 1925).

It has also been observed that "the dominant metaphor of the book [*Main
Street*] is the machine. The villagers sit 'in rocking chairs. . . listening to
mechanical music, saying mechanical things about the excellence of Ford
automobiles.'"95 Again, this is true of other revolt texts (Lewis' 1929 *Dodsworth*
has a car magnate for its central hero). And as noted, Fields is just as taken with
the mechanical, from flivvers and radios to martini shakers that can be attached
to pogo sticks. Fields (both the man and his antihero persona) are just as
enamored of the family motor outing as Will Kennicott (*Main Street*) and
George F. Babbitt. In fact, the Fields-influenced *Comic Supplement* of 1925
beautifully combines a car picnic with the fundamental materialism also
inherent in the stereotypical American village against which these artists were
revolting. That is, after the Jones family finishes its trespassing picnic on the
lawn of a sumptuous estate, Pa (Fields) puts one of the children in the house
for some basics in stealing: "She might just as well start learning how to get
along in the world. Nothing like training children right when they're young."96
Fields' *So's Your Old Man* (1926, loosely adapted from Julian Street's award-
winning, Sinclair Lewis-like short story, "Mr. Bisbee's Princess") combines
many of these issues when it presents Fields as the inventor of unbreakable
automobile glass, living in the most class-conscious of small American towns.
And just as Fields remade *So's Your Old Man* in the 1930s, the comedian
continued his "revolt from the village" theme throughout the decade. His
ongoing attack was somewhat unique, because the Great Depression had
diffused many of the revolt issues, and the pendulum actually swung back (at
times) to the celebration of small-town values, as in Thornton Wilder's *Our
Town* (1938) and the films of Frank Capra. Thus, as stated in a poem of mine:

> While Capra celebrated small-town
> America Fields was busy deflating
> Big wheels on Main Street,
> Making W. C. a red-nosed hero
> To all blue-nose victims.

Carlotta Monti has observed that in private life Fields enjoyed "thrusting at
the mores and hypocrisy of society with a sharp-edged tongue which never cut
two ways."97 Consequently, just as the antiheroic frequently surfaced in the
world of his con men, Fields also addressed small-town hypocrisy in period
costume. And while his "revolt from the village" connections have been
overshadowed by his significance as a universal American figure and a comic

antihero of pioneer status, for many these rebel ties still come to mind first, especially for people who discovered him in the 1960s.

The anti-establishment 1960s were a time, of course, when the equally anti-establishment Fields was rediscovered in a big way. Monti comments on the even bigger dissident the comedian was in real life, where "single-handedly he wanted to fight the entire social system."[98] For instance, the performer who comically railed against income tax in *Fields for President* (1940) was obsessed with beating the tax system in real life.

Fields' two comedy personae could even be said to have offered models for 1960s dissidents. After all, student radical leader Abbie Hoffman's *Steal This Book* (a compendium of ways to rip off the establishment) is really nothing more than a "how-to" book for the con man of the former Now Generation. And while Fields' antihero could never be as direct about his options, he, too, represented a nonconforming spirit, muttering asides and making illegal alcohol. Both Fields personae have "fifth-columnist" tendencies, but they are more apparent in the antihero.

These are the key thrusts of Fields' influence on American humor and popular culture. Yet this is only a survey on the impact of a man probably best described as America's greatest native-born comedian. More needs to be written on a number of subjects, such as his apparent influence on such important, diverse figures in American comedy as film writer-director Preston Sturges and actor Walter Matthau.

For this author, Sturges' greatest film is the screwball classic *The Lady Eve* (1941), which showcases a truly delightful Fieldsian trickster named "Colonel" Harrington (Charles Coburn), who refers to his daughter (Barbara Stanwyck) as "my little minx."[99] The Colonel travels the world fleecing suckers in cards, and to the question, "Is this a game of chance?" one always expects him to drawl Fields' priceless reply, "Not the way I play it, no." In true Fields fashion, the Colonel is accompanied by his beautiful and loving daughter, who manages to fall in love with the story's wealthy young man (Henry Fonda).

Fonda is the son of Mr. Pike (Eugene Pallette), an antiheroic (though wealthy) father in the tradition of Fields' antiheroic neglectful fathers of the 1920s. Appropriately Fieldsian also is the fact that the Pike fortune is from a brewery—"Pike's Pale, the Ale That Won for Yale." Word games, like the Pike advertising jingle or the name of Fonda's bodyguard—Ambrose Murgatroyd (William Demarest, who is equally antiheroic and prefers the nickname "Muggsy")—also put the viewer in a Fieldsian environment.

At the time of *The Lady Eve*, Fields was no longer at Paramount, the parent company for Sturges, but both individuals had been employed for most of the decade by that studio. And both had close ties with producer William LeBaron (in charge of Paramount productions under Y. Frank Freeman at the time of

The Lady Eve). LeBaron was responsible for giving both men much of their creative freedom in a period when studio supervision was generally much tighter. But regardless of how it happened, *The Lady Eve* is very much a Fields-like creation. And the Sturges film world in general reflects much that is Fieldsian, particularly the frequency with which the director satirizes small-town America (see especially *Hail the Conquering Hero*, 1944). Moreover, as comedy historian Raymond Durgnat has suggested, "It's no accident that before Sturges, he [Fields] used Franklin Pangborn and other preferred denizens of the Sturges world."[100]

Such behind-the-scene ties between Fields and Walter Matthau are not as readily apparent, but on screen Matthau frequently seems to borrow. This is most apparent in Matthau's greatest role, his Academy Award-winning performance as the con man lawyer in *The Fortune Cookie* (1965) who exaggerates client Jack Lemmon's injuries for insurance purposes.[101] Other Matthau roles that are reminiscent of Fields are the oddball aristocrat of *A New Leaf* (1971, in which Matthau "frequently delivers his lines like W. C. Fields"[102]), the crotchety ex-vaudevillian of *The Sunshine Boys* (1975, an adaptation of a Neil Simon play), the nonstop-drinking Little League coach of *The Bad News Bears* (1976, unorthodoxically leading a team of comically foul-mouthed problem kids), the initially very reluctant father figure of *Little Miss Marker* (1980, a remake of the Damon Runyon story with Matthau as the bookie), the comically contrary antihero of *Survivors* (1983), Mr. Wilson of *Dennis the Menace* (1993) and his feisty figure from *Grumpy Old Men* (1993).

The general spirit of Fields' outrageousness, such as his bass fiddle having a litter of illegitimate little bass fiddles in *The Barber Shop* (1933) or really putting the toe to Baby LeRoy in *The Old-Fashioned Way*, best lives on today, however, in the films of Mel Brooks. In fact, Fields' belief that comedy needs a certain degree of vulgarity[103] works equally well as a philosophy for Brooks' world.

The Brooks film that best carries on this mood, besides *Blazing Saddles* (1974), is his greatest work to date—*The Producers* (1968, an Oscar winner for best original screenplay). Zero Mostel plays a down-and-out theater con man who goes for one big score by selling more than 100 percent of a play he is sure will fail—"Springtime for Hitler." It is, of course, a hit, and the antiheroic Mostel is "held over" in prison. In addition to this stock Fields situation, Mostel must con an innocent but simple-minded young man (Gene Wilder) into being his partner (shades of Fields conning Grady Sutton into a get-rich scheme in *The Bank Dick*), while Mostel wines and dines little old lady investors—a frequent Fields ploy for raising capital.

Fields is honored, not despite his vulgarity, but by virtue of it. His unorthodox, at times even irresponsible, comedy manner was well earned in both a real life and a screen life that were frequently antiheroic. And unlike the often similar Falstaff, who was eventually banished by a king, Fields films inevitably close with him in a kingly position—before a public bowing with laughter. Fields left a unique comedy heritage for an ever-expanding following. It seems a miracle that so much laughter could be born of so much pain, particularly (like Chaplin) from his early years. But that is often the tradition, the bittersweet beauty, the preciousness, of comedy.

NOTES

1. Harpo Marx (with Rowland Barber), *Harpo Speaks!* (1961; reprinted New York: Freeway Press, 1974), p. 24.

2. Jeanie Williams, "Woody's Film Sparks Pulitzer Tiff," *USA Today*, weekend edition, April 18–20, 1986, 1A.

3. Paul G. Wesolowski, "TGF Reviews Groucho," *The Freedonia Gazette*, Winter 1985, pp. 7–8. This review lists Wesolowski's top five Marx Brothers impersonation stage shows.

4. Martin A. Gardner, "The Marx Brothers: An Investigation of their Films as Satirical Social Criticism," Ph.D. dissertation, New York University, 1970.

5. Joe Adamson, *Groucho, Harpo, Chico and Sometimes Zeppo* (New York: Simon and Schuster, 1973), p. 156.

6. James Thurber, "The Secret Life of Walter Mitty," in *My Life and Welcome to It* (New York: Harcourt, Brace and Co., 1942), pp. 72–81.

7. Groucho Marx, "Press Agents I Have Known," *The New Yorker*, March 9, 1929, pp. 52, 54–55; Groucho Marx, *Memoirs of a Mangy Lover* (New York: Bernard Geis Associates, 1963).

8. Marie Seton, "S. Dalie + 3 Marxes = ," *Theatre Arts*, October 1939, p. 734.

9. Norris W. Yates, *The American Humorist: Conscience of the Twentieth Century* (1964; reprinted Ames, Iowa: Iowa State University Press, 1967).

10. Walter Blair, *Native American Humor* (1937; reprinted San Francisco: Chandler Publishing Co., 1960), p. 169.

11. Thurber, "Der Tag Aux Courses," *Stage*, March 1937.

12. John Grierson, "The Logic of Comedy," in *Grierson on Documentary*, ed. Forsyth Hardy (1947; reprinted Los Angeles: University of California Press, 1966), p. 55. (Marx Brothers segments originally appeared as an *Animal Crackers* review in *The Clarion* of December 1930 and a *Monkey Business* review in the *Everyman* of October 15, 1931.)

13. Gerald Weales, "Duck Soup," in *Canned Goods as Caviar: American Film Comedy of the 1930s* (Chicago: University of Chicago Press, 1985), p. 58; Donald Ogden Stewart, *Mr. and Mrs. Haddock* (New York: George H. Doran Co., 1924), pp. 123–37.

14. Weales, "Duck Soup," p. 58.

15. J. A. Ward, "The Hollywood Metaphor: The Marx Brothers, S. J. Perelman, and Nathanael West," *The Southern Review*, Summer 1976, p. 660.

16. S. J. Perelman, "Week End With Groucho Marx," *Holiday*, April 1952, pp. 59, 126–33. Later anthologized as "I'll Always Call You Schnorrer, My African Explorer" in *The Most of S. J. Perelman* (New York: Simon and Schuster, 1958), pp. 624–31.

17. Weales, "Duck Soup," p. 57.

18. William Troy, *Duck Soup* review, *The Nation*, December 13, 1933, p. 688.

19. Thurber, "The Car We Had to Push," in *My Life and Hard Times* (1933; reprinted New York: Bantam Books, 1947), p. 41.

20. Wes D. Gehring, *Screwball Comedy: A Genre of Madcap Romance* (Westport, Conn.: Greenwood Press, 1986).

21. Thurber, "Destructive Forces in Life," in *Let Your Mind Alone! and Other More or Less Inspirational Pieces* (1937; reprinted New York: The Universal Library, 1973), p. 18.

22. Allen Eyles, *The Marx Brothers: Their World of Comedy* (1966; reprinted New York: Paperback Library, 1971), p. 106.

23. Gehring, *W. C. Fields: Huckster Comedians* (Jackson, Miss.: University of Mississippi Press, 1994).

24. Salvador Dali, "Surrealism in Hollywood," *Harper's Bazaar*, June 1937, pp. 68–69, 132.

25. Eugene Ionesco's *The Shepherd's Chameleon* review, *Time*, December 12, 1960, p. 63; Gardner, "The Marx Brothers," pp. 2–3; Martin Esslin, *The Theatre of the Absurd* (Garden City, N.Y.: Doubleday & Co., 1961), pp. 236–37.

26. Gehring, *American Dark Comedy: Beyond Satire* (Westport, Conn.: Greenwood Press, 1996).

27. For more on this, see Gardner's "The Marx Brothers," p. 94.

28. Lance Morrow, *Accidental Death of an Anarchist* review, *Time*, March 12, 1984, p. 70.

29. *The Freedonia Gazette*, November 1980, p. 17.

30. Patricia Mellencamp, "Jokes and Their Relationship to the Marx Brothers," in *Cinema and Language*, eds. Stephen Heath and Patricia Mellencamp (Frederick, Md.: University Publications of America, 1983), p. 76.

31. Hector Arce, *Groucho* (New York: G. P. Putnam's Sons, 1979). This "official" biography of the comedian by his close friend is also the most detailed look at the Marx Brothers.

32. Thomas H. Jordan, "The Marx Brothers," in *The Anatomy of Cinematic Humor* (New York: Revisionist Press, 1975), p. 90.

33. Ibid., pp. 91–92.

34. Max Wilk, *The Golden Age of Television* (1976; reprinted New York: Delacorte Press, 1977), p. 92.

35. Gilbert Seldes, *The Movies Come From America* (New York: Charles Scribner's Sons, 1937), p. 41.

36. "Mr. Stan Laurel: A Great Comedy Partnership" (obituary), *The Times* (London), February 24, 1965, p. 15a.

37. Walter Kerr, "Laurel and Hardy: The Saving Turnaround," in *The Silent Clowns* (New York: Alfred A. Knopf, 1975), p. 330.

38. John Grierson, "The Logic of Comedy."

39. Leonard Maltin, ed. *The Laurel & Hardy Book* (New York: Curtis Books, 1973), p. 74.

40. Gehring, "The Comic Anti-Hero in American Fiction: Its First Full Articulation," *Thalia: Studies in Literary Humor*, Winter 1979–80, pp. 11–14; Gehring, "Film's First Comic Anti-Heroes: Leo McCarey's Laurel & Hardy," *Ball State University Forum*, Autumn 1979, pp. 46–56; Gehring, *Screwball Comedy: A Genre of Madcap Romance* (Westport, Conn.: Greenwood Press, 1986), pp. 13–35.

41. Siegfried Kracauer *Theory of Film: The Redemption of Physical Reality* (New York: Oxford University Press, 1960).

42. Gerald Mast, *The Comic Mind: Comedy and the Movies*, 2nd edn. (1973; reprinted Chicago: University of Chicago Press, 1979), p. 191.

43. Ibid., p. 192.

44. Hamlin Hill, "Modern American Humor: The Janus Laugh," *College English* (December 1963), p. 174.

45. Mast, *A Short History of the Movies*, 3rd edn. (1971; reprinted Indianapolis: Bobbs-Merrill, 1981), pp. 76–92.

46. Robert Benchley, *From Bed to Worse: Or Comforting Thoughts About the Bison* (New York: Harper & Brothers, 1934), p. 255.

47. Graham Greene, *A Chump at Oxford* review, *Spectator*, February 23, 1940, p. 248.

48. Jordan Young, "Popularity Grows on Borrowed Roots," *Pratfall* 1, No. 5, pp. 7–9 (n.d.).

49. Kenneth McLeish, "Samuel Beckett," in *Arts in the Twentieth Century* (New York: Viking Penguin, 1985), p. 463.

50. Kurt Vonnegut, "Dedication and Prologue" in *Slapstick* (New York: Delacorte Press/Seymour Lawrence, 1976), pp. 1–19.

51. *Planes, Trains and Automobiles* review, *Variety*, November 25, 1987, p. 14.

52. Ray Bradbury, "The Laurel and Hardy Love Affair," *Playboy*, December 1987, pp. 76–78, 210–11. See also Bradbury, *The Toynbee Convector* (New York: Alfred A. Knopf, 1988). A condensed version appeared in the September 1988 *Reader's Digest*, pp. 149–52.

53. Hellel Italie, "Director Martin Brest Is Considered a Bit of a Smart Aleck" (wire service story), *Waterloo Courier* (Iowa), August 10, 1988, p. C-3.

54. Elaine Warren, "He Forgot His Own Name—And Was Hired on the Spot," *TV Guide*, November 5, 1988, p. 11.

55. Robert Lewis Taylor, *W. C. Fields: His Follies and Fortunes* (Garden City, N.Y.: Doubleday, 1949), p. 341.

56. James Reid, "Nobody's Dummy," *Motion Picture*, October 1937, p. 85.

57. "'Poppy' Is Charming" (September 4, 1923), in *New York Times Theatre Reviews, 1920–1926*, Vol. 1 (New York: New York Times and Arno Press, 1971), n.p.

58. Carl Van Doren, "The Revolt From the Village," *The Nation*, October 12, 1921, p. 407.

59. J. B. Priestley, *The English Comic Characters* (New York: Dodd, Mead, 1931), p. 69.

60. Gene Fowler, *Minutes of the Last Meeting* (New York: Viking Press, 1954).

61. *Henry IV, Part II*, Act 4, scene 3, lines 97–105.

62. *The Best of W. C. Fields*, previously released recordings (Columbia, BL 34145), 1976.

63. Carlotta Monti (with Cy Rice), *W. C. Fields & Me* (1971; reprinted New York: Warner Books, 1973), p. 205.

64. Ibid., p. 206.

65. Taylor, *W. C. Fields: His Follies and Fortunes*, p. 242.

66. *Henry IV, Part I*, Act 5, scene 4, lines 52–55.

67. *Henry IV, Part I*, Act 2, scene 4, lines 185–88.

68. Sara Hamilton, "A Red-Nosed Romeo," *Photoplay*, December 1934, p. 33.

69. Monti, *W. C. Fields & Me*, p. 78.

70. *Henry IV, Part I*, Act 2, scene 4, lines 258–61, 263–65.

71. Ibid., lines 268–74.

72. Fowler, *Minutes of the Last Meeting*, p. 184.

73. Ibid.

74. Ibid.

75. Thurber, "The Night the Bed Fell," in *My Life and Hard Times* (1933; New York: Bantam Books, 1947), pp. 19–31.

76. Monti, *W. C. Fields & Me*, p. 184.

77. The domestic private battles of Fields often figure in the biographical literature on the comedian. See Taylor, *W. C. Fields: His Follies and Fortunes*, pp. 256–57.

78. Fowler, *Minutes of the Last Meeting*, p. 257.

79. Ibid., p. 152.

80. Ibid., p. 205.

81. *Henry IV, Part I*, Act 4, scene 4, lines 75, 119, 127–28.

82. This is another oft-reported incident. See Alva Johnston, "Profiles: Legitimate Nonchalance—II," *New Yorker*, February 9, 1935, p. 26; Taylor, *W. C. Fields: His Follies and Fortunes*, pp. 150–51.

83. Taylor, *W. C. Fields: His Follies and Fortunes*, p. 259.

84. *Henry IV, Part 1*, Act 3, scene 3, lines 25–28.

85. Fowler, *Minutes of the Last Meeting*, p. 222.

86. Anthony Channell Hilfer, *The Revolt From the Village: 1915–1930* (Chapel Hill, N.C.: University of North Carolina Press, 1969), p. 5.

87. Carl Van Doren, "Revolt From the Village," *The Nation*, October 12, 1921, p. 407.

88. Monti, *W. C. Fields & Me*, p. 48.

89. Edgar Lee Masters, "Deacon Taylor," in *Spoon River Anthology* (1915; reprinted New York: Collier Books, 1962), p. 80.

90. Van Doren, "Revolt From the Village," p. 407.

91. Hilfer, *Revolt From the Village*, pp. 3–136.

92. Van Doren, "Revolt From the Village," p. 410.

93. Blair, *Native American Humor*, p. 168.

94. Hilfer, *Revolt From the Village*, pp. 162–63.

95. Ibid., p. 163.

96. J. P. McEvoy, *The Comic Supplement* (1925), Billy Rose Theatre Collection, New York Public Library at Lincoln Center, p. 112.

97. Monti, *W. C. Fields & Me*, p. 90.

98. Ibid., p. 53.

99. Douglas McVay, "Elysian Fields," *Film*, Winter 1967, p. 23.

100. Raymond Durgnat, "Suckers and Soaks," in *The Crazy Mirror: Hollywood Comedy and the American Image* (1969; New York: Dell Publishing Co., 1972), p. 145.

101. McVay, "Elysian Fields," p. 23.

102. Pauline Kael, review of *A New Leaf* in *Deeper Into the Movies* (Boston: Little, Brown, 1973), p. 269.

103. Sara Redway, "W. C. FIELDS for Rough HUMOR," *Motion Picture Classic*, September 1925, pp. 32–33, 73.

4

WHERE THERE'S HOPE...
THERE'S ALLEN—WOODY

You see, I wanted to be a detective, too. It only took brains, courage, and a gun. And I had the gun.
Voice-over narrative by baby photographer Ronnie Jackson (Bob Hope) in the film noir spoof *My Favorite Brunette* (1947).

I was thrown out of NYU my freshman year for cheating on my metaphysics final. I looked within the soul of the boy sitting next to me.
Alvy Singer (Woody Allen) in *Annie Hall* (1977)

INTRODUCTION

One of the most dominant comedians of the post-World War II period was Bob Hope, who sometimes teamed with Bing Crosby in the "Road" pictures. Woody Allen, *the* comedian of the modern age (since 1960) is a longtime disciple of Hope. Allen has said, "If I wanted to have a weekend of pure pleasure, it would be to have a half-dozen Bob Hope films. . . . He is a great, great talent."[1] Allen and the Film Society of New York's Lincoln Center conspired to put on a 1979 Hope film retrospective. Allen edited and narrated a 63-minute compilation of clips from 17 Hope films, adding that it was Hope's work that had been his inspiration to enter film comedy. Revisionist movie critic Jeffrey Couchman, writing for the May 6, 1979, *New York Times*, noted that Hope's

> natural comedic asset is his voice, as distinctive in its twang as the voice of either Groucho or W. C. Fields and well suited to his clipped, under-

stated delivery. . . . [T]hese sounds are enhanced by a wonderfully mobile face [including] lips which practically curl around his sloped nose in a sneer of contempt or mock ferocity.

Bob Hope was finally being rediscovered.

Like his early idol, Charlie Chaplin, Hope was born in England, christened Leslie Towns Hope. But whereas the creator of the "Little Fellow" came to America as a young adult, Hope's family resettled when he was a child. Perhaps this immigrant bonding helped him become, with the possible exception of Will Rogers, the entertainer most likened to an American ambassador of goodwill, entertaining troops abroad or hobnobbing with presidents. He has maintained this position while managing to entertain the nation for 50-plus years in vaudeville, radio, television, the movies, and books. This unique position was acknowledged in the mid-1940s: "The gap left by the death of Will Rogers [1935], as a comedian whose barbs at politics and politicians were particularly appreciated in Washington, has been filled. Bob Hope has stepped into the shoes of Will Rogers in this respect."[2]

As with many personality comedians, Hope's films often have a parody foundation—the antihero as fool when trying to copy a real hero. But Hope went beyond the typical spoof. For instance, while most comedians tackle *the* American genre, the western, sometime in their career, Hope made four send-ups of the genre: *The Paleface* (1948), *Fancy Pants* (1950), *Son of Paleface* (1952) and *Alias Jessie James* (1959). The most critically and commercially successful movie of his career was *The Paleface*.[3]

Hope was hardly a slave to the western, however. He sideswiped an assortment of genres, from spoofing Hollywood and the action adventure in the "Road" pictures, to his inspired parody of film noir in *My Favorite Brunette* (1947). While not limited to these movies, the Hope portion of this chapter focuses on *The Road to Utopia* (1945, the best of the "Road" series), *My Favorite Brunette*, and *The Paleface*. Before examining Hope's films, some parody basics need to be established.

Film parody is a comic, distorted, yet generally affectionate imitation of a given genre, auteur (author), or specific work. There are six basic characteristics of the spoof film. First, while parody is frequently humorous even without viewer expertise on the subject under comic attack, it is most entertaining when one is familiar with the parody source.

Second, though the fundamental goal of parody is to be funny, this genre is also an educational tool, something that might be defined as "creative criticism."[4] That is, to create effective parody, one must be thoroughly versed in the subject genre. (It is for this reason that parody is often comically affectionate in nature; the artist is frequently a student of the target genre or auteur.) Thus, parody is the most palatable of *critical approaches*, offering insights through laughter. I frequently teach a genre course in which parody films are used to better define specific genres under discussion.

The "creative criticism" significance of parody is important to keep in mind, because the genre often has been considered as something less than important, as a parasitic growth on true works of art or as a literary elitist form of trivial pursuits, where one needs to know unnecessarily detailed facts before being able to understand the parody. Parody theorist Joe Lee Davis probably best demonstrated the genre's less than lofty image when he drew the following analogy: "As the pun [an abbreviated parody] has been called the lowest form of wit, so parody may often seem the lowest form of literary art."[5] (This is a key reason why Hope's parodies have not always been given the respect they deserve.) Yet it takes just as much creative talent to perceive a given structure and then effectively parody it as it does to create a structure in the first place. Parody is simultaneously something old and something new: Kid a traditional structure, have fun with the content.

Third, in further emphasis on the significance of parody, the genre should not be confused with satire, of which it has sometimes been considered a lesser subcategory. As genre theorist Joseph A. Dane has observed: "The norms in parody and satire are different; parody deals with literary [or cinematic] norms (collective understanding of a text or genre), while satire deals with social norms."[6] Parody has affectionate fun at the expense of a given form or structure; satire more aggressively attacks the flaws and follies of mankind.

So why the confusion? Parody scholar Linda Hutcheon addressed this question in her seminal book, *A Theory of Parody*: "The obvious reason for the confusion of parody and satire, despite this major difference between them, is the fact that the two genres are often used together."[7] (This phenomenon often occurs in Woody Allen's films, which will be addressed later in this chapter.)

Fourth, film parody, like other comedy approaches, is a genre of indeterminate date and location—it is not limited to one period and place, as is a western. But, unlike the other comedy genres, once a specific parody subject has been chosen, time and place and all the icons that go with it (such as six-guns and ten-gallon hats in a western parody) are of the utmost importance.

Because parody is based on a viewer's prior knowledge of a given genre or auteur, it is naturally important to showcase early on (through icons) which particular subject has been chosen. Again, this accents the earlier point that parody focuses on having fun with a given structure or text.

Another triggering device is the use of real footage from the genre being spoofed, as Carl Reiner and Steve Martin did in *Dead Men Don't Wear Plaid* (1982). An additional variation involves cameo appearances by performers strongly associated with the type of film being spoofed. Thus, Bob Hope's film noir parody *My Favorite Brunette* (to be expanded upon later in the chapter) opens with a pivotal cameo from celebrated noir performer Alan Ladd; his western parody *Son of Paleface* included Roy Rogers; Hope's *Alias Jessie James* closes with a corral full of western cameos, ranging from Jay Silverheels (Tonto) to Gary Cooper. A further twist of actor as icon occurs in those film spoofs in which a performer imitates a classic screen persona, as Hope imitates Ladd in *My Favorite Brunette*.

Fifth, film parody repeatedly involves a compounding phenomenon. While spoofing usually has a focus genre or auteur under comic attack, the movie is frequently peppered with eclectic references to other films. For instance, although *Airplane!* (1980) makes parody mincemeat of the *Airport* movies, it still has irreverent time for other film targets, such as the wonderful opening-credit deflating of *Jaws* (1975).

A sixth and final frequent trait of film parody is to self-consciously draw attention to the fact that it is a movie. This does not mean that movies about moviemaking, often now called "genre genre" films, are parodies. To honestly be incorporated into a parody format, this self-consciousness must be used to complement an ongoing attack on a target genre or auteur. An example would be Bob Hope's direct address comments to the camera, especially in the "Road" pictures.

In either case, such self-consciousness represents the ultimate parody prick, since nothing deflates a celebrated genre or auteur faster than a reminder that this is, indeed, only a movie. Moreover, since parody is based on self-consciousness about a given subject, such filmmaking interjections represent a logical culmination of the parody experience—the comic death blow to any vestiges of the viewer's suspension of disbelief. In addition, as implied by theory historian Margaret A. Rose, the self-consciousness is one other way of "signaling" to the audience that this is indeed a parody.[8]

These, then, are the six pivotal characteristics of parody: a humor based on the distorted imitation of a familiar genre or auteur; "creative criticism," or offering educational insights; a distinction from satire as an affectionate attack on structure, not society; a genre of indeterminate time and place; the compounding of more than one target subjects; and self-consciousness about the filmmaking experience.

Hope's *Utopia*

Between 1940 and 1962 Hope and Crosby teamed in seven "Road" films: *Road to Singapore* (1940), *Road to Zanzibar* (1941), *Road to Morocco* (1942), *Road to Utopia* (1945), *Road to Rio* (1947), *Road to Bali* (1952), and *Road to*

Hong Kong (1962). Besides spoofing the action adventure genre, the "Road" pictures are an affectionate parody of Hollywood.

Utopia was originally to be the *Road to Moscow*, but because two then recent Hollywood films on Russia, *Mission to Moscow* and *North Star* (both 1943), had not been commercial hits, production company Paramount decided a new title was needed. It was also a providential change, since the paranoia about communism that followed World War II resulted in the Hollywood blacklisting of many talented artists, all because they might have "red" interests. Even some people involved in the production of *Mission to Moscow* and *North Star* were later hassled by communist witch hunters—and this was during a time when the Soviet Union was a U.S. *ally* (1941–45). With the Moscow destination scrapped, Paramount was stuck with winter sets, and the need for an appropriate story. But like most comedies, the "Road" pictures are not married to a script. As the reviewer for *The New Yorker* wrote: "The plot, if you care, has the boys whooping around Alaska in search of a gold mine, and Miss Lamour [the "Road" show romantic interest] is present as the owner of the property,"[9] It is the late 1890s and gold in the Klondike makes *Utopia* the only period "Road" film, which might contribute to the film's unique status.

All the "Road" pictures spoof the movies but none as effectively as *Utopia*. And it all begins before the film. That is, as *Esquire's* critic noted, humorist Robert Benchley (see Illustration 8) "supplies another element of [parody] importance; [he's] a prologue without portfolio."[10] Prior to the opening credits one sees Benchley standing behind the desk he normally used in his award-winning short-film subjects. Best known for his inspired comic essays, which helped bring the figure of the comic antihero to a broader audience, Benchley had also found major antiheroic success in film and radio. At the time he was arguably America's best-known funnyman.[11] With tongue firmly in cheek he introduces the movie:

> The motion picture which you are about to see is not very clear in spots. As a matter of fact it was made to demonstrate how not to make a motion picture and at the same time win an Academy Award. Now someone in what is known as the Front Office has thought an occasional word from me might help clarify the plot and other vague portions of the film. [chuckling] Personally, I doubt it.

Periodically, Benchley reappears in the corner of the screen and shares bits of comic wisdom, such as "This is a device known as a flashback," or "Did you ever stop to think of one of those dog teams? The lead dog is the only one that ever gets a change of scenery." Appropriately enough, the *New York Tribune's* critic used Benchley as a symbol of the film's parody: "He kids the film as much

8. Robert Benchley—"Mr. Antihero" (c. 1940).

as it kids itself. His ironic explanations of the screen's flashback or calling attention to a group of people as obvious 'extras' underline the superb humor of the show."12 And *Esquire* said, "His cheerfully inane ad libs do more than merely compound the confusion. They give the idiotic events on the screen a certain related reality."13 Years later when Hope was asked about the Benchley comments, as well as other examples of spoofing the movies, he said, "They [audience] love anything that gives them a little mental jerk and they want to be 'with it.' "14 Neither before *Utopia* nor after would the "Road" pictures have such a gifted supporting comedian as Benchley.

In addition to the screen corner appearances of Benchley there are numerous scenes that derail what plot exists and shout out "movie spoof." For instance, there are a talking fish and a talking bear who feels underappreciated ("A fine thing. A fish they let talk. Me, they won't give one stinking line.") This is a perfect commentary on the saturation comedy of the "Road" pictures—anything for a laugh. And while there is a loose plot reason for the fish and bear to be there, the comments are hardly expected. Hope does his own animal sound (wolf) when he has a big kissing scene with Dorothy Lamour's character (Sal), adding in direct address to the viewer, "As far as I'm concerned this picture is over right now."

Duke Johnson (Bing Crosby) and Chester Hooten (Bob Hope) even discuss being off on another "Road" picture as they dogsled across the Klondike. Chester then looks off into the distance and observes, "Get a load of that bread and butter." While Duke is mystified, the camera cuts to a snow-covered mountain that has stars around it—the logo for Paramount, the studio producing the film. At another point a character dressed like a magician strolls through their scene. When asked if he is in the movie, he answers, "No, I'm taking a short-cut to stage 10."

The biggest spoof, of course, is having Hope and Crosby posing as two murderers who have stolen a gold mine map belonging to Dorothy Lamour's character. It's a funny premise that plays even funnier when the film's other figures accept the trick for a while. It is difficult for Chester and Duke, hardly two tough guys, to stay in character. The funniest recovery finds Hope's Chester ordering lemonade in a bar. Immediately recognizing his mistake, he quickly growls to put it "in a dirty glass."

Bing Crosby has said, "The basic ingredient of any *Road* picture is a Rover Boys-type plot, plus music. The plot takes two fellows, throws them into as many jams as possible, then lets them clown their way out."15 As noted in Chapter 1, the "Road" pictures use travel to get Hope and Crosby into as many comic "jams" as possible.

Crosby, however, has left one ingredient out of his "Road" formula. He does not examine the difference between these "two fellows." Though they are both women-chasing con artists (in *Utopia* [see Illustration 9] they have a huckster game called "Ghost-O" that involves a magic box increasing however much money is placed inside), Crosby's Duke is in charge of all the team's misadventures, as is the case in all the "Road" pictures. For example, in *The Road to Morocco* (1942) Crosby's character goes so far as to sell Hope's into slavery.

And the romantic Crosby always gets the girl—Dorothy Lamour—except in *Utopia*. But this lone Hope victory must be qualified. *Utopia* has a framing device, with the opening and closing scenes finding the three stars quite old; the comedy adventure is told in flashback. When elderly Duke drops in on the longtime married Chester and Sal, the couple is taken by surprise because Duke seemed to be a goner at the close of *Utopia*. An earthquake had suddenly opened an abyss separating Duke from Chester and Sal, and Crosby's character was last seen with an angry mob bearing down upon him. Still the skirt-chaser, Duke arrives at Chester and Sal's with two beautiful young "nieces." The topper to this action has Chester and Sal's only child coming into the scene—he is the spitting image of Duke, naturally played by Crosby. Thus, even Hope's one "success" with Dorothy Lamour finds him to have been cuckolded despite help from an earthquake.

Hope's favorite description of his "Road" character came from a 1953 *Saturday Evening Post* article: "Fate is determined to make [him] a jerk. He brags and blusters, but there isn't a child over five who can't outwit him, disarm him or steal his pants."[16] Hope's "Road" character could still be the wise guy, as in his bragging situations. But as Hope observed of these pictures, "We put more emphasis on the 'boob' aspect" of his "Road" character.[17] As a reviewer noted, "Theatre ushers report that spectators all laugh at Hope and identify themselves with Crosby."[18] But Crosby's *Zanzibar* character is most succinct on the subject: "Stick with me and if you live, we're going to do all right" (see Illustration 10).

Part of the inspired saturation comedy effect of *Utopia* could be attributed to the fact that it was scripted by two of Hope's former radio gag writers, Norman Panama and Melvin Frank. They pop up every so often in later Hope projects. For instance, they wrote the script for *Road to Hong Kong*, with Frank producing and Panama directing.

Hope and Crosby did not write and direct their films, but they peppered their scripts with much additional gag material, from themselves and from their radio gag men. (Hope and Crosby had competing radio programs.) Thus, many names might have appeared under script credit. Moreover, like other independent personality comedians mentioned earlier in the text, Hope (the team's designated comedian) was directable, *if* he wanted to be. For instance, probably the best director Hope worked with was Frank Tashlin, who co-scripted and directed *Son of Paleface*. Tashlin comically described how Hope

9. Bob Hope & Bing Crosby on the *Road to Utopia* (1945).

10. One of many "Road" picture "nooses" Crosby put Hope into.

would get his way: "His narrowed eyes squinting [anticipating the future look of an angry Clint Eastwood?] at you down the maligned nose, is a withering experience. Your puttees curl and your megaphone sags [these two objects were once considered standard fare for a director]."[19]

In *Road to Utopia* Hope and Crosby had an especially casual approach to filmmaking, though the production of all the "Road" pictures had an easygoing strategy. Crosby observed, "We had a ball [on the "Road"] pictures. We had directors who let us suit our own schedules."[20]

While the "Road" pictures are famous for the comic asides of Hope and Crosby (*Utopia* included), as noted in Chapter 1 American humor is best known for its visual/slapstick action. The *New York Herald Tribune*'s critic went so far as to credit the visual side of *Utopia* as the key to its success: "Much of the show is premised on the violently witty asides of Crosby and Hope, but it is not the dialogue which sustains the production. It is at its best when pantomime is the springboard for crazy characterizations and ludicrous scenes."[21] Examples include the pickpocket scenes with Hope and Crosby, their reduction to babies when they find out what they turned down from Santa (Claus makes a cameo appearance), and Hope's accidental romancing of a bear.

Though not in *Utopia*, the team's most repeated physical game is their "pattycake" defense. When villains have the duo in a tight spot, Hope and Crosby's characters start playing patty-cake. At a given moment, instead of the normal "patty" to their partner's hand, each punches out the mystified bad guy on his side. When this defense does not work, as in the *Road to Zanzibar*, their characters observe, "They must have seen the [last "Road"] picture."

The final "Road" picture opened in 1962 and by this decade the solo movie careers of Hope and Crosby were in decline. Some critics felt the "Road" pictures, with the exception of the *Road to Utopia*, "haven't worn too well."[22] One explanation for the unique appeal of *Utopia* is that "it tries hardest for those self-spoofing gags which shatter the storyline."[23] No little part of this was the inspired use of Robert Benchley. Other reasons are that it is the only period "Road" picture, and it has a more pronounced use of physical comedy. The volatile 1960s was also a time when the anarchistic comedy of the Marx Brothers, W. C. Fields, and others was rediscovered. In contrast, the late 1940s and 1950s films of Hope and Crosby, Dean Martin and Jerry Lewis, Danny Kaye and others were in "the more conservative thematic structure of affirmative [status quo] comedy."[24] One did not satirize the McCarthy witch-hunting 1950s, with its threat of communists under everyone's bed.

Utopia and the other "Road" pictures are now appreciated by most students of comedy, whether critics or kids. And while some parody references can be obscured by time, the good spoof picture saturates the screen with so much material one has no time to bemoan the occasional parody reference gone astray. Moreover, if the performers in the parody vehicle are memorable stars, such as Hope and Crosby, what might be potentially obscure is anything but. For example, a pivotal source of Hope and Crosby's humor is their continual bickering at each other. The basis for this is a comic "feud" originating in their competing radio programs. No doubt this was inspired by earlier radio feuds between Jack Benny and Fred Allen, or W. C. Fields and Edgar Bergen's Charlie McCarthy. Period fans of the "Road" pictures would have had the added bonus of recognizing this shtick move from radio to screen, but the bickering in and of itself is funny, whether one knows the radio connection or not. Good parody works on the shotgun approach; it peppers a large area of subjects, big and small.

Hope's *My Favorite Brunette*

My Favorite Brunette was especially important to Hope. It was the first movie product of Hope Enterprises Inc., and it was made on a fifty-fifty basis with Paramount studio. The comedian was very happy to be his own boss: "When you're under contract to a certain studio you are obligated to do certain things whether you like it or not. Of course, they will fix it for you, but it is not the way to make pictures today."[25]

The private-eye picture was carefully chosen, possibly influenced by the fact that Hope's favorite reading material was detective stories. He spared no expense, using over a million dollars of his own funds in the project. This added control paid off; the film was a major critical and commercial success, invariably being noted as one of his best.

While the "Road" Pictures spoofed the movies as a whole, *My Favorite Brunette* is primarily a parody of the film noir (literally, black cinema) genre, which was at the height of its popularity in 1947. Film noir, known for its man-in-the-middle detectives, such as Dashiell Hammett's Sam Spade in the *Maltese Falcon* (1941), or Raymond Chandler's detective Philip Marlowe in *Murder, My Sweet* (1944, adapted from *Farewell My Lovely*). Being a detective is not a film noir requirement, but the genre's central male ends up playing detective, regardless of his given screen trade. For instance, *Brunette* finds Hope playing a baby photographer who lives to be a detective.

Film noir is dark in story line, with suffering and death the indifferent norm. The fatalism of German Expressionism, as well as its visual style (the city at night, shiny black surfaces everywhere, unusual camera angles) had a great influence on film noir. The genre represents corruption mixed with healthy doses of sex and psychotic violence.

Film noir, which flourished from the middle 1940s until the early 1950s, was the result of several post-World War II developments. First was the cynical world view born of revelations about the Nazi Holocaust, the developing Cold War, and the use of the atomic bomb. Second, several Jewish directors, who had been active during the period of German Expressionism, had fled Nazi-occupied Europe and eventually found themselves in Hollywood. Third, since the 1930s there had been a school of writing often referred to as "Tough Guy Fiction," with writers ranging from James Cain to Ernest Hemingway, and including Hammett and Chandler. While there was still a Hollywood censorship board, 1940s adaptations of these provocative works were allowed to be closer to the original stories (after World War II, people expected more adult fare). Fourth, with so many men serving in the armed forces, women on the homefront assumed a lot of previously male jobs. When the war was over, there was some tension between returning veterans and the women who had successfully held down the job market. This was no doubt a factor in film noir's strong, dominating, and dangerous women.

Thematically, this genre undercuts the American dream and success story: People who seem to have achieved success have cheated along the way. The dream is just one more American myth. The genre also undercuts the traditional location of the American paradise—California, be it the 1849 gold rush, or the 1930s migration of Dust Bowl farmers. Thus, film noir invariably takes place in California, often in Los Angeles or San Francisco. Appropriately, the genre sometimes rubs shoulders with the film industry. Indeed, the movies are a metaphor for this negative world view. That is, films are not what they seem to be, from the false-front buildings to the stunt men for the stars. The dark comedy/noir classic *The Player* (1992), is about a film studio.

Hope's *My Favorite Brunette* appeared in the noir heyday. It would be difficult to highlight a more thorough genre parody. This film is an excellent example of the aforementioned "creative criticism." Wannabe detective Ronnie Jackson (Hope) has his modest studio next to a real detective's office—with film noir star Alan Ladd in a cameo as private-eye Sam McCloud. This is the beginning of a story-long flashback and voice-over narration (both classic noir devices) by Jackson, who is currently awaiting execution on San Quentin's death row.

Besides the immediate comedy contrast between Hope's essentially cowardly figure and his attempts to be a tough guy, there is a blatant difference in acting styles. Hope is a fully animated, over-the-top comedian. Ladd, like most noir film figures, uses a minimalist style of body and dialogue, with the latter both brief and pithy. Noir is an existentialist world in which protecting one's self means personally exposing very little.

Since Hope's Jackson had a hard time even handling his last photography assignment (a two-year-old child who nearly bites his finger off), one would wager Jackson's chances are less than good to be a private eye. But Hope at his best, as he is here, brings such enthusiasm to this detective dream (he has invented a key-hole camera that has already gotten him kicked out of five hotels) that he naturally gets a chance to play the part. A critic observed, "Bob Hope wanders through the show as though he were improvising every incident. Performing such as this is no trick. It is high artistry."[26]

As he sits in Sam McCloud's office while Ladd's tough guy is gone, Hope tries to imitate Sam by downing some whiskey from McCloud's desk. The comic's response might be compared with humorist Robert Benchley's inspired description of strong drink:

> In . . . seconds the top of the inhaler's head rises slowly and in a dignified manner until it reaches the ceiling where it floats, bumping gently up and down. The teeth then drop out and arrange themselves on the floor to spell "Portage High School, 1930" . . . and a strange odor of burning rubbers fills the room.[27]

Woody Allen borrows Hope's scene for his *Play It Again, Sam* (1972). Fittingly, Allen's character is also trying to imitate a hard-drinking film noir detective— genre icon Humphrey Bogart.

As in most film noir, the catalyst for the hero's (or in this case, the antihero's) entry into the genre is by way of a beautiful, mysterious woman. The *New York Daily Mirror* described it thus: "Hope with his confusion, double-takes, asides to the audience and drooling pursuit of the sultry Dorothy Lamour, makes a highly agreeable detective."[28] Mobsters have kidnapped Lamour's scientist uncle and she desperately wants help from Hope's Jackson, whom she mistakes for Ladd's McCloud.

For the contemporary viewer, *My Favorite Brunette* is a broad take-off on film noir. But there is a second, less acknowledged type of parody that should briefly be touched on with regard to *Brunette*. This second and more subdued approach manages to balance both comic deflation with an eventual reaffirmation of the genre subject being targeted. The latter spoof movies are not as obvious and are often confused with the genre being undercut. An example of this is John Landis' *An American Werewolf in London* (1981), where broad parody (such as the use of songs like "Bad Moon Rising" and several versions of "Blue Moon") alternates with shocking horror (graphic violence and painfully vivid werewolf transformations). This produces a fascinating tension between genre expectations (in this case, horror—to be scared) and a parody that is comic without deflating the characters involved. This is opposed to the more traditional horror parody of *Young Frankenstein* (1974), where, for example, Marty Feldman's Igor, with those eyes and a roving hump, can never be taken seriously. Thus, the reaffirmation approach adds a poignancy not normally associated with parody. One is truly saddened by the death of the American werewolf (David Naughton).

Obviously, *Brunette* belongs to the first broad parody category. But in numerous period reviews there were references that at least flirt with the reaffirmation approach. For example: "In addition to being hilariously funny, the picture is a genuine thriller," and it manages to have "suspense and excitement as well as jokes."[29] This was due in no small part to the casting of two period villains forever linked with the horror genre, Peter Lorre and Lon Chaney, Jr. This observation is made merely to note the enigmatic nature of genre study. Without casting any aspersions on the often inspired nature of genre writing, a formula of sorts exists for each type. Yet, one must allow for variations to occur over time.

At the risk of sounding blasphemous, even pioneer genre writings by pivotal film critics like Robert Warshow (on the western and the gangster film) and James Agee (on comedy) are not without some limitations. Warshow has problems with *My Darling Clementine* (1946), *Kiss of Death* (1947), *High Society* (1952), and *Shane* (1953); Agee has reservations about comedy outside the silent era.[30] Genre criticism exists as a guide for the inquiring mind, highlighting recurring patterns of cultural significance in the arts, and not as a dictator of said patterns. As influential genre author John G. Cawelti has observed, "When genre critics forget that their super texts are critical artifacts and start treating them as prescriptions for artistic creation, the concept of genre becomes stultifying and limiting."[31] Consequently, *Brunette* remains a parody today, but any period suggestions of reaffirmation, the aforementioned "genre thriller," have long since gone.

Continuing this examination of *Brunette* as broad parody, a passing comedy aside by *Newsweek*'s review—"anything Sherlock Holmes can do, Sherlock Hope can do better"[32]—invites a connection between film noir and the antiheroic Hope. The noir private eye is just the opposite of Sherlock Holmes. Sherlock is all-knowing; he can look at a footprint and tell how much change the suspect had in his pants and whether he preferred peach cobbler over pumpkin pie. With his brilliant deductions, the last page of the Holmes story has all the loose ends tied together. Now, while the film noir detective is tough, he is often no further ahead in solving the mystery than a member of the audience, and some questions even go unanswered. In arguably the greatest film noir, the revisionist *Chinatown* (1974), Jack Nicholson's central character is never ahead of the viewer and ends up defeated by John Huston's figure of evil. But, though the "last page" of *Chinatown* is difficult to accept, one has enjoyed the equal-ground nature of the "trip" to the end. Bob Hope can only comically fill the film noir shoes of an Alan Ladd or Jack Nicholson, and thus film noir is parodied. Yet, it is appropriate that Hope should be spoofing a then-new, more vulnerable private eye. Indeed, the *New York Times'* review of *Brunette* included an observation—"as for clarity, what would it want with such as that?"[33]—that could apply to many legitimate examples of film noir.

An additional point with regard to *Brunette* is the mistaken period connection drawn between it and Hope's earlier *My Favorite Blonde* (1942), where the comic is not in search of adventure.[34] While some parallels exist, such as a pretty girl and an antihero with "delusions of courage,"[35] *Blonde's* parody has a different pre-noir target—Alfred Hitchcock's *The Thirty-Nine Steps* (1935). *Blonde* even features the same leading lady of *Steps*, Madeleine Carroll. It is unfortunate that most people think only of Mel Brooks' spoof of the director—*High Anxiety* (1977)—when one mentions parody and Hitchcock. *Blonde* complements Brooks' work, since the Hope vehicle keys on one Hitchcock movie while *High Anxiety* takes a shotgun approach that attempts to refer to as many of the celebrated director's movies as possible. If truth be told, the Hope picture is the better spoof. Brooks' film, due to its broad comic attack, is often uneven in getting laughs. But comparison of these two affectionate but different spoofs of Hitchcock will have to be saved for some future study.

Brunette sometimes seems a model for Woody Allen. For instance, Hope's false bravado on death row (the framing device from which the flashback occurs) anticipates Allen's demeanor in *Love and Death* (1975) as he awaits execution; both characters anticipate a pardon. Consequently, these normally devout cowards act as calm wiseguys. For instance, Hope's Ronnie Jackson, on the verge of his walk to San Quentin's gas chamber, sneers at a penitentiary that has not yet converted to electricity. Even this comment is topped with the closing reaction of the disappointed executioner (Bing Crosby) when Ronnie's last-second pardon arrives. Hope's character responds, "That guy will take any part." "Road" picture footnotes like this, always at Crosby's expense, occur in many of Hope's solo films.

There is also an interesting link between Allen's *Crimes and Misdemeanors* (1989) and *Brunette*. In the Hope film a confession that would clear the antihero of murder charges has been recorded. But a switch is made and when Ronnie plays what he thinks will clear him, he hears a speeded-up version of Betty Hutton singing "Murder He Said," from the film *Happy Go Lucky* (1943), a comic surprise that seems to keep pointing the murder finger at Ronnie. In *Crimes* Allen has a dual-focus narrative, with a murder in one and more comic frustration for his antihero in the other. And at precisely the moment when the decision to murder has been chosen, the film cuts to a theatrical screening of *Happy Go Lucky* and Hutton belting out "Murder He Said." It is an inspired surprise comic transition to the world of Allen's character, a patron at the movies.

A good parody acts as a guide to a genre, and *Brunette* does just that. The film noir woman is sexually manipulative. When Dorothy Lamour's character, Carlotta Montay, mistakes Ronnie for a detective, he is reluctant to take her case. But she comes on to him saying: "We Montays are generous. If you will just find my husband [actually, it is her uncle] I will be so grateful. You'll see." With that promise and the appropriate sexy body language, the word "no" drops out of Ronnie's vocabulary. Period reviews often treated Lamour as just another pretty face: "She is little more than a comely prop in a one-man [Hope] job of bumbling clowning."[36] Though being drop-dead gorgeous is certainly in the genre's femme fatale job description, Lamour goes beyond beauty as a plot catalyst. In part because of the "Road" pictures, she and Hope have excellent screen chemistry. And with no Bing Crosby in sight, save for the cameo, the viewer can finally assume Hope will get the girl. Moreover, despite Carlotta's initial manipulation, Lamour's "Road" picture ties convince the viewer they belong together.

Film noir oozes sexuality, and *Brunette* is saturated with it. When Ronnie finds out Carlotta is not married he drools, "So he's not your husband. Well, did I quote you any rates? I may work cheaper, you know." When Ronnie is being chased and escapes through an apartment building, he buzzes nearly all the apartments to unlock the main door, repeating the line, "Hello, honey, this is Joe." Countless women replying in a "come hither" nature lead Ronnie to observe in the midst of his flight, "I must remember this address." Even events not associated with sex are described in a sexual manner. For example, when Ronnie comes to after being knocked out, he says, "I was playing post office with the floor." (This comic patter after a concussion is also reminiscent of noir classic *Murder, My Sweet* [1944], where Dick Powell as Philip Marlowe is forever responding with a quip after being knocked out by bad guys.)

Another noir characteristic is the suggestion that the femme fatale or a member of her immediate family is mentally unstable. For instance, the younger daughter (Martha Vickers) in *The Big Sleep* (1946) has Humphrey Bogart's Philip Marlowe complaining she tried to sit on his lap—while he was standing up. The period noir films often imply ties to incest, but the era's censorship policy forbade anything that provocative. Only later, when restrictions were dropped, could a noir movie like *Chinatown* (1974) or *The Grifters* (1990) deal directly with incest. In *Brunette*, Ronnie is told Carlotta has mental problems, and has him asking, "Does she snap her cap very often?" Carlotta's waffling on just who is missing, her husband or her uncle, could also be construed as someone being a victim of, or having a propensity toward, incest. Ronnie has to rescue Carlotta from a mental sanitarium, and this requires Hope to act crazy, something he finds upsetting: "I think I do this too well."

Parody films frequently spoof specific films and/or genres in addition to the key genre under attack—rather a nothing-sacred policy. And *Brunette* includes many examples. For instance, when Ronnie is having difficulty climbing a tree, in order to break into a second story window, he mumbles, "It always looks so easy in those *Tarzan* pictures." Later, when he finds himself hanging from a chandelier during a chase, he discovers a bottle and immediately quips "Ray Milland has been here." This is a reference to Millard's Oscar-winning performance as an alcoholic in *Lost Weekend* (1945), forever hiding bottles in odd places.

Film noir often also features a magnificent old mansion in which the decadent heavies reside, or at least appear to live. Ronnie says in voice-over, "It's the kind of house that looks like you can hunt quail in the hallway." But as in Hitchcock's later noir-ish *North By Northwest* (1959), when authorities are brought in by the central character (in this case, Ronnie) the house is empty of boarders. Things are seldom as they seem in film noir, and even the sanity of the lead figure appears to be in question. Whether occupied or not, such a mansion represents old money obtained in shady deals. The decay of such families is sometimes symbolized by age, sickness, or incest. For example, in *The Big Sleep* a hothouse for plants is attached to the mansion, with the wheelchair-bound, elderly patriarch constantly there. Though not as blatant as this, *Brunette* manages to create that ambiance, including a heavy pretending to use a wheelchair.

Even Ronnie's quips have a way of resurfacing in later noir films. For instance, when he finally manages to hold a gun on the diminutive, knife-obsessed Peter Lorre, he cracks, "One move and you're a dead midget." In *Chinatown* Jack Nicholson's character makes the mistake of calling director Roman Polanski's knife-carrying cameo figure a midget and nearly loses his nose. And as *Chinatown*'s wounded private eye observes, "I like my nose and I like breathing through it."

In these and so many other ways, Hope's *Brunette* manages to take apart film noir, one genre component after another. In answer to a later revisionist critic's article titled "Bob Hope: More Than a Gagster?" the answer has to be a resounding—yes![37]

Hope's *The Paleface*

Though Hope was frequently drawn to the western parody, this segment focuses on *The Paleface* because it is the best of the series and arguably the greatest of his non-"Road" pictures. There is, however, a comparison made with the sequel, *Son of Paleface*, because of its different approach to parody.

Life magazine's "Movie of the Week" (January 3, 1949) salute to *Paleface* paid high tribute to Hope's spoofing abilities when it linked them to America's premier genre: an "astute combination of two ingredients which have always served the movies well: a standard cowboy-and-Indian plot and the standard gags and gimmicks of a Bob Hope comedy."[38]

The comedian plays the most antiheroic of characters—a mail-order dentist named Painless Peter Potter. Business is not going well in the Old West (he has a tendency to pull the wrong teeth), so he plans to head East before any unhappy customers return for revenge. (When one tough character gives him just fifteen minutes to get out of town, Painless replies, "The last town gave me twenty minutes.")

This all changes, however, when he meets a sexy Calamity Jane (Jane Russell), who is a secret agent for the government. Her assignment is to discover who is smuggling guns to the Indians. Calamity marries Potter as a cover (a couple apparently going west to homestead) to succeed in her mission. This puts Painless in constant danger, but Calamity always manages to shoot their way out, while making it appear as if Potter is the real hero. Hope's character, not unlike Harry Langdon's silent screen persona and Peter Sellers' later Inspector Clouseau, is oblivious to this assistance. And therein lies much of the comedy, with Painless thinking he is a gunfighter and even searching out danger. Moreover, the comedy ante is heightened all the more when he decks himself out with a cowboy outfit more elaborate than that of a six-year-old with wealthy parents. It quite possibly influenced Dustin Hoffman's *Little Big Man* (1970) costume when his character was going through a gunslinger stage.

The year after *Paleface* came out, film critic James Agee gave Bob Hope and the picture left-handed praise by describing the actor as a "good radio comedian with a pleasing presence."[39] Agee felt the film was a standout for the period but could not rival the classic silent comedies; while a visual gag could be milked for several laughs, he noted, the verbal joke received just one, if that.

In 1952, *Saturday Review* critic Hollis Alpert took Agee to task for those comments when Alpert reviewed the sequel to *Paleface*, *Son of Paleface*.[40] This *Review* essay focused on the sequel but defended the propensity for sight gags in both pictures. Though Alpert does not provide *Paleface* examples, he might have described the inspired marriage sequence. The viewer sees the hands of the minister, Potter, and Russell's new bride in close-up for a single long take. When the reverend calls for the ring, Painless cannot find it and searches several pockets. After the ring has been found, the clergyman explains what it symbolizes. Hope's character then puts the ring back into his vest pocket. The minister's hand impatiently gestures to get the ring back. A confused Potter now retrieves his watch from another pocket and tries to hand that over. Further gesturing from the minister has Potter fishing out the ring again. But now he puts it on one of the reverend's fingers. The exasperated bride grabs the ring and tries to give it back to Painless. But Potter keeps mistakenly arranging his hand so the Jane twice accidentally puts the ring on one of her antiheroic husband's digits. Losing patience, Jane slaps Painless' hand and personally guides him in the placement of the ring on her finger. Potter then puts his hand over Jane's, as if to say, "I can't chance having the ring come off and go through this ordeal again." At last they are officially husband and wife, though it remains a mere cover for Jane.

Scenes like these do not make Hope another Chaplin, but they should help correct the misconception that he is merely a radio (that is, verbal) comedian. In fact, the ring sequence is reminiscent of Frank Capra's use of visual comedy in sound films. An example is the long-take, close-up scene of title character Jimmy Stewart's hat in *Mr. Smith Goes To Washington* (1939). Smith is very nervous to find himself in conversation with the most beautiful woman he has ever seen. Capra showcases this uneasiness by following Smith's hat from hand to hand, held behind his back, dropped, and more hand to hand movement.

Bob Hope's comedy is often an effective combination of sight and sound. Shortly after the wedding scene, Potter comes into his bedroom thinking Jane is behind a dressing screen. However, it is an Indian, periodically giggling from previously inhaling Potter's dental laughing gas. When Hope's character comes to the screen he affectionately reaches over and touches "her" shoulder saying, "My but you're a muscular little thing, aren't you? Those dresses are awful deceiving." Then Potter rubs "her" arm and the Indian giggles from the laughing gas. Hope's character says, "I'm sorry; I didn't mean to tickle you." He feels "her" hair, observing, "Isn't that sweet, you put your hair up in braids."

Painless says, "Come out Mrs. Potter. ["She" giggles.] I know you're modest. But it's all right. I'll keep my eyes closed." He pulls "her" toward him and as they kiss the Indian whacks him on the back of the head, causing Potter to say, "Boy, can you kiss!" He then passes out on the bed.

In and of itself this is an effective comedy scene. But it goes beyond this. Agee had wanted as much as possible to be milked from a gag, and Hope's mistaken identity scene does just that. But also it includes two other components. The laughing gas had comically been set up earlier in the movie. Part of one's laughter is tied to that earlier dental scene. The laugh is thus being stretched out. Later in the film all we need to hear is a high-pitched giggle to know the gas has been put to comic use again. Along similar lines, the Indian hitting Potter in the back of the head is funny. But it is all the more amusing given that this is precisely what Jane does every time Painless tries to kiss her. She whacks him, and he attributes it to great kissing; then he passes out.

With recognition of these visual skills, it is time to briefly examine Hope's brilliant verbal talent. His comic dialogue ranges from the comic throwaway description of a patient's mouth (a "happy little dungeon") to the elaborate word game he must play in preparing for a gunfight. One cowboy advises Painless that his opponent "draws from the left, so lean to the right." Another bystander tells him, "There's a wind from the east, so you better lean to the west." A third cowboy warns him that his adversary "crouches when he shoots, so stand on your toes." With each additional tip Potter comically repeats them all. But then, as if anticipating the criticism that verbal humor cannot be stretched, Painless attempts to run through the advice one more time and it comes out, "He draws from the left so stand on your toes. There's a wind from the east, better lean to the right. He crouches when he shoots, better aim to the west. He draws from his toes so lean towards the wind." Painless has comically topped the original elaborate directions. Hope's character tops it still one more time by observing, "Ha, ha, I've got it." The addition of a sight gag and a comic aside further stretches this comedy. That is, Potter decides he should take a practice shot before the gunfight, but he misses his target badly. He immediately alibis, however, by licking a finger, holding it up in the air and observing, "Wind shifted."

Scenes such as these are what so influenced Woody Allen. In a review of *Paleface*, movie critic Marilyn Wilson says the "Hope film *persona* is much like the Allen one—the good-hearted but inept man whose main weapon is the wisecrack. . . . Hope's speeches in this film would fit perfectly into one of Allen's early films."[41] Wilson goes so far as to suggest that an offscreen voice that convinces Potter to rescue Jane works much as the Bogart adviser figure in Allen's *Play It Again, Sam.*[42]

Despite the old vaudeville joke about Hollywood being the place where everything is created sequel, it took several years, in spite of *Paleface*'s huge success, before *Son of Paleface* appeared. Regardless, movie sequels are generally interesting both for what they tell the viewer about the original and/or for any new directions that are taken. In *Son of*, Hope plays Junior, the only child of Painless and Jane. He has recently graduated from Harvard and now comes west to retrieve a fortune in gold allegedly left to him by Potter. It is now early in the twentieth century, and young Potter arrives via a noisy horseless carriage. It makes for a great sight and sound gag. The viewer has been led to believe that gun-shooting desperadoes are about to descend on the town. When this offscreen automobile backfires several times, one merely assumes the plot is preceding on course. And then one sees Potter, Jr. in this bright red vehicle, complete with the full-length slicker, goggles, gloves, and cap. The viewer is amused at the comic trickery, and Hope's costume adds to the fun.

Though sequels are often panned for not capturing the unique qualities of the original, *Son of* also found great critical and commercial success. Broader in its parody than *Paleface*, *Son of* plays more along the "anything goes" philosophy that later became synonymous with the parody world of Mel Brooks. For the time period, as at least one critic observed, the movie "comes so close to the style of those old "Road To—" pictures . . . you might almost shut your eyes (if you can manage) and think you are enjoying one of the same."[43]

Before the movie opens the viewer is reminded of *The Road to Utopia*'s prologue with Robert Benchley. Bob Hope does voice-over narration of what to expect from the film and then on the screen is footage of Bing Crosby driving an automobile at night. Hope observes, "Ah, ah, what's this? This is an old character actor on the Paramount [film studio] lot we try to keep working. He's supporting a large family, but I guarantee this fellow will not be in the picture tonight." Hope's voice-over occasionally returns during the film, such as his commentary about the statue of his father which graces the main street of Paleface Potter's western hometown, Sawbuck Pass. Chiseled onto the statue's base are the words "He won the West." Hope says, "If he won it, he was using loaded dice."

Like the "Road" pictures, *Son of* is peppered with Hollywood film references. For instance, when an old tintype photographer suddenly appears for no discernible reason and Junior states, "Who do you think you are, Cecil B. DeMille?"—that is precisely who it is. Later, when Potter's son attempts a lengthy horseless-carriage trip across the desert, two buzzards alight on the back seat. Junior orders, "Hey, Martin and Lewis [Dean Martin and Jerry Lewis, period comedy team for Paramount], no hitchhiking; it's a state law!" Speaking of law, when this picture was made (1952), Hollywood still had a censorship code. Consequently, during one flirtatious scene young Potter's dialogue briefly cannot be heard. Immediately, Junior turns to the camera in direct address and says, "You should have heard that line." It is reminiscent of a fifth columnist moment in *Never Give a Sucker an Even Break* (1941), when W. C. Fields (playing himself) is in a soda fountain that resembles a bar. He turns to the camera and observes, "This scene's supposed to be a saloon, but the censor cut it out. It'll play just as well." Both gags are effective, but Hope's version has a surprise element, since the viewer's first assumption is the soundtrack has gone dead.

As with *My Favorite Brunette*'s inclusion of film noir star Alan Ladd, *Son of* includes a western star, Roy Rogers, playing himself. But there is a decided difference. Ladd's detective is revered by Bob Hope's wannabe private eye. Rogers' secret agent cowboy is seen as something of a joke by Potter Junior. This is largely based on Rogers' preference for horses, particularly his famous Trigger, to women. He even sings a ballad about the subject, titled "Four-Legged Friend." Obviously, this situation plays on the old western stereotype of the special bond between a cowboy and his horse. But Rogers' macho quotient is further comically damaged when he turns down the sexual advances of Jane Russell, who is again co-starring with Hope. For the oversexed Junior (just like Dad), Rogers' disinterest is incomprehensible. In fact, at one point in the film Junior gives Rogers a look that goes well beyond comic pity, almost as if to suggest that Rogers *loves* his horse. (Of course, one should give Rogers credit for leaving himself open to such spoofing.) Ironically, Junior later spends time in bed with Trigger, as he and the horse have a lengthy fight over the covers; the horse ends up the winner. This is just another example of how much broader the parody is when contrasted with *Paleface* or especially *My Favorite Brunette*.

With Rogers' preference for Trigger, Junior wins Jane Russell's Mike (she is a good bad girl in each picture) by comic default, which sets up the film's biggest laugh and inspired close. Mike has had to serve a long prison term. Thus, the ending is a fast-forward to parole day. Junior (once again in driving attire) and Mike seem to have been married before she was incarcerated. As Roy and Junior await her release, Rogers observes that it must have been difficult biding one's time all those years. Hope's character answers, "I saw Mike on visiting days but it wasn't any fun talking to the woman you love through a wire screen." Mike soon exits prison and after a short delay, four little boys follow. An incredulous Rogers asks, "Yours?" But unlike the close to *Utopia*, where Hope's character has obviously been cuckolded, these children are his, as evidenced by their wearing early motoring garb identical to Junior's. As Rogers and the viewer ponder the making of babies and wire screen, Hope's character states, "Let's see' em top this on television!" (By the early 1950s, when *Son of* was made, the new medium of television had begun to cut into movie attendance.)

As the credits close on *Son of*, the viewer sees Roy Rogers riding off into the sunset (a classic western conclusion), while Potter Junior drives his new family east in his horseless carriage. Junior, like his father, prefers the comforts of civilization. Indeed, Painless Potter sings the Academy Award-winning song of 1948—"Buttons and Bows"—whose East versus West lyrics decidedly embrace the former. Potter had planned to return to the East when Calamity Jane essentially kidnapped him West. Fittingly, Painless takes part of the wagon train off-course when he pays more attention to singing "Buttons and Bows" than following the correct fork in the road. (The popular song again resurfaces in *Son of*.) Dentist Potter does, however, represent one of the basic pioneer types going west—the young professional (maybe *semi*-professional in his case) looking for a ready market of less demanding customers. It is precisely this kind of western immigrant that needs the protection of the stereotypical good guy cowboy. Thus, when Potter, thanks to the shooting of Jane, is mistaken for just that capable cowboy type, the parody success of *Paleface* is heightened. As a footnote, Hope brings off the dental humor most impressively. Numerous comedians have not fared as well when dealing with this subject, whether W. C. Fields in *The Dentist* (1932) or Red Skelton in *A Southern Yankee* (1948). Laurel & Hardy are not much more successful in their dental comedy *Leave 'Em Laughing* (1928). But the saving grace for this team is the introduction of laughing gas. Possibly Hope took a page from this sketch, because the best part of his *Paleface* "dental work" also involves laughing gas. In fact, the use of laughing gas becomes a comic motif in Hope's picture.

The East-West dichotomy is expanded in *Son of,* because it is 1896 and the standard period associated with the western genre (post-Civil War to the turn of the century) is fast approaching. Junior accents this further by arriving in an early automobile and forever referring to his eastern alma mater Harvard (the letter "H" is plastered over everything he wears or owns). And there is never any doubt about Junior returning to "Boston, Mass." Moreover, at exit time Potter is just as comically incompetent as when he arrived from Harvard. In contrast, most western spoofs involve comic characters who either prefer the West (such as Buster Keaton in *Go West*, 1925) and/or have grown from the experience (like Jerry Lewis in *Pardners*, 1956). It is not until Mel Brooks' *Blazing Saddles* (1973) that another spoof of the genre both left the West (literally breaking out into Los Angeles reality) and learned little from the experience.

CONCLUSION

This portion of the chapter has been an examination of Bob Hope at his antiheroic spoofing best, from the "Road" to film noir and way out West. With that high-pitched growling sound Hope makes when he perceives how handsome he is or his fleeting moments of courage, it is difficult to dislike his persona. (His misperception on personal looks is often accompanied, as it was in *Paleface*, with a winningly egocentric line like "What are you doing to that glorious beast [Jane Russell's character]?" Comedy historian and theorist Raymond Durgnat has observed:

> Hope's characterization is a rich and relevant one. He has spasms of Harold Lloyd's optimism, [Eddie] Cantor's jitteriness, [W. C.] Fields's disillusionment, and a Don Duryea desperation, while his bouts of childlike bluff and hopeful cunning expertly transpose into farcical terms the comic vices of salesmanlike opportunism.[44]

Hope is a key player in the development and acceptance of American humor's antihero/wise-guy formula. He also represents a key comedian in the transition of 1940s film comedy to the modern (post–1960) era. And as this chapter suggests, he has greatly influenced the work of the pivotal Woody Allen.

WOODY ALLEN

Woody Allen is the first comedian equal to the "Chaplin disease." Like the creator of the Tramp, Allen also writes, directs, and stars in his films. And as did Chaplin, Allen has been able to sustain quality works for decades. He has also continued to experiment with his art, frequently embracing darker subjects—despite the public's reluctance to support such change. And like Chaplin, his personal life has been rocked by sexual scandal. Both comedians rose to film fame with vulnerable underdog antiheroes. But whereas Chaplin's Tramp was capable if he chose to be (see Chapter 2), Allen's persona was the ultimate dysfunctional comic character. Still, with time both artists embraced stronger screen figures.

In this chapter three phases of Allen's career are examined through the trilogy *Play It Again, Sam* (1972), *Annie Hall* (1977), and *Crimes and Misdemeanors*. *Sam* finds Allen at his best as the ultimate antihero Allan Felix (even his name sounds like an incapable cartoon figure). *Annie Hall*, his inspired and most celebrated work (winner of four Oscars, including Best Picture), is an autobiographical love story that first takes him from comic situations to three-dimensional characters. *Crimes* finds Allen wonderfully balancing dual storylines of black humor. The comic narrative showcases the antiheroic Allen of old. But the dramatic narrative is the darkest world view: learning to live with murder. These unlikely companion pieces are nicely interwoven. Allen's balancing act is his best example of the serious themes the artist has preferred since *Annie Hall*.

Play It Again, Sam

Fantasy has always been associated with the comedy world of Woody Allen. The pervasiveness of his comic antihero stance—which Maurice Yacowar[45] focuses on as the comic outsider—in his films, short stories, and stand-up comedy recordings—has come to represent a pivotal view of the frustrations of modern society. And fantasy has been crucial in these presentations, be it the short sketches from *Everything You Always Wanted to Know About Sex But Were Afraid to Ask* (1972, where antihero consistency is maintained even when he appears as a sperm), or the moment of supreme self-satisfaction in *Annie Hall* (1977), when Allen suddenly pulls Marshall McLuhan out of nowhere to put down a pompous intellectual. Director Allen even underlines the fantasy magic of this moment by then giving his comedy character the direct address line, "Boy, if life were only like this."

For the student of comedy, it is quite natural to link the frustrations and fantasies of Allen's world with an earlier author who helped bring the comic antihero to centerstage in American humor, James Thurber. In fact, if one's sense of a comedy chronology were a bit shaky, it would seem logical to note the Woody Allen-like nature of James Thurber's classic fantasy, "The Secret Life of Walter Mitty":

> Captain Mitty stood up and strapped on his huge Webley-Vickers automatic. "It's forty kilometers through hell, sir," said the sergeant. Mitty finished one last brandy. "After all," he said softly, "What isn't?" The pounding of the cannon increased. There was the rat-tat-tatting of machine guns. . . . Something struck his shoulder. "I've been looking all over this hotel for you," said Mrs. Mitty. "Why do you have to hide in this old chair?"[46]

It is important to keep in mind, however, that the Allen fantasy does not always represent the escape from frustration associated with Walter Mitty's secret life. For example, in *Bananas* (1971) Allen dreams that the monks carrying him on a cross are beaten out of a parking place by a second cross-toting group of monks; one fantasy in *Play It Again, Sam* (1972) even has Bogart being shot by Allen's ex-wife.

Frustration in comedy fantasy is, of course, nothing new. Charlie Chaplin was shot in the heaven scene from *The Kid* (1921), after he has succumbed to sin; and in the more modern variation on this in *The Seven Year Itch* (1955), Tom Ewell gets conflicting fantasy messages from heaven and hell about what to do when upstairs neighbor Marilyn Monroe comes visiting. Goodness wins—if you can call that a victory.

What is so unique about Allen's depiction of frustration in the fantasy world is that it occurs so often. In fact, *Sleeper* (1973), where Allen is defrosted in a Big-Brother-like world 200 years in the future, might be termed a science fiction fantasy of frustration—a comic nightmare. As John Brosnan has noted, Allen had completed science fiction trial runs for *Sleeper* (see Illustration 11) the previous year (1972) with some of the episodes from *Everything You Wanted to Know About Sex but Were Afraid to Ask*, particularly one involving a giant, mobile, killer breast.[47]

But apart from underlining the deep-seated nature of his comedy persona's frustration (which can cause real-world problems to show up in his fantasies), this aspect of Allen's imaginary world does not offer the viewer much new insight. However, when examined in tandem with truly escapist fantasy

11. Woody Allen and Diane Keaton on the set of *Sleeper* (1973).

elements in his work (also the more dominant), some rather interesting insights are revealed.

This is best exemplified in *Play It Again, Sam*, which Allen described as "fun to write because it dwelt on fantasies and I could write all these romantic things you could not live out in real life."[48] By casting Bogart (played by Jerry Lacy) in a number of the fantasy scenes, Allen raised viewer identification to the last degree. And without discarding occasional fantasy frustration, he was able to construct a story around such traditional Woody Allen requirements as his relationship with women, movie history, and personal identity. The film has no fewer than 18 often lengthy fantasy scenes (his longest and most consistently integrated use of film fantasy at the time) and is his most effective balancing of the fantastic and the real for both comic effect and maximum viewer identification.

The film opens with Allen in a theater watching the close of *Casablanca* (1942). As the film cuts back and forth between Bogart on screen and its antihero audience member, it is clear that Allen, like a Bob Hope figure, has momentarily become Bogart. He underlines this after the close of *Casablanca* (and his first fantasy) by saying, "Who'm I kidding? I'm not like that. I never was, I never will be. Strictly movies." For the next several minutes the film avoids fantasy, allowing the viewer to become acquainted with the real-world situation of Allen's character. It is familiar ground: Allen is a film journalist who is feeling especially frustrated sexually because his wife has recently divorced him. Most of this information is provided through two flashback scenes with his ex-wife (Susan Anspach), which help prepare the viewer for the next bit of fantasizing.

When Allen asks himself, "What's the secret to being cool?" Bogart appears and essentially tells Allen to toughen up. The "naturalness" of Bogart's appearance is helped by the fact that Allen's apartment is like a Bogart museum, with posters from *Casablanca* and *Across the Pacific* (another Bogart film, 1942) dominating, while smaller bits of Bogart memorabilia, stills, and books, lie scattered about. Allen, like an updated Bob Hope, tries Bogart's prescription of bourbon and soda and passes out. The result: His depression continues.

Next enter his supportive friends (Diane Keaton and Tony Roberts), who make it a point to play matchmaker. But Allen is so depressed now that his third fantasy occurs. It is a short vision of his ex-wife on a wild date with a Hell's Angel type, while she sneers about Allen, "He fell off a scooter once. And broke his collarbone."

His friends manage to get him a date, and as Allen dresses, Bogart again appears. His message is be more earthy; tone down the mouthwash, deodorant, after-shave, and baby powder, or "you're gonna smell like a French cat house." Encouraged by Bogart, mimicking Bogart's mannerisms and inflections, and with a reflection of a Bogart poster in the mirror before him, he fantasizes the seduction of his blind date—curing her of frigidity. This is very much like a misguided pose of Bob Hope's persona.

As might be expected, however, the blind date is a horrible failure, as are his next several interactions with different women, from a suicidal girl who is interested in Jackson Pollock, to a drug user who nearly gets Allen's face redesigned by taking him into a bikers' night spot (more Hell's Angel types). This series of failures is reminiscent of the comment by Shelley Duvall's character in *Annie Hall*: "Sex with you is really a Kafkaesque experience," and is the longest passage of the film without a fantasy break. However, fantasies occur regularly for the rest of the film, starting with an appearance by his ex-wife, who tells him, "You're not the romantic type."

After she goes, Allen does not exactly negate her message when he ponders, "I wonder if she actually had an orgasm in the two years we were married—or did she fake it that night?" In fact, there is more of the same in the next scene, when Allen calls the home of a girl he took out in high school 11 years ago and finds that she has still left explicit directions with her parents not to give Allen her number.

By this point the viewer has started to realize, though it has not yet become apparent to Allen's character, that this frustrated outsider happens to have a lovely rapport with Diane Keaton. Since she is married to his best friend, she is the only girl he has not been trying to impress—a classic example of the success of being yourself. And since her nonstop businessman husband is also a "phone man" (a continuing gag finds him constantly calling his answering service to leave new numbers where he can be reached), Keaton and Allen have lots of time together.

To top off the logical nature of their budding relationship is the fact that, despite her beauty, Keaton is as insecure as Allen; this is compounded by her husband's marital neglect. That all of this should culminate naturally in an innocent affair has been foreshadowed in the comically touching scene in which he gives her a plastic skunk for her birthday, the skunk being her favorite animal.

It is not long, therefore, before his next fantasy (the seventh), finds him briefly imagining the seduction of Keaton. Appropriately enough, this fantasy is immediately followed by feelings of guilt, which just as logically bring Jerry Lacy's Bogart to the rescue, trying to downplay the guilt. This soon becomes the most important fantasy since the *Casablanca* opening because Allen's ex-wife then appears and proceeds to argue with Bogart about what Allen should do. It is a pivotal fantasy because it brings together for the first time the two poles of Allen's fantasy world—the castrating ex-wife and the macho legend—who later battle for control of Allen's real world. The scene is given an added comic touch by taking place in a supermarket (which Allen accents at the fantasy's close by saying, "Fellas, we're in a supermarket!"). From this point on, his imagination will become much more active.

On the way home from the market Allen fantasizes how much easier it would be if his friends were getting divorced, and if Roberts had asked him to take care of Keaton. The fantasy, though very brief, maintains an otherwise beautiful consistency with the rest of the movie by having Roberts leave by plane (echoing the *Casablanca* opening airport scene and anticipating its return at the close), and also by continuing and topping all previous telephone numbers at which he could be reached—he is meeting an Eskimo lover at "Frozen Tundra six, nine two nine oh."

At home now, preparing for a dinner date with Keaton (Roberts is out of town on business), Allen imagines all his advances being misunderstood, with the cry of rape quickly dispatching this nightmare fantasy. Understandably sobered, he plays it very detached upon Keaton's real arrival.

Bogart soon appears as sort of an on-the-job date counselor. It will represent his longest scene thus far in the film, as well as his funniest. Allen, like Buster Keaton in *Sherlock Jr.* (1924), effectively uses this example of a "real" screen love to guide his own life. And once again the mise-en-scène of Allen's apartment enhances the effectiveness and believability of Bogart stepping out of the shadows to coach Allen. Bogart posters seem to turn up in every shot, and bits of room décor ape the Moroccan set design of the original *Casablanca*, from the beaded curtain in the kitchen to the living room's rattan chair and shutters. But just as Allen is about to become Bogart's A student, the ex-wife appears and guns the teacher down. Needless to say, this is a bit disconcerting to pupil Allen, especially since the fantasy assassination takes place right over the living room couch on which he is courting Keaton. However, Bogart's pointers are not wasted, because everything comes to pass; thus, a long take of one very passionate Allen-Keaton kiss is intercut (once again courtesy of Allen's imagination) with a similar Bogart-Bergman kiss from *Casablanca*.

The next scene finds Allen and Keaton in bed the morning after, and though we seem to have returned to total reality (that is, if you can accept Allen's character in bed with anyone), the cue still seems to be taken from Bogart—a huge film poster of *Across the Pacific* appears over the bed, completely dominating the couple. This morning-after scene opens with a close-up of the poster, in which Bogart is "scoring" a one-two punch, as if suggesting a sexual pun on what has occurred the night before.

Allen and Keaton decide they have found something good and that Roberts must be told. Since Keaton insists she will tell him, Allen has time alone to imagine how his best friend will respond. Thus, Allen's next three fantasies represent different possible reactions from the cuckolded husband. The first fantasy (thirteenth overall) is a monocle-and-pipe parody of two English gentlemen discussing things ever so rationally. Allen defuses any hostility by giving Roberts a terminal disease and closes the scene with proper British civility—a toast and "cheers."

Cuckolded-husband fantasies two and three are both movie parodies and do not run quite so pleasantly for interloper Allen. The first plays upon Allen's guilt and finds Roberts walking into the sea as in the first two versions of *A Star Is Born* (director Allen will use the scene again, this time seriously, in *Interiors*, 1978). In *Play It Again, Sam*, however, any lingering melancholy is undercut by Roberts' parting soliloquy on the beach: "Why didn't I see it coming? Me, who had the foresight to buy Polaroid at eight and a half."

In the final fantasy of this trilogy it is Allen, however, who bites the dust. Passing a theater playing the Italian film *Le Coppie* (with a large display poster acting as a backdrop for the fantasy opening), Allen imagines Roberts as a humiliated, hot-tempered Italian out for revenge. The knife-wielding husband corners Allen, a most unlikely baker, who tries to defend himself with some of the limpest dough ever to put in a movie appearance. The little baker never has a chance.

Allen is, however, suddenly and comically jarred back to reality when, outside his apartment, he runs into Roberts. Though Allen fears the worst, Roberts only senses trouble but does not suspect his friend. He pours out his love for Keaton to Allen, and then leaves our comic antihero Romeo with even more guilt. Not surprisingly, Allen decides he cannot break up the marriage. Thus, his primary anxiety becomes how to let Keaton down easily. This will not be simple, he says, since "I was incredible last night in bed. I never once had to sit up and consult the manual."

The next two fantasies occur as Allen rushes to the airport to tell Keaton he has reconsidered, while Keaton is rushing to the airport to tell her husband she has reconsidered (he is, of course, just rushing off on more business). In the first fantasy, Keaton takes Allen's decision poorly, and it quickly turns into a melodrama parody, with Keaton asking for a mysterious letter (*Casablanca's* letters of transit?), and then pulling a gun. The fantasy closes just as Allen screams, "Don't pull the trigger, I'm a bleeder."

This near-disaster then cuts directly to Allen's second fantasy on the ride to the airport—Bogart is his cab driver, ready to give him more pointers and settle him down. Bogart stops the car and shows Allen how to break it off with a "dame" (appropriately, again played by a gun-toting Keaton). This, along with Bogart's praise of Allen's sacrifice "for a pal," prepares Allen for the big romantic finish with Keaton.

This final fantasy brings us full circle to the film's opening, only this time instead of cutting back and forth between fantasizing audience member Allen and the projected image of *Casablanca*, both the situation (romantic triangle preparing for airport farewell) and the mise-en-scène (incoming fog and the separate starting of the plane's propellers) of *Play It Again, Sam* actually recreate *Casablanca*. Then, when the plane is safely away, Bogart assumes the original Claude Rains role by joining Allen in his walk into the enveloping mist.

Unlike earlier fantasies, however, in which Allen blindly tried to ape the complete Bogart persona, the closing scene uses the Bogart legend as a point of reference to aid Allen in the final liberation and acceptance of his own identity. That is, Allen essentially plays the part on his own; Bogart is not giving him cues from the wings, as he did earlier in the apartment. And though Allen does restate part of Bogart's farewell speech from *Casablanca*, it is the act of a mature person merely using past experience, rather than the alienated incompetent in search of a style that opened the movie. Still, a sense of Bob Hope bravado remains.

Allen's character summarizes it quite nicely when he says, "I guess the secret's not being you [Bogart]; it's being me." As if to keynote this, Bogart and Allen break up their stroll at the close; after the former's "Here's looking at you, kid," Allen walks off into the darkness of the night (and into his future?) alone, but not quite so lonely.

These are the eighteen fantasies in *Play It Again, Sam*. Like antihero Walter Mitty, the fantasies have at times provided Allen with unique adventure (hobnobbing with Bogart) in what is otherwise a rather banal life. At the same time, as noted, there have been balancing fantasy frustrations. Yet the key difference here between Allen's fantasy life and Mitty's lies not so much in the latter point (important as it may be) but rather in the fact that Allen's comedy persona (unlike Thurber's) is allowed to take his fantasy beyond mere distraction, using it to learn both to be himself and to accept himself. At the close of *Manhattan* (1979), Allen's girlfriend echoes that same message when she tells him, "You have to have a little faith in people."

In achieving this level of maturity, the Allen film persona no doubt needed both poles of fantasy, from the confidence Bogart could provide to the occasional fantasy frustration that kept his values in perspective—which eventually steered him away from being just a Bogart clone. And this final narration has become the norm for much of his later work, be it the eventual touching acceptance of Annie (Keaton) as friend instead of lover in *Annie Hall*; the realization late in *Stardust Memories* (1980) that the real joys of life can be locked in the most simple moments; the message of *A Midsummer Night's Sex Comedy* (1982) to seize the opportunities of life; finding the capacity to forgive at the close of *Broadway Danny Rose* (1984); and the touchingly upbeat conclusion of *Hannah and Her Sisters* (1986), which celebrates the fundamentals of comedy and life itself—marriage and an approaching birth. None of these situations, of course, leaves him with any real answers to life's eternal questions (the same might be said of the Chaplin-like exit of Woody in *Play It Again, Sam*), but they do leave his character in a much healthier state of mind for coping with the darker side of existence.

In terms of comedy theory, the dominant element in *Play It Again, Sam* is the fantasy identification with Bogart and a situation in which the viewer could relate to having him as a special tutor. The actions of this film fall under what genre theorist Northrop Frye calls the "drama of the green world," with the green world representing the ideal romance of another place, such as our imagination. More specifically this type of "comedy begins in a world represented as a normal world, moves into the green world, goes into a metamorphosis there in which the comic resolution is achieved, and returns to the normal world."[49] In *Play It Again, Sam*, Allen's character has moved from a frustrated normal existence to a fantasy "green world" apprenticeship with Bogart (certainly a key romantic ideal to anyone immersed in film culture). A metamorphosis takes place in which Allen learns to accept himself, and then he returns to the normal world (necessitating the solo walk off at the film's close) after Bogart has tendered something of a "graduation" toast by way of his "Here's looking at you, kid." Through this interaction with one of the legends of cinema history, director Allen has tapped a seemingly universal romantic fantasy among the viewing public.

Moreover, Allen accents the universality of the Bogart figure by the realistic manner in which this macho symbol appears and interacts with today's most prominent example of the comic antihero. This is nothing like the white ball of light that heralds the arrival of the good witch Glinda in *The Wizard of Oz* (1939), or even the special glossy setting one associates with the goddess of death in *All That Jazz* (1979). Bogey just drops in at Allen's apartment, appears at your typical A & P, and turns up behind the wheel of a cab.

This realistic tone in the fantasy scenes is consistent with the majority of other such excursions in Woody Allen's films. It also might help explain the tendency for Allen's more exotic fantasies never to reach the final print stage, from his playing a spider caught in Louise Lasser's "black widow" web (shot for *Everything . . .*), to the giant chess game using real people (shot for *Sleeper*)[50] with Allen appropriately playing a white pawn about to be sacrificed but not without a lovely bargaining argument: "Hey, fellas, it's only a game. We'll all be together later in the box."[51] The generally natural tone of these fantasies, particularly the Bogart scenes, might best be classified as what Siegfried Kracauer labels "fantasy established in terms of physical reality."[52] That is, the plot of *Play It Again, Sam* takes "the existence of the supernatural [in this case Bogart] more or less for granted, its presence does not simply follow from these visuals. . . . [T]he spectator must from the outset conceive of them as tokens of the supernatural."[53]

Thus, even to relate to the fact that a fantasy is in progress whenever Bogart appears, one must already be a practicing member of the modern world's biggest fantasy club—the film-going public. And by getting the joke (Allen's inadequacies and Bogart's giving home lessons in self-assertiveness), we go a long way toward becoming part of it. Who has not felt similar inadequacies, at least in comparison to our favorite cinema superhero, whether Bogart or 007?

Allen represents his own best example of such a fantasy world of daydreams peopled with cinema heroes even as a child: "I remember seeing *Tom, Dick and Harry* advertised and saying, 'I can't wait to see that.' It was one of those things that became a part of my conscious, because I lived in the movies and identified with that."[54]

His comedy persona in *Play It Again, Sam* restructures part of his life to use the "experience" of his film fantasy existence, slipping in and out of this other world as someone else might do with an old pair of shoes. An example is the farewell break with Diane Keaton that uses the *Casablanca* model for its inspiration. All this activity tends to flirt with the tongue-in-cheek message of Oscar Wilde's delightful "critical" essay, "The Decay of Lying": "Paradox though it may seem . . . life imitates art far more than art imitates life."[55] That is, by so immersing himself in Bogart with posters, movies, books, and other assorted memorabilia, Allen's screen persona both consciously and subconsciously tried to imitate film art, the world of Bogey. Allen stops trying to be Bogart only when he inadvertently achieves romantic success with Keaton by simply being himself. His closing walk-off symbolizes a literal as well as physical break with Bogart. And thus his posture changes from trying to ape art to constructively applying it to a less-than-perfect lifestyle.

This "be yourself" lesson parallels the closing message of America's favorite fantasy, *The Wizard of Oz*; there, too, the viewer is reminded by Dorothy's refrain, "There's no place like home," that individual happiness can be found only within oneself. For this reason, Allen's *Purple Rose of Cairo* (1985) has the saddest of conclusions. Overworked Depression-era waitress and film fan Mia Farrow does not live happily ever after with movie idol Jeff Daniels, who had literally stepped off the screen at her local theater. The heartbreaking close comes about because Farrow cannot move beyond the mere fantasy escape level of the movies, just as Daniels' AWOL screen shadow does not know how to act in real life. The film's last image of Farrow has her alone again, at the movies.

Fantasy for the Allen comedy persona has a continuing duality that he struggles with in each film (will he use fantasy as mere escape, or as a step toward maturity?), and much of this section has examined the struggle in the light of an opening reference to Thurber's most celebrated short story, the escapist "Secret Life of Walter Mitty." To come full circle, however, an apt closing observation on this duality might best be drawn from Allen's own most celebrated short story, "The Kugelmass Episode," which won the O. Henry Award as best short story of 1977 (early in 1978, *Annie Hall* [1977] won an Academy Award for best picture).

"The Kugelmass Episode," rather reminiscent of the Mitty story, examines the life of an unhappily married professor (Kugelmass) out to put some excitement back in his life, preferably on a sexual level. His adventure, or escape, comes in the form of a fantasy-like invention that can transport a subject into the world of the written word. For Kugelmass, this means an opportunity to date "any of the women created by the world's best writers."[56] Walter Mitty could not have gone for it any faster. Thus, Kugelmass ends up having an affair with Emma Bovary. But there are complications when the invention breaks down, causing the frustrated professor mental and financial ruin. Therefore, when the crisis is over, he swears off these fantasy time trips, happy that at least his wife has not found out and grateful that "I learned my lesson."[57]

But Kugelmass's maturity is short-lived, and he tries another "trip" (this time into *Portnoy's Complaint*), but the fantasy quickly becomes an eternal comic nightmare. The machine shorts out and is destroyed, the operator-inventor dies of a heart attack on the spot, and poor Kugelmass, instead of finding himself projected into *Portnoy's Complaint*, turns up in "an old textbook, *Remedial Spanish* . . . running for his life over a barren, rocky terrain as the word tener ('to have')—a large and hairy irregular verb—races after him on its spindly legs."[58] Quite clearly, Allen is warning us that total fantasy escape can be dangerous (as it is later in *Purple Rose*) if it is not directed toward character growth as in *Play It Again, Sam*. Otherwise, we might end up like Kugelmass, forever running away.

Annie Hall

Newsweek wrote: "Woody Allen became a national hero when his movie *Annie Hall* won four Academy Awards—for best picture, for Allen as best director, for Allen and Marshall Brickman as best original screenwriters, for Diane Keaton as best actress."[59] But this had been standard *Annie Hall* commentary since its April 1977 release. *Time* called it Allen's "breakthrough movie."[60] *Variety* likened it to the warm "believability" of the classic Tracy-Hepburn comedies.[61] The *New York Times* said Allen was the "only American film maker who is able to work seriously in the comic mode without being the least bit ponderous."[62] Moreover, the latter publication added, as Annie Hall,

Miss Keaton emerges as the comedian's Liv Ullman, then the frequent star of Ingmar Bergman's films, the director most admired by Allen.

The film story is the fictional "fictional?" treatment of the on-again, off-again, year-long affair/mentorship of Annie Hall (Diane Keaton) and Alvy Singer (Allen), a tale of loss and recovery of dignity. Though the comedian minimized the ties to his real-life relationship with Keaton, here one might best embrace that age-old advice, "Trust the tale, not the teller." Besides their previous mentor/romantic connection, Alvy plays a Jewish, twice-divorced, successful comedian—precisely Allen's status. He even uses some of his original stand-up comedy material when Singer has a Midwest performance date. When he time-trips back to one of his elementary classrooms, the date on the board is his birthday. (Since he is being given a hard time by his teacher even on his birthday, it further accents his comic attack on education.) Allen even uses actual footage of himself on a Dick Cavett talk show to flesh out Alvy's character. Moreover, all the personal idiosyncrasies of the artist chronicled over the years, from his nonstop analysis/therapy to his dislike of California, are included in the film. Keaton's family name is Hall, and she was then very much the rummage-sale attired (those were her own clothes) Annie of the picture, complete to the la-de-dah speech pattern and the screwball WASP nature. Keaton's father called it "eighty-five percent true—even to [wife] Dorothy and my mother ["Grammy" Hall]."[63] Consequently, critics were nearly unanimous in calling it Allen's most personal film.[64] In conjunction with this "factual" material, Allen showed a marked propensity for using real people. The Marshall McLuhan character he pulls out from behind a theater sign is the real McLuhan, being used to put down a pompous professor. When Annie goes out for a people-watching walk, the "winner of the Truman Capote look-alike contest" actually is Capote, just as Cecil B. DeMille really is DeMille in Bob Hope's *Son of Paleface.*

Annie Hall is probably Allen's most pivotal film, as well as his most influential. Though not widely addressed at the time, the movie is most significant as a major transition work in the art-house film movement.

During the 1950s, when television had taken much of the traditional movie audience out of the theater, a small but growing segment of viewers began to patronize what came to be called the "art houses." These were theaters in large metropolitan areas and/or near universities that showed only foreign films by uniquely individual auteurs, such as Allen's patron saint of the movies, Bergman. While many directors caught the attention of this distinct slice of the American audience, such as Italian directors Roberto Rossellini (of neo-realism fame) and Federico Fellini, for many Bergman constituted a one-man movement. With classics like *Wild Strawberries* (1957) or *the Seventh Seal* (1957), where a disillusioned knight returning from the Crusades attempts to solve life's mysteries by playing chess with Death, the intelligentsia had challenging literary material to digest at the movies. And although the censorship code was crumbling in 1950s American films, many restrictions about sexuality and adult subject matter still applied, something to which foreign films were exempt.

Allen (born in 1935) has credited this 1950s development as a crucial part of his cinema development, though he seems to have been a student of all films, be they from Bob Hope or Bergman, since the beginning. His special affinity for Bergman is a natural outgrowth of this era.

Most genre films work on a visual "lived problem" level.[65] That is, the soldiers must hold the fort against attacking Indians, or earthlings are at war with invading Martians. In contrast, art-house movies address raised problems, cerebral questions difficult to portray in a visual manner: What is the meaning of life? Is there a God? How does the ethical person live? How will I make my life meaningful? These hard-to-visualize, abstract universals apply to everyone. Consequently, when Bergman did the *Seventh Seal*, he caught the viewer's attention by doing an unusual visual, casting a character as Death. Of course, the art-house director need not be quite so dramatic. In a film like *Dead Poets Society* (1989) a charismatic prep school teacher (Robin Williams) gives his students a different vantage point on life by having them stand on his desk, or having them imagine the aspirations of all those trophy case pictures of long-dead students. The goal here and in other art-house films is to "seize the day," to make the most of life.

According to art film historian and theorist William C. Siska, *Annie Hall* became "the crossover film between the art cinema and the popular film. . . . [I]ts box-office success, although not of blockbuster proportions, showed that the art was acceptable, under certain circumstances, to the mass audience."[66] This was accomplished in part due to the acceptance of modernistic techniques by both the Hollywood establishment and the public in general. This is most obvious in the nonlinear progression of the story, which is guided by romantic memories instead of chronology. Allen's character tells the audience as much in the movie's direct address opening, where his figure informs us he plans to explore the failure of his relationship with Annie.

Allen uses numerous modernistic techniques, such as from flashbacks that include the contemporary figure providing a running commentary on the past and comic subtitles that reveal what Singer and Hall are really thinking as they struggle to make small talk early in the relationship. Woody and a co-star appear briefly as characters in an animated *Snow White*, the first film he saw as a child (more reality-based material). Another effective device is the use of the split screen, providing a comic dichotomy between their families and their therapy sessions. As funny as they are, their water and-oil dissimilarity telegraph the eventual breakup of their relationship.

The most amusing device finds Allen wandering through his past, including a return to fourth grade, which begins by addressing his early sexual drive and closes with his still little classmates informing us of how they are now employed, ranging from a plumber to someone who is "into leather." For a time Allen's character is even a cartoon figure (see the previous paragraph), and this says nothing of how he randomly stops people during the movie to ask about plot points. For a personally realistic story, one is still constantly aware of the filmmaker. This greatly assists in the incorporation of the art house questions noted earlier. Like the title of the Allen film *Love and Death* (1975), these topics surface frequently in his work but no more effectively than in *Annie Hall*.

Despite Allen's ties with the art-house movement, there is still a reluctance by many fans to accept him in this domain. Even Allen has observed, "I've put myself in the area of kind of doing art films—but they're not perceived as art films because I'm a local person, I'm an American [Hope, not a foreign Bergman], and I've been known for years as a commercial entity [a successful personality comedian]."[67] Yet since *Annie Hall*, Allen's work is more likely to be sprinkled with cerebral questions than laugh lines. This is not to suggest it began only with *Hall*. Though it is clearly the transitional work, earlier films like *Love and Death* (a parody, in part, of *The Seventh Seal*) are not without art-house questions as well. For instance, Allen has his *Love and Death* characters argue whether it can ever be ethical to kill someone for a greater good.

Beginning with *Annie Hall*, Allen's film endings tend to be more bleak. With *Hall* the relationship eventually fails. The absence of a Hollywood happy ending is closer to art-house film reality: Life is ambiguous, and there is no one given storyline, let alone a happy one. Allen suggests just this earlier in the movie when he gives the romantic play-within-the-film a happy conclusion, that you try to get things right in art because you don't in real life.

Allen's direct-address close to *Hall* (coming full circle from a similar opening) has sometimes wrongly been criticized for its absurdity. The comedian Singer relates how he tells a psychiatrist that his brother thinks himself a chicken. But when the doctor asks why he didn't turn him in, the answer comes back: "I would, but I need the eggs." The punchline reinforces the absurdity of persisting in trying to form relationships, because they never seem to last.

While most period critics did not immediately recognize the *Annie Hall* art-house connection, a handful did. Critic Joe Queenan likened Allen's film to French existentialist novelist Albert Camus, observing: "Camus, like Woody, was a master of Posing the Big Question."[68] And reviewer Vincent Canby conducted a mock but affectionately humorous interview, titled "Woody Allen Is the American Bergman."[69] *Annie Hall* as art film does manage, however, to avoid one frequent dark component of the genre. The art movie pushes for such a full commitment that some characters are not able to handle the stress. For example, in the British film *Educating Rita* (1983) the title character's (Julia Walters) roommate works very hard to soak up culture in every form, from music to the theater. But when she realizes she does not have the talent to create art of any kind, she attempts suicide. A variation of this occurs in *Dead Poets Society* when Robin Williams' teacher encourages his students to be all they can. One young man comes alive to the joy of acting. In his case, the talent exists, but his martinet father forbids it. He wants his son to follow the more steady traditional path of law or medicine. Aware that there was no possibility of defeating his father and that the artistic passion of his life is to be denied, the boy kills himself. In Allen's film the failed relationship creates pain, but his character uses art (the play within the film) to enable him to work through the problem. Unlike Rita's friend, he does have the talent, and he is without the restrictions imposed by the father of *Dead Poets Society*. But it is important to remember that as much as "seize the day" could be the motto of the art-house film, it is a gala that can be self-destructive. The power of art does not always make up for the limitations of life.

Allen's success as an art-house filmmaker is due in part to a playful spoofing of the genre, too, an affectionate heading that says, "I need not get too deep dish." For example, when Allen's character visits Annie's Midwestern home, her brother Dwayne (Christopher Walken) invites Alvy into his room. The subject is suicide:

> Can I make a confession? As an artist, I think you'll understand. Sometimes, at night, when I'm driving, I see these two bright headlights coming toward me from the opposite direction and I have this sudden impulse just to turn the wheel quickly, and head on into the oncoming car. I can hear the glass shattering and see the flames rising up out of the spilling gasoline.

Allen's Alvy replies, "OK, I have to go now, Dwayne, because I'm due back on the planet Earth." The humor builds quickly when it turns out Dwayne will be driving Alvy and Annie to the airport that night during a pounding thunderstorm. The art film's fascination with suicide has briefly and comically been addressed by a minor character. Allen has made the film true to a genre characteristic without derailing the movie with a lengthy, serious pondering of the subject.

Allen also does a parody on the ever-present dark side of the art-house film:

> See, life is forever divided up into the horrible and the miserable. The horrible are the terminal cases—blind, crippled. How they make it through life is absolutely amazing. The miserable is everyone else. As you go through life, you should be thankful that you're miserable because you've very lucky to be that.

Allen still acknowledges life's inherent unfairness, but the comic plea for some joy allows one to not become totally morose.

Allen's Alvy also does a spoof variation on the art-house film's propensity for an academic setting, be it *Dead Poet Society*'s prep school, or Rita's university professor/mentor in *Educating Rita*. The often troubling "raised problems" of the genre can be depressing, and thus frequently are avoided by the individual. But higher education is immersed in such questions. Consequently, by placing an art-house story in an academic setting, it becomes a more acceptable location for examining such troubling questions.

In contrast, Alvy gives a more mixed message about education. He completely writes off elementary school: "We had a saying that those who can't teach, teach gym. Those who couldn't do anything come to our school." And while Alvy recommends that Annie take some college classes, he soon retracts his advice when he suspects she and a professor are getting romantically involved. The one professor the viewer sees is the pompous individual from the movie queue that Alvy must shut up by the brief introduction of Marshall McLuhan. Allen, a college dropout, has a hard time accepting the merits of education, even as a basic art-house film component.

Alvy does, however, use his own indirect slant on acceptable education. He becomes the teacher/mentor, with his own unusual slant on recommended reading lists—books with death in the title, such as Thomas Mann's classic novella, *Death in Venice* (1913). A passage from the text, though not noted in the film, sums up Allen's perfectionist, nonstop work ethic as an artist and the fear of not creating: "He whose preoccupation is with excellence longs fervently to find rest in perfection; and is not nothingness a form of perfection."[70] One is tempted to add the comment of Alvy as a child refusing to do his homework: "The universe is expanding and the universe is everything, so if it's expanding, eventually it will break apart and that will be the end of everything." In *Death in Venice*, the neurotic young Alvy, and Allen the artist, one is dealing with internal and external pressures (real or imagined) which cripple creativity.

An additional slant on Alvy as mentor would be to liken this art film to an updated *Pygmalion*, remaking a young woman into "my fair lady." But the difference here is that Alvy's student eventually blossoms (for Annie, it is through her singing) and needs her freedom. Consequently, there is no romantic ending, though a friendship remains.

Besides the transition *Annie Hall* made for the art-house film—bringing it to a larger audience, while not compromising an artist's deep-felt need to express himself or herself—the movie provided other firsts for the director. Allen observed, "It was a major turning point for me. I had the courage to abandon . . . just clowning. . . . I will try and make some deeper films and not be as funny in the same way."[71] The statement says two things. First, for once Allen went beyond the spoofing situations of his earlier movies. He likened this to attempting to get inside "Alvy's mind a lot of times."[72] Moreover, "for the first time, on public view, Woody expresses a genuine unhappiness with himself. This time his neuroses cost him a relationship."[73] Second, Allen's statement promises darker, more dramatic movies for his future. This is something he accomplished in his next film, *Interiors* (1978), about a distraught gentle family and their three troubled adult children, ruled by a castrating mother. For many it seems like a second-rate Bergman. It received radically diverse reviews, ranging from praise to damnation: "Perhaps the single worst movie ever made by a major American film maker."[74] I note this reaction because Allen was entering a period best titled, by the general audience, anyway, "I liked his earlier funny films better." In fact, the comment was so common in the late 1970s that Allen himself used a variation of it in *Stardust Memories* (1980). He made it self-deprecatingly more amusing by giving the line to an extraterrestrial, implying that Allen's alleged comedy decline was known throughout the universe. This period, continuing to the time of this writing, finds Allen writing radically different properties—dramatic, comic, and sometimes a mix (see the section on *Crimes and Misdemeanors*, 1989, later in this chapter).

Annie Hall provided another first for Allen: "Like Buster Keaton, Woody Allen has made one of the rare comedies in existence about a well-heeled hero."[75] One need go no further than Allen's idol, Charlie Chaplin, to discuss the screen clown as the poor underdog. Chaplin's Tramp remains the definitive screen persona as a homeless person. And the vast majority of comic figures since that time have scrimped to get by; W. C. Fields' huckster leaves town one step ahead of his landlady, and Bob Hope and Bing Crosby are forever on the "road" ahead of their creditors.

When Allen noted of *Annie Hall*, "I had the courage to abandon . . . just clowning," this was the sort of thing to which he was referring. A "well-heeled hero" is less sympathetic than the underdog, and there is less likelihood that viewers will relate to the character. Naturally, Allen's Alvy still wins us over by his comic manner; by the character's more accomplished nature, Allen lets the antiheroic nature be readily passed to Keaton's Annie. For once he is neither the central person in his work nor even the pivotal antihero. This comedy torch has been passed to Annie, something she demonstrates immediately after their tennis match. When Alvy compliments Annie on her tennis she replies with a verbal slapstick worthy of eccentric comedian Gracie Allen: "Oh, yeah? So do you. Oh, God, what a [making sounds and laughing], what a dumb thing to say, right? I mean, you say it, 'You play well' and right away . . . I have to say well. Oh, oh . . . God, Annie [she gestures with her hand]. Well . . . oh, well . . . la-de-da, la-de-da, la-la." And she turns around and moves toward the door.

The grooming of Keaton's comedy persona as antihero had begun in those earlier Allen films in which she had co-starred: *Play It Again, Sam, Sleeper,* and *Love and Death.* But it is fleshed out to perfection in *Annie Hall,* a role for which Keaton won an Oscar for best actress. Moreover, for the first time she is the focus of the film, a decision made in the editing, because the footage worked best keying upon her. Otherwise, one might have had a film titled *Annie Hall and Alvy Singer.*

To come full circle, the winning antiheroic nature of Keaton in the key role better allows the "well-heeled" nature of Allen's character to be accepted. There is less comic pressure placed upon him to carry the movie. This certainly helps explain why *Annie Hall* is almost completely devoid of slapstick. Earlier Allen films were peppered with it, especially his Harold Lloyd-like character in *Sleeper.* But, like the mixed critical response to *Interiors,* Allen's slapstick sequences in his earlier films had received a lukewarm response. While his verbal wit was always stronger than his physical humor, it is hard to avoid the inspired slapstick of *Sleeper.* Still, for the first time he severely cut back on the physical humor in *Annie Hall,* consistent with his decision to take comedy risks in this movie.

The only physical humor of note in *Annie Hall* represented another comedy risk—improvising a scene. The setting is a kitchen with runaway lobsters. Annie and Alvy play at being terrified of these creatures, as well as being concerned about dinner, when one lobster crawls behind the refrigerator. The spontaneity of the scene comes across perfectly. Indeed, it is so effectively captured that a variation of the scene is repeated later in the film when Alvy is dating someone else. The other woman finds nothing funny about "frighten-ingly" trying to corral lobsters and Alvy further realized what a loss his breakup with Annie was.

An additional first for Allen's *Annie Hall* is the preponderance of ethical stances he addresses. It was not that his earlier films had completely lacked such issues; for example, *Love and Death* questions everything from individual murder to full-scale war. Yet, each subject is treated more as a platform for another joke, not as a serious ethical point. In contrast, Alvy dislikes Annie's smoking pot, especially before sex, because the whole person does not seem to be there. At one such point a double-exposure allows Annie's inner, ghostlike being to get up from the bed and sit down on a chair, watching them. Alvy likens this removed phenomenon to not wanting his comedy club audiences stoned: "If I get a laugh from a person who's high, it doesn't count. You know, 'cause they're always laughing." He is also upset that his best friend (Tony Roberts), a TV star, lays in a laugh track each week for his show. An additional entertainment complaint is the preponderance of award shows. Alvy observes, "They give away awards for everything: 'For the World's Biggest Fascist—Adolf Hitler!' " Possibly his increased ethical awareness was precipitated in part by the movie he had done just prior to *Annie Hall*, *The Front* (1976). Though Allen neither wrote nor directed the film, he played the lead in this moving attack on the post–World War II "Red" scare period, with its inquisition-like communist witch-hunting of the House Un-American Activities Committee (HUAC) and Senator Joseph McCarthy. Anyone with leftist tendencies in the 1940s was threatened with being blacklisted from film in the reactionary 1950s. Since Allen seldom accepts roles in movies he does not control, this would suggest just how strong his artistic principles could be.

Another first for Allen's *Annie Hall* is how much he utilized direct address. Besides the opening and closing examples, the film is inundated with scenes of Alvy talking directly to the camera. Direct address is new neither to Allen nor cinema itself; Bob Hope frequently utilized this in his work. But the sheer number of instances demonstrates Allen's willingness to take a chance. Of course, unlike other "formalist" techniques (when an artist draws attention to himself, such as through slow motion, speeded-up action), direct address has a way of further pulling the viewer into the action. It is as if viewer and comedian have a special joke between them that excludes other cast members.

As a side note to *Annie Hall*, shortly before the film was released, Allen had a similar comic essay published in the *New Republic*.[76] Only one period critic seems to have noted this. *New Republic* reviewer Stanley Kauffman described the piece, "The Lunatic's Tale," as a "cartoon abstract" of the film.[77] It merits comment for several reasons. First, as did "The Kugelmass Episode" and *Play It Again, Sam*, the article underlines Allen's artistic versatility. Second, the essay provides another perspective on the same theme, only in a different medium. Third, "The Lunatic's Tale" is one more example of the Benchley/Thurber influence on Allen. For example, one of Thurber's most celebrated drawings has a woman perched on a bookshelf. And when a bullet passes through Mrs. Fitelson's apartment it causes this Allen character "to leap straight upward onto her bookshelf and remain perched there."[78] The main difference between *Annie Hall* and the essay is that the former ends on a more positive note—acceptance of Annie as a friend. In contrast, as the title suggests, "The Lunatic's Tale" finds the central antihero as one of those crazies who wears a pinwheel hat and knapsack while skating down Broadway. As with the *Play It Again, Sam*–"The Kugelmass Episode" comparison, Allen seems to provide slightly more hope in his films than in his comic essays.

Crimes and Misdemeanors

In *Crimes and Misdemeanors* (see Illustration 12) Allen takes two movie plots—comic and dramatic—and successfully merges them into a provocative black comedy. The serious story (the *Crimes* of the title) involved a successful, philanthropic ophthalmologist named Judah Rosenthal (Martin Landau), who is being badgered by his mistress Dolores Paley (Anjelica Huston) into making their relationship public. She also threatens to reveal that he sometimes embezzles from his charity work. She must be stopped—but how? Judah talks to his best friend and family rabbi Ben (Sam Waterston). Sweet and saintly, Ben, who is tragically going blind, counsels confession to Judah's wife and a forgiving world. But just as the doctor cannot help Ben's failing eyesight, Judah cannot accept the approach recommended by the rabbi. Instead, Judah goes to his ne'er-do-well brother Jack (Jerry Orbach), whose business ties include mob connections. Jack suggests a simple murder. Judah is initially shocked and disgusted, but eventually this is the route he takes.

The comic story (the title's *Misdemeanors*) focuses on small-time failing documentary filmmaker Cliff Stern (Woody Allen). He is unhappily married (to Joanna Gleason) and currently working on a project he hates but cannot afford to pass up, a profile of his pompous ass of a brother-in-law Lester (Alan Alda). Lester is a shallow but successful television producer who loves the sound of his own voice. Woody's character has more "conscience than talent,"[79] and cannot help sabotaging the project. For instance, he is fired after his editing juxtaposes Lester pontificating with footage from a Mussolini speech. Cliff's real passion is with a film he is doing on an optimistic Jewish philosopher who survived the Holocaust. He is supported in this project by television producer Halley Reed (Mia Farrow), who is quickly becoming the love of his life. (As a side note on this film, Alvy in *Annie Hall* courted Annie with a steady diet of the Holocaust-related film *The Sorrow and the Pity*, 1970.) Cliff loses Halley to Alan Alda's wheeler-dealer producer. But even more surprising, Cliff loses his pet project when his philosopher, who so strongly embraces life, inexplicably commits suicide, leaving a darkly comic note about simply going out the window.

In the end, after much guilt, Landau's character finds that he can live with his murderous deed, and his life prospers. In contrast, Allen's antihero loses on all counts, and the kind rabbi goes completely blind. Baseball manager Leo Durocher's axiom about "Nice guys finish last" has never been so true. Before

12. Woody Allen, director, on the set of *Crimes and Misdemeanors* (1989).

examining the film further as a dark comedy, there are several carryover themes from *Annie Hall* that need to be addressed.

First, though Allen mixes the dramatic and the comic in *Crimes*, his humor, as in *Annie Hall*, avoids mere gags to prop up a weak story. It is not merely humor for its own sake but rather a carrier for the tale. For instance, the movie's most praised laugh is an inspired one-line summary of Cliff's failed marriage: The last woman he has been in was the Statue of Liberty.

Second, like *Annie Hall*, *Crimes* also works very effectively on an art-house level. As the *Los Angeles Times* observed, the movie "reaffirms Allen's status as the most persistently personal, original and provocative of all U.S. film makers."[80] *Commonwealth* discussed the movie's "existential flavor,"[81] while the *Christian Century* more explicitly noted, "If the eye of God sees everything, when does retribution finally occur? And if God doesn't exist, why are we weighed down with guilt?"[82] Like any good art-house movie, *Crimes* works upon an extended metaphor, that of sight and sin. In addition to Landau's character being an eye doctor whose rabbi friend is going blind, the film abounds with sight references. After the murder of Judah's mistress, her lifeless eyes stare at him as he combs her apartment for evidence that might link him to the crime. When Judah returns to his childhood home he has a flashback to his youth and his father telling him the eyes of God are always on him. Just as Judah was evidently blind to his father's teachings, Ben's faith in all people "blinds" him even before he actually loses his eyesight. Gifted film critic and scholar Richard Schickel comically sums up the significance of such references when he states: "By visiting this affliction [blindness] on the only character in his movie who remains close to God [the rabbi], Allen is suggesting that if the Deity himself is not dead, then he must be suffering from severely impaired vision."[83] Also, vision of the godly absence thereof (literal and figurative) plays an important symbol for all the conflicts that confront the film's characters. The most provocative question on vision is: If God is represented by the rabbi Ben, does Ben's eventual blindness mean God is sightless, too? Judah literally gets away with murder.

Third, although the dramatic element in *Crimes* received the lion's share of the press, the comic element is pivotal to the film's overall success. Allen's character is a "modern Everyman, all of us, aware of our smallness in a universe drawn too terrifying to grasp as tragedy. A wisecrack and a shrug ease the pain or fear and enable us to go on."[84]

Fourth, despite the darker route Allen has taken since *Annie Hall*, his films still furnish some hope. Among the large cast of *Crimes*, Allen allows his character the joy of mentoring his niece Jenny (Jenny Nichols). Age ten or 12, "schooling" for Cliff is getting her to revival house screenings of classic Hollywood films from the 1930s and 1940s. In addition showing a warm and caring side to Cliff, clips from the movies also serve as a transitional device between the world of Judah and Cliff. For example, after a serious scene between Landau's character and his frantic mistress, Allen cuts to Alfred Hitchcock's screwball comedy *Mr. and Mrs. Smith*, with the title characters in a real fight. Thus, the movie Cliff and Jenny are attending comically mirrors the prior dramatic scene.

At its most basic, however, Allen's film embraces dark comedy. The latter genre has three interrelated themes: man as beast, the absurdity of the world, and the omnipresence of death.[85] *Crimes* depicts a less than idealistic view of mankind in several ways. Landau's apparent pillar of the community is anything but, and Alda's "great" television producer uses his position to constantly harass women, something Allen's Cliff comically records for his aborted documentary. One of the genre's most pervasive ways of undercutting any concept of man's nobility is portraying his obsession with sex. This sexual negation of man has three variations. First, it is difficult to attach any significance to man's lofty ideals when serious subjects of concern are constantly displaced by sex. Thus, Alda's Lester quickly switches from his theories of comedy to offering attractive young women possible positions in his upcoming sitcoms. Second, sex also represents an absence of control. In *Crimes* Cliff's wife Wendy suffers through a shocking "date" when her friend from the personal ads achieves sexual satisfaction only by tying Wendy up and defecating upon her. As dark comedy director Luis Buñuel observed, "Sex—which respects no barriers and obeys no laws—can at any moment become an agent of chaos."[86] Third, black comedy frequently makes direct links between sex and death, the ultimate lack of control. Thus, when Judah's lover becomes too demanding he has her "removed," like a toy he has become tired of playing with. The fact that sex frequently symbolizes the only solace even for the genre's nominal good guy (Allen's Cliff) is a further comment upon the pitiful condition of modern man, especially since his wife has been having headaches for over a year.

The second theme of dark comedy (unlike populist comedy's rational-world fantasy of a Frank Capra, where justice prevails because of a man-of-the-people leader), is that the world is only an absurd environment, where the individual does not count. This absurdity is most obviously showcased by the fact that black humor's antiheroes often are not so much participants in the genre as they are unwilling spectators in a terrible, ongoing joke called life. This leaf-in-the-wind characterization is nicely showcased in the life and hard times of Cliff Stern, the antihero whose strong-sounding name seems to mock him. Allen's documentary filmmaker's only career accomplishment seems to have been a third-place finish in a minor midwestern movie competition. He is fired from his big film break, the profile of Lester, essentially because he has ethics.

His marriage is failing and the promise of a new love is lost when Lester somehow convinces Farrow's Halley to marry him—the same woman who had once agreed with Cliff on Lester's shallowness.

Dark humor absurdity is usually presented in two ways—through the chaos of an unordered universe and through the flaws of mortal man. *Crimes* has it both ways. The first and most fundamental simply has man being victimized for merely trying to exist, such as Cliff or his lonely sister Barbara.

For all the comic frightfulness of an unordered universe, man has been a strong contributor to the absurdity of the black comedy world. *Pogo* cartoonist Walt Kelly summarized this nicely with his delightful axiom, "We have met the enemy and he is us." This manmade absurdity is the result of both general species incompetence and its perpetuation in human institutions. People prefer the mind-candy world of Lester's television sitcoms to the serious subjects offered by filmmakers like Cliff.

The often absurd actions and policies of establishment institutions (here, the media) are constantly under attack in black comedy. Their status as targets is due to the fact that they routinely profess (such as through Lester's sitcoms) that it is a rational world. Just as Allen's *Annie Hall* character is shocked that his best friend would add a laugh track to his hit television show, Cliff is bothered by the pap Lester successfully cranks out.

The third theme of black humor focuses upon the awful finality of death. In this genre, death means the end. To paraphrase a popular axiom of the genre: "Life is awful, and then you die." Death is the final joke of a futile life. Black comedy merely obtains more mileage out of the terrible finality of death by laughing at it. There are no *final* happy endings, as Buñuel implies with the title of his autobiography—*My Last Sigh* (see Note 86)—unless one is rooting for Judah. Black comedy attacks the related taboos, those sacred things that give meaning to death (such as religion, when Judah's atheist aunt baits his very devout father) and reveal the less than dignified elements of a pitiful life (Anjelica Huston's Dolores lies lifeless on her apartment floor). The portrayal of black comedy death is also a compendium for all the genre's themes (man as beast and the absurdity of life) and subthemes (undercutting institutions).

There are four basic lessons to be learned or reaffirmed in the genre's obsession with death. First, death is a terrible absurdity. How can a once vital, passionate human being be reduced to so much "garbage" in death? Yet that is black comedy's great revelation. Second, the casual randomness with which death frequently appears underlines both the world's absurdity and the insignificance of man. Judah's brother Jack arranges the murder through mob contacts as though he were ordering a sandwich. It is reminiscent of celebrated film critic Robert Warshow's reading of Chaplin's *Monsieur Verdoux* (1947), which produced an axiom that could be applied to any number of these smaller black comedies: "Business is like murder and therefore murder is only a kind of business."[87]

The third lesson to be gained from the genre's obsession with death is the popularity of suicide in black comedies. Suicide further accents man's earthly dilemma in six ways. First, it dramatically demonstrates that the genre's disregard for life actually begins with the individual; witness the exit out a window of Cliff's seemingly optimistic philosopher Sol Rosenthal. Second, suicide is that rare activity where the black comedy individual can initiate the event instead of being the passive recipient. How ironically fitting, however, that this act results in the total negation of the individual. Third, life is full of pain, and suicide provides a way around this, as the title to *M.A.S.H.*'s theme song suggests, "Suicide Is Painless." That this escape has always been an alternative to life's suffering is underscored by director Ernst Lubitsch titling a pioneer black comedy with Shakespeare's celebrated wording for suicide: *To Be or Not to Be*. Fourth, on a metaphorical level, suicide is an apt phrase for the literal implementation of the death-wish-like tendency of modern man to rush toward an apocalypse of his own making. Fifth, suicide is a modest example of something black comedy frequently showcases on a broader and more terrible scale—man playing God. Sixth, black comedy suicides, or the attempts, often reveal that randomness is just as strong in suicide as in the frustrating lives it seeks to end. Thus, Sol's suicide occurs years after his survival of the Holocaust, and at a time when his optimistic philosophy is seemingly at its strongest.

The fourth basic lesson to draw from the genre's obsession with death demonstrates man's callousness to shock. When murder becomes the casual suggestion for the messy end of an affair, human values have become debased. Jack's nonchalant answer to Judah's problem is chillingly reinforced later in the movie. When Judah expresses some guilt over the crime, his brother comforts him with words to the effect that it is just one more robbery (the cover for the murder) that ends with a death. No big deal.

These three interrelated central themes of black comedy—man as beast, the absurdity of the world, and the omnipresence of death—are all terrible realities that threaten the veneer of rationality that "civilized" man too often accepts as the norm. Black comedy screams, "Think about it!" as it scrambles one's complacency by juxtapositioning humor and drama. Of course, "thinking about" the unanswerable is like applying the genre's motto, "things are never what they seem in this irrational world." But it does allow the individual to make his or her own separate peace.

Moving beyond the themes to general characterizations of dark comedy further enhances an understanding of *Crimes*. To accomplish this task, the movie will be compared with its generic opposite—the populist films of Frank Capra, such as *Mr. Deeds Goes to Town* (1936), *Mr. Smith Goes to Washington*

(1939), *Meet John Doe* (1941), and *It's a Wonderful Life* (1946). A basic definition of populism is that the people are inherently good, yet the superior and majority will of the common man is forever threatened by a usurping, sophisticated, evil few.

In these Capra films, family is of the utmost importance. One has only to think of Jimmy Stewart's George Bailey in *It's a Wonderful Life* to understand that the family is the beginning and end of everything that is good in populist life. In contrast, Cliff is on the verge of divorce, his sister is divorced, and the only seemingly model family has an adulterous murderer for a father. *Crimes* is not without family attempts: The rabbi loves his daughter, and Woody mentors his niece lovingly. But the general picture is one of family instability. Indeed, even the brother who arranges the murder is not on good terms with the family, including Judah.

Populism assumes a mythic dimension. Capra's heroes frequently take on a Christ-like persona, with phrases like "30 pieces of silver," or "They're crucifying him." To make this more palatable in the cynical post-World War II era, Capra added fantasy and a direct "heavenly" connection to *It's a Wonderful Life*. In fantasy one is more likely to suspend the sense of disbelief. For instance, no one questions the "fact" that witches fly in *The Wizard of Oz* (1939). In contrast, *Crimes* is of the real world. The early moments of the movie suggest Judah might be mythic; the good doctor and philanthropic family man is being celebrated at a large gala dinner. But Allen soon shows that Judah has feet of clay. There is no mythic person here.

The populist movie is linear in nature. One event happens at a time. This type of narrative underlines the rational world view of the genre. Allen's *Crimes* is constantly cross-cutting the dual focus storyline. This disjointedness reinforces dark comedy's message that reality does not come with a plotline. The editing can sometimes be used for dark comedy shock effect.

In a populist film the ending is invariably upbeat, such as family and friends coming to the rescue of George Bailey in *It's a Wonderful Life*. Dark comedy usually has just the opposite close. For example, at the end of *Crimes* Cliff finds himself drinking apart from the guests at a wedding party. Judah wanders by and a conversation begins. (This is the only time the film's two major characters meet.) Cliff is still devastated by the loss of Mia Farrow's Halley to Lester. Cliff kiddingly tells Landau's character he is planing a murder, meaning Alan Alda's Lester. Woody Allen's antihero is merely playing Walter Mitty, because murder is just not in his makeup. The irony here is that Cliff is thinking out loud to a real murderer. The irony increases when Judah tells Cliff a "story" about someone getting away with murder. This dark close is all the more biting since it is played against the backdrop of a wedding, a traditional happy ending for some genres of comedy and symbolic of new beginnings. Allen has never given his antihero such a bleak close. This ending does, however, represent a more realistic conclusion, a theater of the real. And it is only one of a few films in which he has not gotten the girl.

In a populist film the hero and the people usually are triumphant, such as in *Mr. Smith Goes to Washington* (1939). In a dark comedy like *Crimes* the antihero Allen is constantly buffeted about, and the people do not come to the rescue. As *Newsweek* critic Jack Kroll noted, "*Crimes* represent the domestication of evil: 'good' people make murderous decisions as if conscience simply had been exhausted."[88] In dark comedy one can depend on no one. That is the reason Cliff is so devastated by Halley's romantic defection to Lester. She had seemed to be his perfect soul mate. They agreed on everything, from their love of afternoon movies (it feels like playing hooky), to Lester being a pompous ass. To lose her in this manner—and to Lester—is especially difficult.

To take this one step further, the populist hero does not take advantage of his rise from the people. And he leaves his position of power as soon as possible, seemingly because of his unselfish desire for anonymity. Dark comedy frequently showcases a character who is quite willing to play God, such as Judah and his brother.

Populism invariably has a sense of the past, regardless of the period in which it is set. It works because stories of a rational world view are invariably set in what often is perceived as a simpler time. Dark comedy is generally of the now, or the near future, such as *Clockwork Orange* (1971). It is on the cutting edge of today's dark world, whether in high-profile murder cases or killers who also eat their victims. Murder is an all too common statistic; there are over 500 murders committed annually in New York City, the location for *Crimes*. As Charlie Chaplin's title character observes in *Monsieur Verdoux* (1947), "Numbers sanctify." One accepts and/or becomes numb to such a heinous but frequent act as murder, and the banality of murder becomes the norm.

Crimes and dark comedy's 180-degree swing from populism brings one full circle to this section's opening on the art-house movie, but here it is applied to ethics. Instead of dwelling on questions like "Is there a God?" or "Is evil ultimately punished?" one should ponder the ethics of art. For example, should an "artist ever sell out by working on a commercially viable project that he or she finds aesthetically offensive in order to make enough money to work on his or her true artistic endeavor?"[89] Allen's Cliff is put in just this position when he agrees to the movie about his brother-in-law. Cliff needs money for his philosophical film. This ethical question has been around as long as there have been artists. In the twentieth century, acclaimed filmmaker Orson Welles was constantly appearing in mediocre movies to subsidize his own very personalized cinema projects, such as his last great film, *Falstaff* (also released as *Chimes at*

Midnight, 1969). Nobel Prize-winning novelist William Faulkner often wrote formula action adventure Hollywood films to subsidize his serious writing.

At first Allen's character succumbs to temptation. However, from early in the project, though unbeknownst to the viewer, he has been taking unflattering film footage of his brother-in-law's womanizing and a funny editing exercise in which newsreel movie footage of Mussolini is juxtaposed with Lester. Naturally, Lester is less than happy with this portrait and fires Cliff. Allen's character has taken the high ethical road by compiling film he knows Lester is not going to like. This is reminiscent of the *Annie Hall* scene in which Allen's figure criticizes a television friend for adding a false laugh track to a sitcom. Unfortunately, as with so much in *Crimes*, Cliff has done the right thing . . . and been fired. Good is not rewarded, while sin goes unpunished.

Beyond the question of an artist selling out to fund his own work, what of his general world view? One can best judge Cliff by noting a line early in the film that surfaces again near its close. In the first situation Cliff has taken his niece to an old movie where a murder is being plotted. Though entertaining Cliff says, "This only happens in the movies." Yet that is the precise thing Judah is doing. Then late in the film Judah tells Cliff an "idea" for a film—Judah's personal tale of murder. Cliff tells Judah that he would have the murderer turn himself in. Judah responds, "Yes, but this is real life. . . . You've seen too many movies. . . . If you want a happy ending, go see a Hollywood movie."

Critic Kenneth M. Chanko noted, "The scene works in context, revealing Cliff to be a hopeless—even naive—romantic, and it also can be read as self-criticism on the part of Allen-as-artist."[90] That is, has Allen avoided such serious issues in his past films because he, too, had been naive? The answer would have to be a definite no, though Allen would seem to have found himself artistically by mixing equal parts drama and comedy. Or, as one *Crimes* reviewer titled his piece, "Comedy 50, Tragedy 50."[91]

CONCLUSION

This portion of the chapter has addressed three pivotal films in the career of Woody Allen. *Play It Again, Sam* presents his movie persona at its antiheroic best. Fantasy, often a key element in his movies, is showcased most broadly here, where his "fairy godmother" turns out to be a spirited Humphrey Bogart. *Annie Hall*, besides being such a personal Allen film, is significant for being a watershed *American* art-house picture.[92] It is an important transitional movie for bringing a more mainstream audience to a genre often considered too ponderous for the average viewer. In addition, *Annie*, like *Sam*, finds Allen transferring part of his antiheroic persona to frequent co-star Diane Keaton's character. This makes for a refreshing antiheroic twist, something Allen does more of in later films, such as in *Manhattan* (1980). *Crimes and Misdemeanors* breaks new ground by intertwining a dramatic and a comic storyline, making even the most somber ethical questions more palatable with dark comedy laughter. It is for these reasons that this Allen trilogy represents key markers in the most ambitious of movie careers. Like Chaplin, he is forever pushing the comic envelope, to grow as an artist.

NOTES

1. Leonard Maltin, *The Great Movie Comedians* (New York: Crown Publishers, 1978), p. 185.

2. William Robert Faith, *Bob Hope: A Life in Comedy* (New York: G. P. Putnam's Sons, 1982), p. 185.

3. Bob Hope and Bob Thomas, *The Road to Hollywood* (Garden City, N.Y.: Doubleday, 1977), p. 127.

4. Joe Lee Davis, "Criticism and Parody," *Thought*, Summer 1951, p. 180.

5. Ibid., p. 185.

6. Joseph A. Dane, "Parody and Satire: A Theoretical Model," *Genre*, Summer 1980, p. 153.

7. Linda Hutcheon, *A Theory of Parody* (New York: Methuen, 1985), p. 43.

8. Margaret A. Rose, *Parody II Meta-Fiction* (London: Croom Helm, 1979), pp. 25–26.

9. *Road to Utopia* review, *The New Yorker*, March 2, 1946, p. 81.

10. Jack Moffitt, "Back to Utopia," *Esquire*, April 1946, p. 63.

11. Wes D. Gehring, *Mr. "B" or Comforting Thoughts About the Bison: A Critical Biography of Robert Benchley* (Westport, Conn.: Greenwood Press, 1992).

12. *Road to Utopia* review, *New York Herald Tribune*, February 28, 1946, no page cited.

13. Moffitt, "Back to Utopia," p. 63.

14. Brooks Riley, "Words of Hope," *Film Comment*, May-June 1979, p. 24.

15. Bing Crosby (with Pete Martin), *Call Me Lucky* (New York: Simon and Schuster, 1953), p. 95.

16. Bob Hope (with Melville Shavelson), *Don't Shoot It's Only Me* (New York: G. P. Putnam's Sons, 1990), p. 34.

17. Ibid., p. 34.

18. Moffitt, "Back to Utopia," p. 63.

19. Frank Tashlin, "*Son of Paleface* Went Thataway," *New York Times*, October 5, 1952.

20. Faith, *Bob Hope*, p. 183.

21. *Road to Utopia* review, *New York Herald Tribune*.

22. Raymond Durgnat, *The Crazy Mirror: Hollywood Comedy and the American Image* (1969; reprinted New York: Dell. 1972), p. 170.

23. Ibid.

24. Henry Jenkins, *What Made Pistachio Nuts?: Early Sound Comedy and the Vaudeville Aesthetic* (New York: Columbia University Press, 1992), p. 282.

25. Charles Thompson, *Bob Hope: Portrait of a Superstar* (New York: St. Martin's Press, 1981), pp. 78–79.

26. Howard Barnes, *My Favorite Brunette* review, *New York Herald Tribune*, March 20, 1947, no page cited.

27. Robert Benchley, "Carnival Week in Sunny Las Los," in *The Treasurer's Report and Other Aspects of Community Singing* (New York: Grosset & Dunlap, 1930), p. 41.

28. *My Favorite Brunette* review, *New York Daily Mirror*, March 30, 1946, p. 16.

29. Ibid.; "Laughing with and at," *Commonweal*, April 4, 1947, p. 614.

30. Robert Warshow, "The Gangster as Tragic Hero" (1948) and "Movie Chronicle: The Westerner" (1954), in *The Immediate Experience*. Ed. Sherry Abel (New York: Atheneum, 1962), pp. 127–33 and 135–54; James Agee, "Comedy's Greatest Era" (1949), in *Agee on Film*, Vol. 1 (New York: Grosset and Dunlap, 1969), pp. 2–19.

31. John G. Cawelti, "The Question of Popular Genres," *Journal of Popular Film and Television*, Summer 1985, pp. 55–56.

32. "Everybody's Favorite Hope," *Newsweek*, March 31, 1947, p. 92.

33. Bosley Crowther, *My Favorite Brunette* review, *New York Times*, March 20, 1947, p. 38.

34. Ibid.

35. *My Favorite Brunette* review, *Time*, March 31, 1947, p. 99.

36. Barnes, *My Favorite Brunette* review.

37. Jeffrey Couchman, "Bob Hope: More Than a Gagster?" *New York Times*, May 6, 1979, Section 2, pp. 1,15.

38. "Movie of the Week: *The Paleface*," *Life*, January 3, 1949, p. 61.

39. Agee, "Comedy's Greatest Era," p. 18.

40. Hollis Alpert, "The Wild Man Is Coming," *Saturday Review*, August 9, 1952, p. 36.

41. Marilyn Wilson, "*The Paleface*," in *Magill's Survey of Cinema*, second series, Vol. 4, ed. Frank Magill (Englewood Cliffs, N.J.: Salem Press, 1981), p. 1852.

42. Ibid.

43. Bosley Crowther, review of *Son of Paleface*, *New York Times*, October 2, 1952, p. 32.

44. Durgnat, *The Crazy Mirror*, p. 171.

45. Maurice Yacowar, *Loser Take All: The Comic Art of Woody Allen*, expanded edn. (New York: Frederick Unger, 1991).

46. James Thurber, "The Secret Life of Walter Mitty," in *The Thurber Carnival* (New York: Harper and Brothers, 1945), p. 52.

47. John Brosnan, *Future Tense: The Cinema of Science Fiction* (New York: St. Martin's Press, 1978), p. 218.

48. Eric Lax, *On Being Funny: Woody Allen and Comedy* (New York: Manor Books, 1975), p. 68.

49. Northrop Frye, *Anatomy of Criticism* (Princeton: Princeton University Press, 1973), p. 182.

50. Ralph Rosenblum and Robert Karen, *When the Shooting Stops . . . the Cutting Begins: A Film Editor's Story* (New York: Penguin, 1979), p. 261.

51. Ibid.

52. Siegfried Kracauer, *Theory of Film: The Redemption of Physical Reality* (New York: Oxford University Press, 1960), p. 90.

53. Ibid., p. 91.

54. Lax, *On Being Funny*, p. 69.

55. Oscar Wilde, "The Decay of Living," in *Critical Theory Since Plato*, ed. Hazard Adams (Chicago: Harcourt Brace Jovanovich, 1971), p. 680.

56. Woody Allen, *Side Effects* (New York: Random House, 1980), p. 44.

57. Ibid., p. 54.

58. Ibid., p. 55.

59. Jack Kroll, "Woody Funny, but He's Serious," *Newsweek*, April 24, 1978, p. 62.

60. Richard Schickel, "Woody Allen's Breakthrough Movie," *Time*, April 25, 1977, p. 70.

61. *Annie Hall* review, *Variety*, March 30, 1977.

62. Vincent Canby, "Somber Comedy," *New York Times*, April 21, 1977, C-22.

63. Stephen J. Spignesi, *The Woody Allen Companion* (Kansas City: Andrews and McMeel, 1992), pp. 158–59.

64. For example, see Note 60.

65. William C. Siska, "The Art Film," in *The Handbook of American Film Genres*, ed. Wes D. Gehring (Westport, Conn.: Greenwood Press, 1988), p. 354.

66. Ibid., p. 363.

67. Eric Lax, *Woody Allen* (New York: Knopf, 1995), p. 197.

68. Joe Queenan, "Whine, Women, and Song," *Movieline*, May 1991, p. 44.

69. Vincent Canby, "Woody Allen Is the American Bergman," *New York Times*, April 24, 1977, p. 19.

70. Thomas Mann, *Death in Venice* (1913; reprinted New York: Vintage Books, 1963), p. 31.

71. Stig Bjorkman, *Woody Allen on Woody Allen* (New York: Grove Press, 1993), p. 75.

72. Ibid., p. 88.

73. Foster Hirsch, *Love, Sex, Death and the Meaning of Life* (New York: McGraw-Hill Book Co., 1981), p. 87.

74. Ibid., p. 89.

75. Penelope Gilliatt, "Woody at His Best Yet," *The New Yorker*, April 25, 1977, p. 138.

76. Woody Allen, "The Lunatic's Tale," in *Side Effects* (New York: Random House, 1980), pp. 71–78.

77. Stanley Kauffman, *Annie Hall* review, *New Republic*, May 14, 1977, p. 22.

78. Allen, "The Lunatic's Tale," p. 77.

79. Stuart Klawans, *Crimes and Misdemeanors* review, *The Nation*, November 13, 1989, p. 575.

80. Charles Champlin, "Woody Wooing a New Muse With 'Crimes,'" *Los Angeles Times*, October 17, 1989, Section 6, p. F-1.

81. Tom O'Brien, *Crimes and Misdemeanors* review, *Commonweal*, December 15, 1989, p. 706.

82. "Woody Allen and the Wages of Sin," *Christian Century*, November 1, 1989, p. 991.

83. Richard Schickel, "Postscript to the '80s," *Time*, October 16, 1989, p. 82.

84. Richard A. Blake, "Scales," *America*, December 9, 1989, p. 429.

85. Wes D. Gehring, *Dark Humor: Beyond Satire* (Westport, Conn.: Greenwood Press, 1996).

86. Luis Buñuel, *My Last Sigh*, trans. Abigail Israel (1982; reprinted New York: Random House, 1984), p. 14.

87. Robert Warshow, "*Monsieur Verdoux*," in *The Immediate Experience* (1962; reprinted New York: Atheneum, 1972), p. 213.

88. Jack Kroll, "Comedy 50, Tragedy 50," *Newsweek*, October 16, 1989, p. 67.

89. Spignesi, *The Woody Allen Companion*, p. 213.

90. Kenneth M. Chanko, *Crimes and Misdemeanors* review, *Films in Review*, December 1989, p. 614.

91. Kroll, "Comedy 50, Tragedy 50," p. 67.

92. Siska, "The Art Film," pp. 353–70.

5

EPILOGUE

Laurel: "Say, who do you think I am, Cinderella? You know, if I had any sense I'd leave!"

Hardy: "Well, it's a good thing you haven't!"

—*Helpmates* (1932)

Life doesn't imitate art; it imitates bad television.

Rain (Juliette Lewis) in Woody Allen's
Husbands and Wives (1992)

Unlike Rain's comment above, for many of us life seems to imitate comic art, particularly the frustrations of the comedian. Like the Laurel & Hardy comment cited, the comedic figure often suffers even when trying to do the right thing. In contrast to tragedy, comedian comedy seems much more universally pertinent to the individual banalities we all quietly (and sometimes not so quietly) suffer.

As noted earlier in the text (see the Preface), much of my writing has been influenced by film genre theorist Jim Leach's call for dividing comedy into more than one genre.[1] This book addresses the most basic and obvious of the comedy types—the personality comedian.[2] If one were to draw a large umbrella as representative of all comedy genres, populism and dark humor would be on opposite edges (see previous chapter). In contrast to these two comedy extremes (which through sentimentality or shock values often do not seem funny to some viewers), personality comedy sits right in the middle, on top of the umbrella. There is no question about laughter here. In comedy theory this is known as the "release and relief" approach. The expectation is for nonstop laughter, from film frame one. And that is what makes this comedy genre the most demanding.

For the same "keep them laughing" catharsis, comedian comedy often embraces the saturation, machine-gun patter of a Groucho Marx or a Robin Williams, such as the latter's radio scenes in *Good Morning, Vietnam* (1987). A visual variation of the saturation approach could best be exemplified by any of the mirror sequences in Chaplin's *The Circus* (1928), when there seem to be several Charlie figures on the lam. Through special effects, such as in Buster Keaton's short subject *The Playhouse* (1921), and Michael Keaton's (no relation) feature *Multiplicity* (1996), saturation comedy can also be achieved without a mirror. But returning to mirror "multiplicity," *the* dramatic example is Orson Welles' *The Lady From Shanghai* (1946), with a husband and wife shooting at their many images in a house of mirrors. Woody Allen's *Manhattan Murder Mystery* mirror sequence seems a combination of *The Circus* and *Shanghai*. The saturation effect can also be done via editing, such as Groucho's call for help in *Duck Soup* (1933), when his country is losing the war. The "assistance" comes by way of brief film clips of numerous things in motion, from speeding fire trucks to monkeys scampering across a jungle rope bridge.

Verbal or visual saturation is also complemented by a natural personality comedian tendency. For instance, when Harpo Marx takes to a bicycle and honks his horn in the pursuit of blondes in *Monkey Business* (1931), "it suggests the clown's immediate responsiveness to bodily desire without regard to social custom or self-restraint."[3]

This occasional anti-social nature of the clown recalls an observation by celebrated genre critic Robert Warshow on the gangster: "He is what we want to be and what we are afraid we may become."[4] Comedian comedy is broad enough to provide two variations on that statement. The most universal, as suggested earlier, would be: The comic is what we do *not* want to be but are afraid we have become. In other words, comedy is often praised by the viewer saying, "That's happened to me." Examples would be Laurel & Hardy's frustration of being tied up in a long traffic jam in *Two Tars* (1929), or John Candy trying to take off his coat while driving in *Planes, Trains and Automobiles* (1987). Part of the audience's laughter is based on someone else's playing the fool. But for the more aggressive comedian, such as Groucho Marx's con man or W. C. Fields' huckster, the paraphrasing of Warshow might read: The comic is what we want to be and what we are afraid we'll *never* become. For instance, when someone calls W. C. Fields' character a drunk in *It's A Gift* (1934), the comedian immediately answers, "I'm drunk and you're crazy. But I'll be sober tomorrow and you'll be crazy for the rest of your life." Or, when the minister of war in *Duck Soup* (1933) tells Groucho's character, "Sir, you try my patience!" the mustachioed one answers, "I don't mind if I do. *You* must come over and try mine sometime." For most of us, the perfect comeback, if it comes at all, arrives hours or days too late.

While the gift of laughter is celebration enough for a viewer, tracing a personality comedian's influence on other comedians and/or popular culture in general provides further insight into the genre. Ideally, such a familiarization better allows one to evaluate new and/or different examples of the genre. Most important, such a schematic overview may provide unique personal insight for the individual viewer.

Thankfully, the personality comedian is no longer limited to a refrain once used to describe Laurel & Hardy and Bob Hope (and no doubt others): "Nobody loved them but the public." Yet, there is never too much to learn about one's own response to this most basic of comedy genres.

NOTES

1. Jim Leach, "The Screwball Comedy," in *Film Genre and Criticism*, ed. Barry K. Grant (Metuchen, N.J.: Scarecrow Press, 1977), p. 75.

2. See my genre books: *Screwball Comedy: A Genre of Madcap Romance* (Westport, Conn.: Greenwood Press, 1986); *Populism and the Capra Legacy* (Westport, Conn.: Greenwood Press, 1995); and *Dark Comedy: Beyond Satire* (Westport, Conn.: Greenwood Press, 1996).

3. Henry Jenkins, *What Made Pistachio Nuts? Early Sound Comedy and the Vaudeville Aesthetic* (New York: Columbia University Press, 1992), p. 227.

4. Robert Warshow, "The Gangster as Tragic Hero," in *The Immediate Experience* (1962; reprinted New York: Atheneum, 1972), p. 131.

13. Geraldine Chaplin and the author at a 1989 Paris conference celebrating the 100th anniversary of her father's birth.

APPENDIX: SELECTED FILMOGRAPHY

FILMS MENTIONED AND/OR EXAMINED IN THE TEXT

1911 *The New Stenographer* (app. 10 minutes)
No director or writer credit. Star: John Bunny.

1912 *Umbrellas to Mend*, or *Mr. Niceman's Umbrella* (app. 10 minutes)
No director or writer credit. Star: John Bunny.

1912 *Cure For Pokeritus* (app. 10 minutes)
No director or writer credit. Star: John Bunny.

1912 *Bunny and the Dogs* (app. 5 minutes)
Director: Larry Trimble. No writer credit. Star: John Bunny.

1912 *Bunny All at Sea* (app. 10 minutes)
Director: Larry Trimble. No writer credit. Star: John Bunny.

1912 *Who Stole Bunny's Umbrella?* (app. 5 minutes)
Director: Fred Thompson. No writer credit. Star: John Bunny.

1913 *Pickwick Papers* (app. 20 minutes)
Director: Larry Trimble. Adapted from Charles Dickens. Star: John Bunny.

1914 *Making a Living* (app. 10 minutes)
Director: Henry Lehrman. Story: Reed Huestis. Star: Charlie Chaplin.

1914 *Bunny's Birthday* (app. 5 minutes)
Director: George D. Baker. No writer credit. Star: John Bunny.

1914 *Hearts and Diamonds* (app. 20 minutes)
Director: George D. Baker. No writer credit. Star: John Bunny.

1914 *The Rounders* (app. 5 minutes)
Director/story: Charlie Chaplin. Stars: Chaplin and Fatty Arbuckle.

1915 *The Tramp* (app. 20 minutes)
      Director/story: Charlie Chaplin. Star: Chaplin.

1915 *The Bank* (app. 20 minutes)
      Director/story: Charlie Chaplin. Star: Chaplin.

1916 *The Floorwalker* (app. 20 minutes)
      Director: Charlie Chaplin. Story: Chaplin, Vincent Bryan. Star: Chaplin.

1916 *The Fireman* (app. 20 minutes)
      Director: Charlie Chaplin. Story: Chaplin and Vincent Bryan. Star: Chaplin.

1916 *The Vagabond* (app. 20 minutes)
      Director: Charlie Chaplin. Story: Chaplin and Vincent Bryan. Star: Chaplin.

1916 *One A. M.* (app. 20 minutes)
      Director/story: Charlie Chaplin. Star: Chaplin.

1916 *The Count* (app. 20 minutes)
      Director/story: Charlie Chaplin. Star: Chaplin.

1916 *The Pawnshop* (app. 20 minutes)
      Director/story: Charlie Chaplin. Star: Chaplin.

1916 *Behind the Screen* (app. 20 minutes)
      Director/story: Charlie Chaplin. Star: Chaplin.

1916 *The Rink* (app. 20 minutes)
      Director/story: Charlie Chaplin. Star: Chaplin.

1917 *Easy Street* (app. 20 minutes)
      Director/story: Charlie Chaplin. Star: Chaplin.

1917 *The Immigrant* (app. 20 minutes)
      Director/story: Charlie Chaplin. Star: Chaplin.

1917 *The Cure* (app. 20 minutes)
      Director/story: Charlie Chaplin. Star: Chaplin.

1917 *The Adventurer* (app. 20 minutes)
      Director/story: Charlie Chaplin. Star: Chaplin.

1918 *A Dog's Life* (app. 30 minutes)
      Director/story: Charlie Chaplin. Star: Chaplin.

1918 *Shoulder Arms* (app. 40 minutes)
      Director/story: Charlie Chaplin. Star: Chaplin.

1921 *The Kid* (app. 60 minutes)
      Director/story: Charlie Chaplin. Star: Chaplin.

1921 *The Playhouse* (app. 20 minutes)
      Director/story: Buster Keaton and Eddie Cline. Star: Keaton.

1922 *Cops* (app. 20 minutes)
      Director/story: Buster Keaton and Eddie Cline. Star: Keaton.

1922 *Pay Day* (app. 20 minutes)
      Director/story: Charlie Chaplin. Star: Chaplin.

1922 *Daydreams* (app. 30 minutes)
      Director/story: Buster Keaton and Eddie Cline. Star: Keaton.

1923 *The Pilgrim* (app. 50 minutes)
Director/story: Charlie Chaplin. Star: Chaplin.

1923 *Safety Last* (78 minutes)
Director: Fred Newmeyer and Sam Taylor. Story: Hal Roach, Sam Taylor, and Tim Whelan. Star: Harold Lloyd.

1924 *Sherlock Jr.* (45 minutes)
Director: Buster Keaton. Story: Clyde Bruckman, Joseph Mitchell, and Jean Havez. Star: Keaton.

1924 *The Navigator* (app. 60 minutes)
Director: Buster Keaton and Donald Crisp. Story: Clyde Bruckman, Joseph Mitchell, and Jean Havez. Star: Keaton.

1925 *The Gold Rush* (82 minutes)
Director/story: Charlie Chaplin. Star: Chaplin.

1925 *The Freshman* (70 minutes)
Director: Sam Taylor and Fred Newmeyer. Story: Sam Taylor, John Grey, Ted Wilde, Tim Whelan, Clyde Bruckman, Lex Neal, Jean Havez, and Brooks B. Harding. Star: Harold Lloyd.

1925 *Sally of the Sawdust* (104 minutes)
Director: D. W. Griffith; based on Dorothy Donnelly stage play *Poppy*. Star: W. C. Fields.

1926 *Tramp, Tramp, Tramp* (app. 60 minutes)
Director: Harry Edwards. Story: Arthur Ripley and Frank Capra. Star: Harry Langdon.

1926 *The Strong Man* (app. 70 minutes)
Director: Frank Capra. Story: Arthur Ripley. Star: Harry Langdon.

1927 *The General* (74 minutes)
Director/story: Buster Keaton and Clyde Bruckman. Star: Keaton.

1927 *Long Pants* (app. 60 minutes)
Director: Frank Capra. Story: Arthur Ripley. Star: Harry Langdon.

1927 *College* (65 minutes)
Director: James Horne. Story: Carl Harbaugh and Bryan Foy. Star: Buster Keaton.

1927 *The Battle of the Century* (app. 20 minutes)
Director: Clyde A. Bruckman. Story: Hal Roach. Stars: Laurel & Hardy.

1928 *The Circus* (72 minutes)
Director/story: Charlie Chaplin. Star: Chaplin.

1928 *Steamboat Bill, Jr.* (71 minutes)
Director: Charles "Chuck" Reisner. Story: Carl Harbaugh. Star: Buster Keaton.

1928 *Their Purple Moment* (app. 20 minutes)
Director: James Parrott. No story credit. Stars: Laurel & Hardy.

1928 *Should Married Men Go Home?* (app. 20 minutes)
Director: James Parrott. Story: Leo McCarey. Stars: Laurel & Hardy.

1928 *Two Tars* (app. 20 minutes)
Director: James Parrott. Story: Leo McCarey. Stars: Laurel & Hardy.

1929 *That's My Wife* (app. 20 minutes)
Director: Lloyd French. Story: Leo McCarey. Stars: Laurel & Hardy.

1929 *A Perfect Day* (app. 20 minutes)
Director: James Parrott. Story: Hal Roach and Leo McCarey. Stars: Laurel & Hardy.

1929 *The Hoose-Gow* (app. 20 minutes)
Director: James Parrott. Story: Leo McCarey. Stars: Laurel & Hardy.

1929 *The Cocoanuts* (96 minutes)
Directors: Robert Florey and Joseph Santley. Screenplay: Morrie Ryskind, from the George S. Kaufman and Ryskind play. Stars: The Marx Brothers.

1929 *They Had to See Paris* (95 minutes)
Director: Frank Borzage. Screenplay: Sonya Levien, based on a Homer Cray story. Star: Will Rogers.

1930 *So This Is London* (89 minutes)
Director: John Blystone. Screenplay: Sonya Levien, from the Arthur Goodrich play. Star: Will Rogers.

1930 *Hog Wild* (app. 20 minutes)
Director: James Parrott. Story: Leo McCarey. Stars: Laurel & Hardy.

1930 *Animal Crackers* (98 minutes)
Director: Victor Heerman. Screenplay: Morrie Ryskind. Stars: The Marx Brothers.

1931 *City Lights* (87 minutes)
Director/story: Charlie Chaplin. Star: Chaplin.

1931 *Monkey Business* (77 minutes)
Director: Norman McLeod. Screenplay: S. J. Perelman and William B. Johnstone. Stars: The Marx Brothers.

1932 *Horse Feathers* (68 minutes)
Director: Norman McLeod. Screenplay: Bert Kalmar, Harry Ruby, S. J.Perelman, and William B. Johnstone. Stars: The Marx Brothers.

1932 *The Music Box* (app. 30 minutes)
Director: James Parrott. Dialogue: H. M. Walker. Stars: Laurel & Hardy.

1933 *Twice Two* (app. 20 minutes)
Director: James Parrott. No story credit. Stars: Laurel & Hardy.

1933 *International House* (70 minutes)
Director: Edward Sutherland. Screenplay: Francis Martin and Walter DeLeon. Star: W. C. Fields.

1933 *Tillie and Gus* (58 minutes)
Director: Francis Martin. Screenplay: Walter DeLeon and Francis Martin, from a Rupert Hughes story. Star: W. C. Fields.

1933 *Duck Soup* (70 minutes)
Director: Leo McCarey. Screenplay: Bert Kalmar and Harry Ruby. Stars: The Marx Brothers.

1934 *The Old Fashioned Way* (66 minutes)
Director: William Beaudine. Screenplay: Garnett Weston and Jack Cunningham, from a Charles Bogle (Fields) story. Star: W. C. Fields.

1934 *Judge Priest* (70 minutes)
Director: John Ford. Screenplay: Dudley Nichols and Lamar Trotti, based on Irvin S. Cobb stories. Star: Will Rogers.

1934 *It's a Gift* (73 minutes)
      Director: Norman McLeod. Screenplay: Jack Cunningham, from a Charles Bogle (Fields) story. Star: W. C. Fields.

1935 *Mississippi* (80 minutes)
      Director: Edward Sutherland. Screenplay: Francis Martin and Jack Cunningham, from the Booth Tarkington play, *The Magnolia*. Star: W. C. Fields.

1935 *David Copperfield* (133 minutes)
      Director: George Cukor. Screenplay: Howard Estabrook, from Charles Dickens' novel. Star: W. C. Fields.

1935 *The Man on the Flying Trapeze* (65 minutes)
      Director: Clyde Bruckman. Screenplay: Ray Harris and Sam Hardy, from a story by Charles Bogle (Fields) and Sam Hardy. Star: W. C. Fields.

1935 *Steamboat 'Round the Bend* (90 minutes)
      Director: John Ford. Screenplay: Dudley Nichols and Lamar Trotti, from the Ben Lucien novel. Star: Will Rogers.

1935 *A Night at the Opera* (92 minutes)
      Director: Sam Wood. Screenplay: George S. Kaufman and Morrie Ryskind. Stars: The Marx Brothers.

1936 *Modern Times* (85 minutes)
      Director/story: Charlie Chaplin. Star: Chaplin.

1936 *Poppy* (75 minutes)
      Director: Edward Sutherland. Screenplay: Waldemar Young and Virginia Van Up (see *Sally of the Sawdust* entry, 1925, the first film adaptation of the play). Star: W. C. Fields.

1937 *Way Out West* (65 minutes)
      Director: James W. Horne. Screenplay: Charles Rogers, Felix Adler, and James Parrott. Stars: Laurel & Hardy.

1937 *A Day at the Races* (109 minutes)
      Director: Sam Wood. Screenplay: George Seaton, Robert Pirosh, and George Oppenheimer. Stars: The Marx Brothers.

1938 *Room Service* (78 minutes)
      Director: William A. Seiter. Screenplay: Morrie Ryskind, from the John Murray and Allen Boretz play. Star: The Marx Brothers.

1939 *You Can't Cheat an Honest Man* (76 minutes)
      Director: George Marshall. Screenplay: George Marion Jr., Richard Mack, and Everett Freeman, from a Charles Bogle (Fields) story. Star: W. C. Fields.

1939 *At the Circus* (87 minutes)
      Director: Edward Buzzell. Screenplay: Irving Brecher. Stars: The Marx Brothers.

1940 *My Little Chickadee* (83 minutes)
      Director: Edward Cline. Screenplay: Mae West and W. C. Fields. Stars: W. C. Fields and Mae West.

1940 *Road to Singapore* (84 minutes)
      Director: Victor Schertzinger. Screenplay: Don Hartman and Frank Butler. Stars: Bob Hope and Bing Crosby.

1940 *The Great Dictator* (126 minutes)
      Director/story: Charlie Chaplin. Star: Chaplin.

1940 *The Bank Dick* (74 minutes)
      Director: Edward Cline. Screenplay: Mahatma Kane Jeeves (Fields). Star: W. C. Fields.

1940 *A Chump at Oxford* (63 minutes)
      Director: Alfred Goulding. Screenplay: Charles Rogers, Felix Adler, and Harry Langdon.
      Stars: Laurel & Hardy.

1941 *Road to Zanzibar* (92 minutes)
      Director: Victor Schertzinger. Screenplay: Frank Butler and Don Hartman. Stars: Bob
      Hope and Bing Crosby.

1941 *Hellzapoppin* (84 minutes)
      Director: H. C. Potter. Screenplay: Nat Perrin and Warren Wilson. Stars: Ole Olsen and
      Chic Johnson.

1942 *My Favorite Blonde* (78 minutes)
      Director: Sidney Lanfield. Screenplay: Don Hartman and Frank Butler. Star: Bob Hope.

1942 *Road to Morocco* (83 minutes)
      Director: David Butler. Screenplay: Frank Butler and Don Hartman. Stars: Bob Hope
      and Bing Crosby.

1945 *Road to Utopia* (90 minutes)
      Director: Paul Jones. Screenplay: Norman Panama and Melvin Frank. Stars: Bob Hope,
      Bing Crosby, and Robert Benchley.

1945 *Wonder Man* (98 minutes)
      Director: H. Bruce Humberstone. Screenplay: Don Hartman, Melville Shavelson and
      Phil Rapp. Star: Danny Kaye.

1946 *The Time of Their Lives* (82 minutes)
      Director: Charles Barton. Screenplay: Val Burton, Walter DeLeon, and Bradford Ropes.
      Stars: Abbott & Costello.

1947 *The Sin of Harold Diddlebock* (89 minutes)
      Reissued as *Mad Wednesday* (1950, 77 minutes). Director/screenplay: Preston Sturges.
      Star: Harold Lloyd.

1947 *Monsieur Verdoux* (122 minutes)
      Director/story: Charlie Chaplin. Star: Chaplin.

1947 *My Favorite Brunette* (87 minutes)
      Director: Elliott Nugent. Screenplay: Edmund Beloin and Jack Rose. Star: Bob Hope.

1947 *Road to Rio* (100 minutes)
      Director: Norman Z. McLeod. Screenplay: Edmund Beloin and Jack Rose. Stars: Bob
      Hope and Bing Crosby.

1948 *The Fuller Brush Man* (93 minutes)
      Director: S. Sylvan Simon. Screenplay: Frank Tashlin and Devery Freeman. Star: Red
      Skelton.

1948 *A Southern Yankee* (90 minutes)
      Director: Edward Sedgwick. Screenplay: Harry Tugent (gag assistance by Buster Keaton).
      Star: Red Skelton.

1948 *The Paleface* (91 minutes)
      Director: Norman Z. McLeod. Screenplay: Edmund Hartmann and Frank Tashlin. Star:
      Bob Hope.

1950 *Fancy Pants* (92 minutes)
Director: George Marshall. Screenplay: Edmund Hartmann and Robert O'Brien, from the Harry Leon Wilson novel. Stars: Bob Hope and Lucille Ball.

1951 *The Lemon Drop Kid* (91 minutes)
Director: Sidney Lanfield. Screenplay: Edmund Hartmann and Robert O'Brien, from a Damon Runyon story. Star: Bob Hope.

1952 *Son of Paleface* (95 minutes)
Director: Frank Tashlin. Screenplay: Frank Tashlin, Robert L. Welch, and Joseph Quillan. Star: Bob Hope.

1952 *Limelight* (143 minutes)
Director/story: Charlie Chaplin. Star: Chaplin.

1952 *Road to Bali* (90 minutes)
Director: Hal Walker. Screenplay: Frank Butler, Hal Kanter, and William Morrow. Stars: Bob Hope and Bing Crosby.

1955 *The Seven Year Itch* (105 minutes)
Director: Billy Wilder. Screenplay: Wilder and George Axelrod, from the Axelrod play. Star: Marilyn Monroe.

1956 *The Court Jester* (101 minutes)
Director/screenplay: Norman Panama. Star: Danny Kaye.

1956 *Pardners* (90 minutes)
Director: Norman Taurog. Screenplay: Sidney Sheldon. Stars: Dean Martin and Jerry Lewis.

1959 *Some Like It Hot* (119 minutes)
Director: Billy Wilder. Screenplay: Wilder and I. A. L. Diamond. Stars: Marilyn Monroe, Tony Curtis, and Jack Lemmon.

1959 *Alias Jesse James* (92 minutes)
Director: Norman Z. McLeod. Screenplay: William Bowers and Daniel D. Beauchamp. Star: Bob Hope.

1960 *Bellboy* (72 minutes)
Director/screenplay: Jerry Lewis. Star: Lewis.

1962 *Road to Hong Kong* (91 minutes)
Director: Norman Panama. Screenplay: Panama and Melvin Frank. Stars: Bob Hope and Bing Crosby.

1963 *The Nutty Professor* (107 minutes)
Director/screenplay: Jerry Lewis. Star: Lewis.

1963 *It's A Mad, Mad, Mad, Mad World* (154 minutes)
Director: Stanley Kramer. Screenplay: William and Tania Rose. All star cast.

1966 *Texas Across the River* (101 minutes)
Director: Michael Gordon. Screenplay: Wells Root, Harold Greene, and Bel Starr. Star: Dean Martin.

1969 *Take the Money and Run* (85 minutes)
Director: Woody Allen. Screenplay: Allen and Mickey Rose. Star: Allen.

1971 *Bananas* (82 minutes)
Director: Woody Allen. Screenplay: Allen and Mickey Rose. Star: Allen.

1972 *Everything You Always Wanted to Know About Sex (But Were Afraid to Ask)* (87 minutes)
      Director/story: Woody Allen. Star: Allen.

1972 *Play It Again, Sam* (87 minutes)
      Director: Herbert Ross. Screenplay: Woody Allen, based on Allen's play. Star: Allen.

1973 *Sleeper* (88 minutes)
      Director: Woody Allen. Screenplay: Allen and Marshall Brickman. Star: Allen.

1975 *Love and Death* (85 minutes)
      Director/story: Woody Allen. Star: Allen.

1976 *The Front* (94 minutes)
      Director: Martin Ritt. Screenplay: Walter Bernstein. Star: Woody Allen.

1976 *Silver Streak* (113 minutes)
      Director: Arthur Hiller. Screenplay: Colin Higgins. Stars: Gene Wilder and Richard
      Pryor.

1977 *Annie Hall* (94 minutes)
      Director: Woody Allen. Screenplay: Allen and Marshall Brickman. Star: Woody Allen.

1977 *Smokey and the Bandit* (96 minutes)
      Director: Hal Needham. Screenplay: James Lee Barrett, Charles Shyer, and Alan Mandel.
      Star: Burt Reynolds.

1979 *Manhattan* (96 minutes)
      Director: Woody Allen. Screenplay: Allen and Marshall Brickman. Star: Woody Allen.

1979 *Richard Pryor—Live in Concert* (78 minutes)
      Director: Jeff Margolis. Material by Richard Pryor. Star: Pryor.

1980 *Stardust Memories* (91 minutes)
      Director/story: Woody Allen. Star: Allen.

1980 *Stir Crazy* (111 minutes)
      Director: Sidney Poitier. Screenplay: Bruce Jay Friedman. Stars: Gene Wilder and Richard
      Pryor.

1981 *Stripes* (105 minutes)
      Director: Ivan Reitman. Screenplay: Len Blum, Dan Goldberg, and Harold Ramis. Star:
      Bill Murray.

1982 *Richard Pryor Live on the Sunset Strip* (82 minutes)
      Director: Joe Layton. Material by Richard Pryor. Star: Pryor.

1982 *Dead Men Don't Wear Plaid* (89 minutes)
      Director: Carl Reiner. Screenplay: Phil Robinson. Star: Steve Martin.

1982 *A Midsummer Night's Sex Comedy* (88 minutes)
      Director/screenplay: Woody Allen. Star: Allen.

1982 *48 Hrs.* (97 minutes)
      Director: Walter Hill. Screenplay: Roger Spottiswoode, Hill, Larry Gross, and Steven E.
      deSouza. Star: Eddie Murphy.

1983 *The Man With Two Brains* (93 minutes)
      Director: Carl Reiner. Screenplay: Reiner, Steve Martin, and George Gipe. Star: Martin.

1983 *National Lampoon's Vacation* (98 minutes)
      Director: Harold Ramis. Screenplay: John Hughes. Star: Chevy Chase.

1983 *Richard Pryor Here and Now* (83 minutes)
      Director: Richard Pryor. Material by Pryor. Star: Pryor.

1984 *The Lonely Guy* (90 minutes)
      Director: Arthur Hiller. Screenplay: Ed Weinberger and Stan Daniels, based on Bruce Jay Friedman's novel *The Lonely Guy's Book of Life*. Star: Steve Martin.

1984 *Broadway Danny Rose* (86 minutes)
      Director/screenplay: Woody Allen. Star: Allen.

1984 *All of Me* (93 minutes)
      Director: Carl Reiner. Screenplay: Reiner, George Gipe, and Steve Martin. Star: Martin.

1984 *Beverly Hills Cop* (105 minutes)
      Director: Martin Brest. Screenplay: Daniel Petrie Jr. Star: Eddie Murphy.

1985 *The Purple Rose of Cairo* (82 minutes)
      Director/screenplay: Woody Allen. Stars: Mia Farrow and Jeff Daniels.

1985 *Lost in America* (91 minutes)
      Director: Albert Brooks. Screenplay: Brooks and Monica Johnson. Star: Brooks.

1985 *Pee-wee's Big Adventure* (90 minutes)
      Director: Tim Burton. Screenplay: Phil Hartman, Paul Reubens, and Michael Varhol. Star: Reubens as Pee-wee.

1985 *Spies Like Us* (109 Minutes)
      Director: John Landis. Screenplay: Dan Aykroyd, Lowell Ganz, and Babaloo Mandel. Stars: Aykroyd and Chevy Chase.

1986 *Hannah and Her Sisters* (106 minutes)
      Director/screenplay: Woody Allen. Star: Allen.

1987 *Outrageous Fortune* (100 minutes)
      Director: Arthur Hill. Screenplay: Leslie Dixon. Stars: Bette Midler and Shelley Long.

1987 *Roxanne* (107 minutes)
      Director: Fred Schepisi. Screenplay: Steve Martin (update of *Cyrano de Bergerac*). Star: Martin.

1987 *Planes, Trains and Automobiles* (93 minutes)
      Director/screenplay: John Hughes. Stars: Steve Martin and John Candy.

1987 *Good Morning, Vietnam* (120 minutes)
      Director: Barry Levinson. Screenplay: Mitch Markowitz. Star: Robin Williams.

1988 *Midnight Run* (122 minutes)
      Director: Martin Brest. Screenplay: George Gallo. Stars: Robert De Niro and Charles Grodin.

1989 "Oedipus Wrecks" (in *New York Stories*, 123 minutes)
      Director/screenplay: Woody Allen. Star: Allen.

1989 *Parenthood* (124 minutes)
      Director: Ron Howard. Screenplay: Lowell Ganz and Babaloo Mandel. Star: Steve Martin.

1989 *Crimes and Misdemeanors* (104 minutes)
      Director/screenplay: Woody Allen. Star: Allen.

1989 *Harlem Nights* (115 minutes)
      Director/screenplay: Eddie Murphy. Stars: Murphy and Richard Pryor.

1991 *City Slickers* (112 minutes)
Director: Ron Underwood. Screenplay: Lowell Ganz and Babaloo Mandel. Star: Billy Crystal.

1991 *Father of the Bride* (101 minutes)
Director: Charles Shyer. Screenplay: Frances Goodrich, Albert Hackett, Nancy Meyers and Shyer (remake of the 1950 film, based on Edward Streeter's novel). Star: Steve Martin.

1993 *Groundhog Day* (103 minutes)
Director: Harold Ramis. Screenplay: Ramis and Danny Rubin. Star: Bill Murray.

1993 *Manhattan Murder Mystery* (105 minutes)
Director: Woody Allen. Screenplay: Allen and Marshall Brickman. Star: Allen.

1994 *Ace Ventura: Pet Detective* (87 minutes)
Director: Tom Shadyac. Screenplay: Jack Bernstein, Tom Shadyac, and Jim Carrey. Star: Carrey.

1994 *Dumb and Dumber* (106 minutes)
Director: Peter Farrelly. Screenplay: Peter Farrelly, Bennett Yellin, and Bobby Farrelly. Stars: Jim Carrey and Jeff Daniels.

1994 *The Mask* (101 minutes)
Director: Charles Russell. Screenplay: Mike Webb. Star: Jim Carrey.

SELECTED BIBLIOGRAPHY

Adamson, Joe. *Groucho, Harpo, Chico and Sometimes Zeppo*. New York: Simon and Schuster, 1973.

Agee, James. "Comedy's Greatest Era" (1949). In *Agee on Film*, Vol. 1. New York: Grosset and Dunlap, 1969.

Allen, Woody. "The Lunatic's Tale." In *Side Effects*. New York: Random House, 1980.

Alpert, Hollis. "The Wild Man Is Coming." *Saturday Review* (August 9, 1952), p. 36.

Alsop, Joseph, Jr. "Surrealism Beaten at Its Own Game." *New York Herald Tribune* (December 15, 1935). In *A Night at the Opera* file. Billy Rose Theatre Collection, New York Public Library at Lincoln Center, New York.

Anderson, Joseph L., and Donald Richie. *The Japanese Film: Art and Industry*, 1959; reprinted New York: Grove Press, 1960.

Andrew, J. Dudley. *The Major Film Theories*. New York: Oxford University Press, 1976.

Andrews, Bart. *The Story of I Love Lucy*, 1976; reprinted New York: Popular Library, 1977.

Annie Hall review. *Variety* (March 30, 1977), p. 19.

Arce, Hector. *Groucho*. New York: G. P. Putnam's Sons, 1979.

Armes, Roy. *Patterns of Realism: A Study of Italian Neo-Realist Cinema*. New York: A. S. Barnes, 1971.

Arnheim, Rudolf. *Film as Art*, 1933; reprinted Los Angeles: University of California Press, 1971.

Bair, Deirdre. *Samuel Beckett*. New York: Harcourt Brace Jovanovich, 1978, p. 48.

Balázs, Bela. *Theory of the Film* (trans. Edith Bone). 1952; reprinted New York: Dover Press, 1970.

Bazin, André. "The Virtues and Limitations of Montage." In *What Is Cinema?* Vol. 1 (trans. and ed. Hugh Gray), 1958; reprinted Los Angeles: University of California Press, 1967, p. 52.

——— . "Charlie Chaplin." In *What Is Cinema?* Vol. 1 (trans. and ed. Hugh Gray), 1958; reprinted Los Angeles: University of California Press, 1967, p. 150.

——— . "The Myth of Monsieur Verdoux." In *What Is Cinema?* Vol. 2 (trans. and ed. Hugh Gray), 1958; reprinted Los Angeles: University of California Press, 1971, pp. 102–103.

——— . "The Grandeur of Limelight." In *What Is Cinema?* Vol. 2 (trans. and ed. Hugh Gray), 1958; reprinted Los Angeles: University of California Press, 1971, p. 136.

Benchley, Robert. "Carnival Week in Sunny Las Los." In *The Treasurer's Report and Other Aspects of Community Singing.* New York: Grosset & Dunlap, 1930.

——— . "Johnny-On-The-Spot." In *From Bed to Worse: Or Comforting Thoughts About the Bison.* New York: Harper & Brothers, 1934.

Bjorkman, Stig. *Woody Allen on Woody Allen.* New York: Grove Press, 1993.

Blair, Walter. *Native American Humor.* 1937; reprinted San Francisco: Chandler, 1960.

Blake, Richard A. "Scales." *America* (December 9, 1989), p. 429.

Bowman, William. *Charlie Chaplin: His Life and Art.* 1931; reprinted New York: Haskell House, 1974.

Bradbury, Ray. "The Laurel and Hardy Love Affair." *Playboy* (December 1987), pp. 76–78, 210–11.

——— . *The Toynbee Convector,* New York: Alfred A. Knopf, 1988.

Brosnan, John. *Future Tense: The Cinema of Science Fiction.* New York: St. Martin's Press, 1978.

Buchalter, Gail. "What Failure Taught Me." *Parade* (January 15, 1995), p. 4.

"Bunny Back at Lyceum Again." *Indianapolis News* (January 15, 1915), p. 11.

Bunny in Funnyland review. *Chicago Tribune* (October 11, 1914), Section 8, p. 2.

Bunny, John. "Famous 'Movie' Comedian Dies in Brooklyn." *Indianapolis Star* (April 27, 1915), p. 6.

Bunny, John. *Bunnyisms.* New York: Vitagraph (circa 1914). In the John Bunny file, Billy Rose Theatre Collection, New York Public Library at Lincoln Center, New York.

Buñuel, Luis. *My Last Sigh* (trans. Abigail Israel). 1982; reprinted New York: Random House, 1984.

Cahn, William. *Harold Lloyd's World of Comedy.* London: George Allen and Unwin, 1966.

Canby, Vincent. "Somber Comedy." *New York Times* (April 21, 1977), C-22.

——— . "Woody Allen Is the American Bergman." *New York Times* (April 24, 1977), p. 19.

Cawelti, John G. "The Question of Popular Genres." *Journal of Popular Film and Television* (Summer 1985), pp. 55–56.

Champlin, Charles. "Woody Wooing a New Muse with 'Crimes.'" *Los Angeles Times* (October 17, 1989), Section 6, p. F-1.

Chanko, Kenneth M. *Crimes and Misdemeanors* review. *Films in Review* (December 1989), p. 614.

Chaplin, Charles. *Charlie Chaplin's Own Story.* Indianapolis: Bobbs-Merrill, 1916.
_____. "Pantomime and Comedy." *New York Times* (January 25, 1931), Section 8, p. 6.
_____. *My Autobiography.* 1964; reprinted New York: Pocket Books, 1966.
Chaplin, Charlie, Jr. *My Father, Charlie Chaplin.* New York: Random House, 1960.
Charlie Chaplin Up in the Air. Chicago: M. A. Donohue, 1917.
Cotes, Peter, and Thelma Niklaus. *The Little Fellow: The Life and Works of Charles Spencer Chaplin,* 1951; reprinted New York: Citadel, 1965.
Couchman, Jeffrey. "Bob Hope: More Than a Gagster?" *New York Times* (May 6, 1979), Section 2, pp. 1, 15.
Crosby, Bing, and Pete Martin. *Call Me Lucky.* New York: Simon and Schuster, 1953.
Crowther, Bosley. *My Favorite Brunette* review. *New York Times* (March 20, 1947), p. 38.
_____. *Son of Paleface* review. *New York Times* (October 2, 1952), p. 30.
Dali, Salvador. "Surrealism in Hollywood." *Harper's Bazaar* (June 1937), pp. 68–69, 132.
Dane, Joseph A. "Parody and Satire: A Theoretical Model." *Genre* (Summer 1980), p. 153.
Davis, Joe Lee. "Criticism and Parody." *Thought* (Summer 1951), p. 180.
"Death of Mr. John Bunny." *Saturday Review* (April 1915), p. 5d.
Denby, David. "Introduction." In *Awake in the Dark: An Anthology of American Film Criticism, 1915 to the Present.* New York: Vintage Books, 1977.
Dickens, Charles. *Oliver Twist.* 1841; reprinted New York: Times Mirror, 1961.
Dunham, Harold. "John Bunny." *Silent Picture* (Winter 1968–69), p. 12.
Durgnat, Raymond. "Suckers and Soaks." In *The Crazy Mirror: Hollywood Comedy and the American Image.* 1969; reprinted New York: Dell Publishing, 1972.
Eastman, Max. *Heroes I Have Known: Twelve Who Lived Great Lives.* New York: Simon and Schuster, 1942.
"Ebony Interview With Eddie Murphy." *Ebony* (July 1985), p. 46.
Eisenstein, Sergei. "Word and Image." *The Film Sense* (trans. and ed. Jay Leyda). 1942; reprinted New York: Harcourt, Brace and World, 1947.
Esslin, Martin. *The Theatre of the Absurd.* Garden City, N.Y.: Doubleday, 1961.
"Everybody's Favorite Hope." *Newsweek* (March 20, 1947), p. 92.
Ewer, Frederick. *Bertolt Brecht: His Life, His Art, and His Times.* 1967; reprinted New York: Citadel Press, 1969, p. 386.
Eyles, Allen. *The Marx Brothers: Their World of Comedy.* 1966; reprinted New York: Paperback Library, 1971.
Faith, William Robert. *Bob Hope: A Life in Comedy.* New York: G. P. Putnam's Sons, 1982.
Ferguson, Otis. *A Night At The Opera* review. *New Republic* (December 11, 1935), p. 130.
Fiske, Minnie Maddern. "The Art of Charles Chaplin." *Harper's Weekly* (February 6, 1916), p. 494.
Fowler, Gene. *Minutes of the Last Meeting.* New York: Viking Press, 1954.

Frye, Northrop. *Anatomy of Criticism*. Princeton, N.J.: Princeton University Press, 1973.

Gardner, Martin A. "The Marx Brothers: An Investigation of Their Films as Satirical Social Criticism." Ph.D. dissertation, New York University, 1970.

Gehring, Wes D. "Film's First Comic Anti-Heroes: Leo McCarey's Laurel & Hardy." *Ball State University Forum* (Autumn 1979), pp. 46–56.

———. "The Comic Anti-Hero in American Fiction: Its First Full Articulation." *Thalia: Studies in Literary Humor* (Winter 1979–80), pp. 11–14.

———. *Leo McCarey and the Comic Anti-Hero in American Film*. New York: Arno Press, 1980.

———. "Charlie Chaplin and the Progressive Era." *Indiana Social Studies Quarterly* (Autumn 1981), pp. 10–18.

———. *Charlie Chaplin: A Bio-Bibliography*. Westport, Conn.: Greenwood Press, 1983.

———. *W. C. Fields: A Bio-Bibliography*. Westport, Conn.: Greenwood Press,1984.

———. *Screwball Comedy: A Genre of Madcap Romance*. Westport, Conn.: Greenwood Press, 1986.

———. "W. C. Fields: The Copyright Sketches." *Journal of Popular Film and Television* (Summer 1986), pp. 65–75.

———. *The Marx Brothers: A Bio-Bibliography*. Westport, Conn.: Greenwood Press, 1987.

———. *Handbook of American Film Genres*. Westport, Conn.: Greenwood Press, 1988.

———. *Laurel & Hardy: A Bio-Bibliography*. Westport, Conn., 1990.

———. *"Mr. B" or Comforting Thoughts About the Bison*. Westport, Conn.: Greenwood Press, 1992.

———. *Groucho and W. C. Fields: Huckster Comedians*. Jackson, Miss.: University of Mississippi Press, 1994.

———. *Populism and the Capra Legacy*. Westport, Conn.: Greenwood Press, 1995.

———. *American Dark Comedy: Beyond Satire*. Westport, Conn.: Greenwood Press, 1996.

Gill, Sam. "John Bunny." In *The Silent Comedians* (ed. Richard Dyer MacCann). Metuchen, N.J.: Scarecrow Press, 1993, p. 29.

Gilliatt, Penelope. "Woody at His Best Yet." *The New Yorker* (April 25, 1977), p. 138.

Greene, Graham. *A Chump at Oxford* review. *Spectator* (February 23, 1940), p. 248.

Grierson, John. "The Logic of Comedy." In *Grierson on Documentary*. (ed. Forsyth Hardy). 1947; reprinted Los Angeles: University of California Press, 1966.

Hall, Mordaunt. *Tramp, Tramp, Tramp*. In *New York Film Reviews*, 1913–1931. New York: New York Times and Arno Press, 1970.

———. *Long Pants* review. In *New York Film Review, 1913–1931*. New York: New York Times and Arno Press, 1970.

Halliwell, Leslie. *Double Take and Fade Away*. London: Gragton Books, 1987.

Haskins, Jim. *Richard Pryor: A Man and His Madness*. New York: Beaufort, 1984.

Hilfer, Anthony Channell. *The Revolt From the Village: 1915–1930*. Chapel Hill, N.C.: University of North Carolina Press, 1969.

Hill, Hamlin. "Modern American Humor: The Janus Laugh." *College English* (December 1963), p. 174.

Hirsch, Foster. *Love, Sex, Death, and the Meaning of Life.* New York: McGraw-Hill Book Co., 1981.

Hope, Bob, and Bob Thomas. *The Road to Hollywood.* Garden City, N.Y.: Doubleday, 1977.

Hope, Bob, and Melville Shavelson. *Don't Shoot, It's Only Me.* New York: G. P. Putnam's Sons, 1990.

Huff, Theodore. *Charlie Chaplin.* 1951; reprinted New York: New York Times, 1972.

Hutcheon, Linda. *A Theory of Parody.* New York: Methuen, 1985.

Ionesco's *The Shepherd's Chameleon* review. *Time* (December 12, 1960), p. 63.

Italie, Hellel. "Director Martin Brest Is Considered a Bit of a Smart Aleck" (wire service story). *Waterloo Courier* (Iowa), (August 10, 1988), p. C-3.

Jacobs, Lewis. *The Rise of the American Film.* 1939; reprint. New York: Teachers College Press, 1971.

Jenkins, Henry. *What Made Pistachio Nuts? Early Sound Comedy and the Vaudeville Aesthetic.* New York: Columbia University Press, 1992.

"John Bunny Again." *Indianapolis Star* (January 10, 1915), p. 12.

"John Bunny Dies; Movie Funmaker." *New York Times* (April 27, 1915), p. 13.

"John Bunny in the Flesh." *Indianapolis News* (November 10, 1914), p. 4.

Johnston, Alva. "Profiles: Legitimate Nonchalance-II." *The New Yorker* (February 9, 1935), p. 26.

Jordan, Thomas H. "The Marx Brothers." In *The Anatomy of Cinematic Humor.* New York: Revisionist Press, 1975.

Kael, Pauline. *A New Leaf* review. In *Deeper Into the Movies.* Boston: Little, Brown, 1973.

Kauffman, Stanley. *Annie Hall* review. *New Republic* (May 14, 1977), p. 22.

Kerr, Walter. "Laurel and Hardy: The Saving Turnaround." In *The Silent Clowns.* New York: Alfred A. Knopf, 1975, Chap. 34.

Klawans, Stuart. *Crimes and Misdemeanors* review. *The Nation* (November 13, 1989), p. 575.

Kracauer, Siegfried. *Theory of Film: The Redemption of Physical Reality.* New York: Oxford University Press, 1960.

Kroll, Jack. "Woody Funny, but He's Serious." *Newsweek* (April 24, 1978), p. 62.

_____. "Comedy 50, Tragedy 50." *Newsweek* (October 16, 1989), p. 67.

Lahue, Kalton C. *World of Laughter: The Motion Picture Comedy Short, 1910–1930.* 1966; reprinted Norman, Okla.: University of Oklahoma Press, 1972.

Lanier, Henry Wysham. "The Coquelin of the Movies." *World's Work* (March 1915), p. 576.

"Laughing With and At." *Commonweal* (April 4, 1947), p. 614.

Lax, Eric. *On Being Funny: Woody Allen and Comedy.* New York: Manor Books, 1977.

_____. *Woody Allen.* New York: Knopf, 1995.

"Lyceum—'John Bunny-Himself.'" *Indianapolis Star* (November 10, 1914), p. 15.

"Lyceum [Theatre]—John Bunny." *Indianapolis Star* (January 15, 1915), p. 15.

Lyon, James K. *Bertolt Brecht in America*. Princeton, N.J.: Princeton University Press, 1980.

Lyons, Gene, and Peter McAlevy. "Crazy Eddie." *Newsweek* (January 7, 1985), pp. 53, 55.

McCaffrey, Donald W. *Four Great Comedians: Chaplin, Lloyd, Keaton, Langdon*. New York: A. S. Barnes, 1968.

———. ed. *Focus on Chaplin*. Englewood Cliffs, N.J.: Prentice-Hall, 1971.

McDonald, Gerald D. *The Picture History of Charlie Chaplin*. New York: Nostalgia Press, 1965.

McDonald, Gerald D., Michael Conway, and Mark Ricci, eds. *The Films of Charlie Chaplin*. New York: Bonanza Books, 1965.

McEvoy, J. P. *The Comic Supplement* (1925). Billy Rose Theatre Collection, New York Public Library at Lincoln Center, New York.

McGerr, Celia. *René Clair*. Boston: Twayne, 1980.

McLean, Albert F. *American Vaudeville as Ritual*. Lexington, Ky.: University of Kentucky Press, 1965.

McLeish, Kenneth. "Samuel Beckett." In *Arts in the Twentieth Century*. New York: Viking Penguin, 1985.

Maltin, Leonard, *The Laurel & Hardy Book*. New York: Curtis Books, 1973.

———. *The Great American Comedians*. New York: Crown Publishers, 1978.

———. *Of Mice and Magic: A History of American Animated Cartoons*. New York: New American Library, 1980.

Mann, Thomas. *Death in Venice*. 1913; reprinted New York: Vintage Books, 1963.

Marx, Arthur. *Red Skelton*. New York: E. P. Dutton, 1979.

Marx, Groucho. "Press Agents I Have Known." *The New Yorker* (March 9, 1929), pp. 52, 54–55.

———. *Memoirs of a Mangy Lover*. New York: Bernard Geis Associates, 1963.

Marx, Harpo, and Rowland Barber. *Harpo Speaks!* 1961; reprinted New York: Freeway Press, 1974.

Masters, Edgar Lee. "Deacon Taylor." In *Spoon River Anthology*. 1915; reprinted New York: Collier Books, 1962.

Mast, Gerald. "More Fun Shops." In *The Comic Mind: Comedy and the Movies* (ed. Gerald Mast). 1973; reprinted Chicago: University of Chicago Press, 1979, Chap. 12.

———. "Comic Climate." In *The Comic Mind: Comedy and the Movies*, 2nd edn. (ed. Gerald Mast). Chicago: University of Chicago Press, 1979, Chap. 1.

———. "The Comics: Mack Sennett and the Chaplin Shorts." In *A Short History of the Movies*, 3rd edn. (ed. Gerald Mast). 1971; reprinted Indianapolis: Bobbs-Merrill, 1981, Chap. 5.

"Men, Women and Children Lost Film Friend When John Bunny Died." *Indianapolis News* (April 27, 1915), p. 3.

Michaels, Jennifer E. "Chaplin and Brecht: The Gold Rush and the Rise and Fall of the City of Mahogany." *Literature/Film Quarterly*, 8, No. 3, 1980, pp. 170–79.

INDEX

About the Author

WES D. GEHRING is Professor of Film at Ball State University. He is the author of numerous books, including *American Dark Comedy: Beyond Satire* (Greenwood, 1996), *Screwball Comedy* (Greenwood, 1986), *Populism and the Capra Legacy* (1995), *Handbook of American Film Genres* (1988), and bio-bibliographies on Laurel & Hardy, W. C. Fields, Charlie Chaplin, and the Marx Brothers.

ISBN 0-313-26185-7

90000>

EAN

9 780313 261855

HARDCOVER BAR CODE